D1093226

TIME AND EVENT

TIME AND EVENT

An Exegetical Study of the Use of *'ēth* in
the Old Testament in Comparison to Other
Temporal Expressions in Clarification of
the Concept of Time

BY

JOHN R. WILCH

LEIDEN
E. J. BRILL
1969

PRINTED IN THE NETHERLANDS

to

MY FATHER

faithful
Pastor
Missionary
Teacher
Example
The Rev. Andrew W. Wilch, Sr.

TABLE OF CONTENTS

PREFACE

This work is an inaugural dissertation presented as partial fulfilment of the requirements for a Doctor of Theology degree from the Evangelisch-theologische Fakultät of the Westfälische Wilhelms-Universität in Münster, Westfalen, Germany. It was accepted by the faculty on May 29, 1965.

For instigation, impetus, encouragement and advice, I am deeply indebted to my chief advisor, Prof. D. Dr. Karl Heinrich Rengstorf, D. D. I also wish to express my appreciation for assistance to my co-advisor, Prof. Dr. Franz Hesse, and to Dr. Günter Mayer and Rev. Erwin Buck of the Institutum Judaicum Delitzschianum, as well as to my friends in Münster who helped with the manuscript. Finally, I am sincerely grateful for the continual encouragement and patience offered by my wife.

Abbotsford, British Columbia, Oculi, 1969   J. R. W.

ABBREVIATIONS

Accd.	Accadian
Arab.	Arabic
Aram.	Aramaic
ATD	*Das Alte Testament Deutsch*, Neues Göttinger Bibelwerk, VR
BCAT	*Biblischer Commentar über das Alte Testament*, Dörffling und Franke, Leipzig
BH	*Apparatus criticus* of the *Biblica Hebraica*, ed.: R. Kittel, 7th ed., augmented by A. Alt, O. Eissfeldt, P. Kahle, PWB, 1951
Bibl.	Biblical
BKAT	*Biblischer Kommentar, Altes Testament*, Verlag der Buchhandlung des Erziehungsvereins Neukirchen, Kreis Moers
BZAW	*Beihefte zur Zeitschrift für die alttestamentliche Wissenschaft*, Töpelmann
CAD	*The Assyrian Dictionary of the Oriental Institute of the University of Chicago*, I. J. Gelb, *et al.*, Augustin, Glückstadt
Can.	Canaanite
CIS	*Corpus Inscriptionum Semiticarum ab Academia Inscriptionum et Litterarum Humaniorum Conditum atque Digestum*, Klincksieck, Paris
D	Deuteronomic source
DC	Damascus Codex
Deut	Deuteronomy
DJD	*Discoveries in the Judaean Desert of Jordan* (Jordan Department of Antiquities, American Schools of Oriental Research, École Biblique et Archéologique Française, Palestine Archaeological Museum), Clarendon, Oxford
DSC	Dead Sea Corpus = DC and the Dead Sea Scrolls
E	Elohistic source
EAT	*Erläuterungen zum Alten Testament*, Calwer Verlag
ed.	editor, edition
Egyp.	Egyptian
EHAT	*Exegetisches Handbuch zum Alten Testament*, Aschendorff, Münster i.W.
Eth.	Ethiopian
EVB	Evangelische Verlagsanstalt, Berlin
GHAT	*Göttinger Handkommentar zum Alten Testament*, VR
HAT	*Handbuch zum Alten Testament*, Mohr, Tübingen
Heb.	Hebrew
HSAT	*Die Heilige Schrift des Alten Testaments*, Hanstein, Bonn
HT	Hebrew Text
HTR	*Harvard Theological Review*, Harvard Univ., Cambridge, Mass.
IAAM	*The Intellectual Adventure of Ancient Man. An Essay on Speculative Thought in the Ancient Near East*, H. Frankfort, et al., Univ. of Chicago, Chicago: 1946
IB	*The Interpreter's Bible*, Abingdon, New York
ICC	*The International Critical Commentary*, Clark, Edinburgh
J	Yahwistic source
JBL	*Journal of Biblical Literature* (The Society of Biblical Literature and Exegesis), Philadelphia
K	*Kethibh*

KAT   *Kommentar zum Alten Testament*
KEHAT   *Kurzgefaßtes exegetisches Handbuch zum Alten Testament*, Hirzel, Leipzig
KHCAT   *Kurzer Hand-Commentar zum Alten Testament*, Mohr
KKHS   *Kurzgefaßter Kommentar zu den Heiligen Schriften Alten und Neuen Testaments sowie zu den Apokryphen*, Beck
LXX   Septuaginta
MS(S)   Manuscript(s)
MT   pointed Massoretic Text of Codex Leningradensis
Mur   Murrabba'at
n.   footnote
NF   Neue Folge
NT   New Testament
OLZ   *Orientalistische Literaturzeitung*, Hinrichs, Leipzig; Akademischer Verlag, Berlin
OT   Old Testament
P   Priestly source
Pal.   Palestinian
Phoen.   Phoenician
PIB   Pontificium Institutum Biblicum, Roma
PWB   Privilegierte Württembergische Bibelanstalt, Stuttgart
Q   *Qeré*
1 QH   Scroll of Hymns
1 QHf   Fragment of a Hymn
1 QM   War Scroll ("The War Between the Sons of Light and the Sons of Darkness")
1 QpHab   Midrash of Habakkuk
1 QS   Manual of Discipline
1 QSb   Scroll of Benedictions
4 QF   Florilegium
4 Ma   Fragment of 1 QM
4 QpIsa b Midrash of Isaiah
4 QpPs 37 Midrash of Psalm 37
4 QT   Scroll of Testimonies
R   redactor (Rd = redactor of D, Rp = redactor of P)
repr.   reprint
RSV   The Revised Standard Version
SAT   *Die Schriften des Alten Testaments in Auswahl übersetzt und für die Gegenwart erklärt*, VR
SBtf   *La Sainte Bible traduite en français* (L'École Biblique de Jérusalem), Cerf, Paris
Sira   Ecclesiasticus, or The Wisdom of Jesus ben Sira (Sirach)
Sum.   Sumerian
SVT   *Supplements to Vetus Testamentum*, Brill, Leiden
Syr.   Syriac
ThB   *Theologische Blätter*, Hinrichs, Leipzig
ThLZ   *Theologische Literaturzeitung*, EVB
ThR   *Theologische Rundschau*, Mohr, Tübingen
ThZ   *Theologische Zeitschrift*, Reinhardt, Basel
TJ   Targum Jonathan
TO   Targum Onkelos
tr.   translation
TWNT   *Theologisches Wörterbuch zum Neuen Testament*, ed.: Gerhard Kittel, 1933-1938, Gerhard Friedrich, 1942 ff.

Ugar.	Ugaritic
VR	Vandenhoek & Ruprecht, Göttingen
ZAW	*Zeitschrift für die alttestamentliche Wissenschaft*, Ricker (1881-1904), Töpelmann (1905- —); Giessen (1881-1933), Berlin (1934 ff.)
ZDMG	*Zeitschrift der Deutschen Morgenländischen Gesellschaft*, Brockhaus, Leipzig
ZThK	*Zeitschrift für Theologie und Kirche*, Mohr, Tübingen

CHAPTER ONE

INTRODUCTION

A. The Need for a Study of the Old Testament
Concept of Time

One of the major problems confronting modern man today is the
problem of *history*. The awareness of the weight of past history upon
the present situation and the course of the future has been awakened
in all walks of life and in every academic discipline. This is no less
true for the study of the Christian Scriptures, where an historical
approach and method of interpretation has become indispensable for
our time. The historical problem in Biblical exegesis is not only
concerned with determining the actual historical facts of the past and
their effect upon the witness to the transmitted religion, but also with
comprehending the views of the witnesses toward their own situation
and adapting their message to the contemporary situation.

It is therefore a natural result of the general mental attitude today
that the historical problem takes a central position in the study of
the Scriptures as a whole as well as in the hermeneutical discussion
in particular. There appears to be unanimity for the principle of an
historical approach in interpreting the Scriptures, although there is
a great deal of disagreement in defining the means of this approach.
For example, even when the concept of a "salvation history" (*Heilsgeschichte*) as a means of interpreting the history of the People of God
for the edification of the contemporary Christian has won consider-
able acceptance, it must endure a variety of conflicting definitions.

It may well be that the difficulty of the historical problem is un-
necessarily magnified. In the earnest concern to arrive at a solution,
some steps in method may be reversed or by-passed. Some concepts,
such as that of "salvation history", which are valid in their applicability to the mental environment of the present, may be founded
upon the supposed viewpoints of the Scriptural witnesses instead of
on the contemporary historical approach to the phenomena of divine
activity and human faith. It is indeed important toward an understanding of the transmitted witness to investigate the nature of the
concept of history exhibited by the witnesses. However, it must be
realized that a concept of history is necessarily made possible and

determined by several primary concepts, particularly the concepts of
time, event, chronology, causality and coherence.

The complexity of the problem of the concept of history in the
Biblical witness is thus much too involved for a single investigation.
Yet, it seems appropriate that a contribution toward a solution be
concerned with the nature of the Biblical concept of *time*. That this
concept is basic toward an understanding of the historical concept
has been frequently recognized. That it has far-reaching implications
has been well expressed by Georges Pidoux: "Toutes les études
consacrées à l'Ancien Testament rencontrent une difficulté majeure,
la notion que les auteurs biblique avaient du temps." [1]

Yet, the previous investigations of the problem of the idea of time
have not proven to be satisfactory, as Masao Sekine has observed:
"Denn ich bin der Meinung, daß man in der Behandlung dieses Problems im allgemeinen begrifflich nicht ganz klar verfahren ist. Dann
möchte ich einen Mangel der bisherigen Untersuchungen darin
erblicken, daß man diese Zeitauffassung des Alten Testaments
meistens nur abstrakt dargelegt hat, ohne sie in der konkreten Exegese
des alttestamentlichen Textes anzuwenden." [2]

With the conviction that abstractness and generality must be
avoided in dealing with the problem of time, it would be advisable
that critical investigation be founded squarely upon a concrete
exegesis of a limited area. Therefore, the present study is limited
primarily to a critical exegetical investigation of the use of the normal
word in the Old Testament for "time", *ʿēth*. A complete study of the
entire concept would include all words of temporal character. Because
this task is far too great for a single study, the consideration of other
words relevant to the concept must be limited to a comparison of
their usage to that of *ʿēth*.

B. Previous Investigations Relevant to the Subject

1. *von Orelli*. Modern investigations of the Old Testament concept
of time go back to the monograph of Conrad von Orelli: *Die hebräischen Synonyma der Zeit und Ewigkeit*, published in 1871. He distinguishes between the concepts of finite and infinite time, represented
by two groups of temporal words. However, he bases his investigation primarily on the philosophical conclusions of Friedrich Adolf

---

[1] "A propos de la notion biblique du temps", 120-125, *RTP* 2 (1952), p. 120.
[2] "Erwägungen zur hebräischen Zeitauffassung", *SVT* 9 (1963), p. 66.

Trendelenburg, who describes time as being only conceivable through a change in circumstances; it is therefore a form produced by motion and recognizable through motion.[1]) Thus he looks for and finds exegetical evidence for interpreting the various words according to different aspects of motion or the lack of it.

Von Orelli does not establish the basic meaning according to the actual use of the words, but according to their etymology and comparison with etymologically related words in other languages. For example, he derives *'antāh* and *'ōnāh* from *'nh*, "meet", and conveniently relates them to other temporal words in the Semitic languages, which all have to do with the time that "meets" or "arrives", and which is therefore to be characterized as the "right time". From this he concludes already that the concept of time is closely interwoven with its content. He then proceeds in like manner to other minor expressions, interpreting each one according to some aspect of motion, that of advancing (*'attīq*), accelerating (*sh'h*), quickness (*rega'*, *petha'*), returning (*'ōd*), circulating (*teqūphāh*, *dōr*, *gīl*, *'ophen*), enclosing (*nqm*), and resting (*cheled*).[2]) Yet, von Orelli diverges from his principle of motion in considering the most significant words for time. *mō'ēd*, *'ēth* and *'iddān* are all to be derived from *y'd*, "determine". Thus *mō'ēd* is the "established, ordered time", *'ēth* is the "right, normal, appropriate time", *'attāh* is the "fixed present moment", and *'iddān* is the "reckoned time". Also, *zemān*, from *zmn*, "determine", is the "denoted, limited" time or date. As an afterthought, a brief discussion of the words for the measurement of time is added, for which no etymological explanation can be offered, except for *shānāh* as "repetition". He concludes that there is no Hebrew word for time in general. The same procedure is then followed in the treatment of the words for infinite time.[3])

The faultiness of von Orelli's methods is revealed in their failure to deal with the subject itself. The presupposition of connecting time with motion, derived from a certain philosophical conception, may only be forced upon Hebrew usage. Only the least important words are affected, and even that through some doubtful interpretations. *'attīq* (1 Chr 4:22), *'ōd* (Gen 29:7, *etc.*), and *gīl* (Dt 1:10) have to do with a condition and not a motion. If they, like *cheled*, represent the opposite

---

[1]) *Logische Untersuchungen* I, 3rd ed., Leipzig: 1870, pp. 156 ff.; von Orelli: *Die hebräischen Synonyma der Zeit und Ewigkeit*, Leipzig: 1871, pp. 13 f.

[2]) *Ibid.*, pp. 15-44.

[3]) *Ibid.*, pp. 45-60, 64-105.

of motion,[1]) the principle of motion becomes meaningless as a basis. Furthermore, *shā'āh* (Dan 4:16) and *rega'* (Num 16:21, *etc.*) refer to a unit of time, and *dōr* to the people or period of a generation (Gen 7:1, Dt 32:7, *etc.*).[2]) This demonstrates further that etymological considerations are often very misleading and do not coincide with the actual usage of words. In accordance with the philological methods practiced for the last thirty years in non-theological disciplines, James Barr states: "The etymology of a word is not a statement about its meaning but about its history." [3]) It is therefore not surprising that the very word used for "time" and for measuring time are relegated by von Orelli to categories that have nothing to do with his philosophical presupposition, and that one major word for the Hebrew idea of time, *yōm*, receives only the briefest mention.[4]) Furthermore, it is not a peculiarity of the Hebrew language that it does not have a word for "time in general"; what language does? [5]) Such a concept belongs to the mentality and not to the vocabulary. Nevertheless, von Orelli's methods and resultant conclusions still find a measure of acceptance in theological study.

2. *Pedersen.* Johannes Pedersen proceeds from the phenomenon of the two Hebrew verb tenses to the conclusion that "the time of the action, which for us is the principal thing, is of no importance to the Hebrew". He further denies the significance of the sun and moon in measuring time, recognizing only their function in governing it. His thesis that time "is identical with substance" is supported by the phrases *kā'ēth chayyāh* (Gen 18:10, 14) and *hā'ēth geshāmīm* (Ezra 10:13). *E.g.*, he translates the latter, "time is rain", and interprets it to mean that "the principal substance of time is rain" in this case (see below, pp. 23-25, 27).[6]) For him, then, time is "the development of the very events" and identical with the actions and fate of a person or people. From these considerations, Pedersen jumps to the conclusion that "times of the same substance are therefore identical". Thus, "history is not considered a long chain of events, divided into

---

[1]) *Ibid.*, pp. 42-44.
[2]) That *dōr* is not at all concerned with the idea of a circle or cyclical repetition see Oswald Loretz: *Qohelet und der Alte Orient*, Freiburg: 1964, pp. 294 f.
[3]) *The Semantics of Biblical Language*, Oxford: 1961, p. 109; see below, pp. 159 f.
[4]) *Op. cit.*, p. 60.
[5]) *Cf.* James Barr: *Biblical Words for Time*, London: 1962, p. 78.
[6]) *Israel, Its Life and Culture*, I-II, Copenhagen: 1926, p. 114.

special periods", but consists of generations distinguished by certain events and people which are fused into a great whole as "concentrated time", that is, "eternity"—'ōlām [1]) (see also below, p. 66).

Apart from the fact that the importance of the temporal aspects of an action does not depend upon the nature of the verbal system but on the nature of the context as a whole, the frequent prominence given to chronology and the measurement of time in the OT is completely overlooked. It is further a crass generalization to presume that the concept of history is merely based on that of generations, and particularly that "eternity"—which is not the regular meaning of 'ōlām (cf. Gen 6:4—"distant time", see below, pp. 17-19)—should comprise a concentration of generations.

3. *Galling.* Kurt Galling borrowed from Paul Tillich's philosophical concept of the "kairos" [2]) in finding evidence of "fulfilled time" in the OT, especially in describing the emphasis by the prophets on the "now" and the "coming". He concludes that the prophets conceived of this "now" as the only time [3]) (see pp. 108 f., 121).

4. *Hempel.* True to the modern trend, Johannes Hempel evaluates OT thought in the category of time much greater than that in the category of space, so that the dominating opposites are not "earthly" and "heavenly", but "now" and "then". He thereby disregards the very strong tendency in the OT to localize all occurrences, even those of future promise. Yet, he realizes that the peculiarity of the OT concept of history is derived from the concept of God and not from a peculiar concept of time [4]) (see pp. 109 f., 121).

5. *Weiser.* The "now" is again stressed by Arthur Weiser, who identifies it as the point from which the prophets regard history. For them, "history" is "eine aktuelle in die Gegenwart hereinragende Wirklichkeit" [5]) (see pp. 103-111).

6. *Delling.* Also influenced by modern philosophy, Gerhard Delling identified the "original" meaning of καιρός for the LXX as the "decisive moment". Thus the purely temporal meaning that is much more common than the original one is pushed into the background as theologically unimportant. This aspect of the "moment" is also

---

[1]) *Ibid.*, pp. 487-491.
[2]) "Kairos I", *Der Widerstreit von Raum und Zeit*, Stuttgart: 1963, pp. 9-28.
[3]) "Die Geschichte als Wort Gottes bei den Propheten", *ThB* 8 (1929), p. 171.
[4]) *Altes Testament und Geschichte*, Gütersloh: 1930, pp. 28-33.
[5]) *Glaube und Geschichte im Alten Testament*, Stuttgart: 1931, pp. 85-87.

found to be the meaning for *ʿēth* and even for *yāmīm*, for periods of time are pressed into moments. It is then concluded that the OT writers were not interested in the course of time, but only in the high-points of history, *ʿittīm* [1]) (see pp. 14, 52, 60, 121, 151-155).

7. *Scott.* R. B. Y. Scott bases his considerations on time in the OT on the single expression, "the Day of Yahweh". The character of this "revealing, transforming, catastrophic moment of divine self-disclosure on the plane of history" necessitates an emphasis on the religious importance of the present. Thus he concludes: "Time contains the total experience. Past and future are extensions of the present, and (so to speak) are *present in* the present" (see pp. 92-95, 109).[2])

8. *H. W. Robinson.* H. Wheeler Robinson supports his definition of *ʿēth* as "occurrence", with an etymology from *ʿnh*, "answer", and its Syriac relative *ʿunaya*, "response" (see pp. 3, 156). According to the OT usage, time is conceived "in the concrete, in its filled content, and not as an abstract idea. 'Time' is that which meets you on your path through life." Robinson systematically assigns a formal character to one-third of the instances, as *bāʿēth hahīʾ*, and then discusses those concerned with phenomena of nature, including phases of human life and the specifications in Ecc 3. A third group concerns social convention or appointment, including fixed and appropriate times, and a final group refers to "God's control of man's time-experience."[3])

This last group indicates the characteristic view of history, referring to the definiteness of concrete event and the actual quality and content of time. Hebrew thus lacks a word to express time in general. Robinson observes further that "God's intervention in the affairs of this world to establish His kingly rule does not involve the suspension of the time-order; . . . the quality of time . . . is always time". Because events are referred directly to God, "the Hebrew time-consciousness is much less interested in the causal relation of events . . .; hence the emphasis is taken off exact chronology and the precise time-sequence" (see pp. 53-59). Koheleth is scolded for lacking a sense of history, and for using *ʿēth* without revealing any progress to a goal (see below, pp. 116 f., 124). Yet, Robinson understands well the prophetic inter-

---

[1]) "καιρός", *TWNT*, III, 1938, pp. 459 f.; *Das Zeitverständnis des Neuen Testaments*, Gütersloh: 1940, pp. 49, 52.

[2]) *The Relevance of the Prophets*, New York: 1944, pp. 149 f.

[3]) *Inspiration and Revelation in the Old Testament*, Oxford: 1946, pp. 109-111. *Cf.* his etymological considerations for temporal words, pp. 120 f.

pretation of history, especially the "constitutive principle" of "the constant incorporation of past, present, and future events into that which claims to be the word of the everliving God". Then, too, the Day of Yahweh "brings to a focus the manifestation of Yahweh's purpose in history" as its pivot rather than its goal.[1]

Robinson takes no particular note of the large number of instances of *ʿēth* that evidently do not coincide with his definition. Neither is he consistent in applying his meaning of "occurrence"—which is actually well chosen—for he continually speaks of "times" and not of "occurrences". He also fails to observe that there ought to be a definite character involved with *ʿēth* if many instances deal with fixed and appropriate times of God's control of them.

9. *Vollborn.* In his comprehensive study, Werner Vollborn intends "das Wesen der Zeit und seine Entfaltung in der Verkündigung des Alten Testaments herauszuarbeiten". His thesis is that "time" is "Ereignis in seinem Vollzug", which he attempts to maintain for all temporal expressions. *ʿēth* is characterized as a certain temporal moment that may be determined for something or may even mean the decisive moment—the moment for the religious decision—in the sense of the Greek καιρός. It is not understood abstractly but from the events; "in dem Geschehen der Ereignisse ist ihre Zeit da" (see pp. 60, 121; *cf.* Am 5:13, p. 85). *yōm* is comprehended from its content; for instance, as the Day of Yahweh it means the totality of the eschatological occurrence, while *yāmīm* signifies its individual acts (see pp. 52, 101). *mōʿēd* tis, somewhat more than *ʿēth*, the determined temporal momen when something occurs (see pp. 66, 89). *qēts* is a closing moment or period (see pp. 113 f.), *'acharīth* is the future intervening time or the eschatological salvation time (see pp. 69 f.), and *qedem* is the distant past.[2]

Vollborn then proceeds to a discussion of the supposed peculiarity of the OT view of time, "die Vergegenwärtigung des Geschehens", that is, „die Aufhebung der Zeit". Using the examples of the Patriarchs and the election of the people in the Exodus, he concludes: "Das AT sieht die Ereignisse nicht im chronologischen Ablauf im Sinne einer kontinuierlichen Linie, das AT konstituiert den zeitlichen Abstand zwischen den Ereignissen nicht, sondern sieht sie gleichsam auf eine Fläche projiziert" (see pp. 72-74). Further, "das AT sieht

---

[1] *Ibid.*, pp. 112, 119-121, 125 f., 144 f.
[2] *Studien zum Zeitverständnis des Alten Testaments*, Göttingen: 1951, pp. 4-80.

die Geschichte vom Aspekt Gottes her, und vor Gott ist alles Geschehen gegenwärtig." The history of the ancestors is included in "today"; Moses is present in the words of Deuteronomy; the Covenant is always understood as being present; and even the concept *zkr* involves a present realization of what is called to mind. The verbal tenses also reflect this idea: "Durch die Verwendung des Imperfektum ist das Vergangene als in die Gegenwart hineinragend begriffen." (see pp. 109 f.) [1]) Similarly, the future is realized in the present through visions, word and symbolical acts, and is seen in the use of the prophetic perfect. Vollborn then identifies this realization of the past and future in the "now" as the "time of decision". This realization "ist Schauen der Ereignisse vom Aspekt Gottes her und eben darin die Aufhebung der menschlichen Zeitkategorien", for "wo Gott ist, da ist keine 'Zeit' mehr, da ist die Zeit aufgehoben" (see pp. 74 f., 102 f.). [2])

10. *Marsh*. John Marsh distinguishes between the concepts of "chronological" and "realistic" time, the latter being dominant in the Bible, but the former applying to modern Western man. This contrast is exhibited in the NT by the distinction between χρόνος and καιρός (see below, p. 14), and is also clearly found in the OT, where "realistic" time is represented by *'ēth*, while "chronological" time lacks a designation and was a late development in Hebrew thought (see pp. 10, 65, 71-75). Realistic time is to be understood in terms of opportunity and fulfillment: "events that happen in time derive their location from two factors—an opportunity (a time, *'ēth* or *kairos*) that presents itself to man, and man's response to the opportunity in appropriate action." Even in historical events, the prophets demanded appropriate response to every situation because God fills it with content. Thus "times are known by their contents". All the references to "that time" in Dt 1-10 look back to the one classic time of God's calling and constituting his people (see pp. 65 f.). He also discusses cases of "day" in "supra-temporal" reference known by the content, particularly by that of God. This may also be true of "year", "season" (*mō'ēd*), "month" and "moment" (*rega'*). The second "classic time" of God's activity in history is his coming intervention; both "times" constituted the Hebrew judgement of contemporary history. [3])

---

[1]) *Ibid.*, pp. 138-209.

[2]) *Ibid.*, pp. 212-266.

[3]) "Time, Season", *A Theological Word Book of the Bible*, New York: 1950, pp. 258-262.

In his more systematical treatment of time, Marsh makes use of Gerhard Delling's high-points (see above, p. 6) and Oscar Cullmann's "line of decisive times" (καιροί)[1] in describing history as a "continuum of times", each filled with its own content and demanding a response. God's basic deeds are an example of time with divine content that is independent of chronological succession and that may be placed into immediate relationship to all points of the following history. Chronological sequence is further avoided in the cult, where the past events become simultaneous with the celebrating congregation. The people of God of all time likewise has recourse to the filled historical moment (ʿēth) of the coming divine intervention. The *tempora* of past, present and future are likewise suspended and united into one salvation occurrence in the proclamation of the prophets (see pp. 7 f., 108-110). Furthermore, since the times are determined by their content, they may be identified with each other when their content is identical (see Pedersen, p. 4, above), such as that of the past Exodus and of the future Return. This "realistic" view of time is constitutive for the OT, for it is able to demonstrate that the true meaning of the historical events for God's revelation in time as the category of fulfilment is free from the limits of chronological time with immediate relationship to the Eternal who breaks into history (see pp. 102-104).[2]

The impression is created that every occurrence of ʿēth (= καιρός) implies an opportunity for responsive action, although it is frequently used for natural events or simply to indicate the relationship of events to each other (see below, pp. 21-28, 34-47). Furthermore, instead of demonstrating the true meaning of the historical event, Marsh robs it of its historicity by removing it from its unique place in chronological time and relegating it to a timeless category that is foreign to man's experience in his finite existence.

11. *Pidoux*. Reference to "concentrated time" (*cf.* Pedersen, above, p. 5) is also made by Georges Pidoux in relating the cult to historical events, particularly in evaluating some events more than others and in preserving the concept of the beginning and end of time.[3] The latter concept is indeed a corollary in a natural sense to an historical

---

[1] *Christus und die Zeit*, 3rd ed., Zollikon: 1962 (1st ed., 1947), p. 51.
[2] *The Fulness of Time*, London: 1952, pp. 19-22, 28, 35 f., 49 f., 63-65, 156 f., 167 f.
[3] *Op. cit.*, p. 123; see below, p. 66 (n. 2).

concept, but the phenomenon of evaluation is a matter of emphasis independent from a peculiar concept of time.

12. *Ratschow*. Philosophical presuppositions were again applied to the problem of time in the OT by Carl Heinz Ratschow, who was concerned with the non-Christian attitude of modern man of "not having time for something". He supports his answer to the modern situation with a study of *'ēth*, which is supposed to represent the Biblical view of time in the sense of the "right time for something". The many instances that clearly refer to temporal relationship are branded as the influence of other ideas of time foreign to that of the OT (see pp. 118, 122-124).[1])

13. *Eichrodt*. The chronological concept in the OT is heavily emphasized by Walther Eichrodt. This is to be seen in the references in Deuteronomy to the differences in generations (6:7; 11:2, 7, 18-21), to the ties of the chosen people to genealogy, that is, to the "time-line", and to the expectancy of a salvation-event in the distinct future (*cf.* 2 Kgs 25:27-30). Besides this perspective for ordered epochs of time, a clear distinction is also made between past, present and future, even by the prophets, who differentiated emphatically between the past and present situations (Isa 1:21 ff.; Jer 2:2 ff.; Hos 11:2), as well as between the past and the completely new character of the future divine event (Isa 43:18; 63:16; Jer 23:7 f.). There is no bursting of the limits of time or flight into a salvation beyond all time (see p. 110). Man's position for decision looks back to the past as well as forward to the future. Although the "kairoi" of God's acts of revelation are inwardly bound together into a salvation history without being identified with the general temporal sequence, they may nevertheless be given a place in the "time-line". It is within history that God is at work. At each point of the "time-line", he is present with his call for decision—the opportunity to prepare for his impending salvation. The subservience of historical time for a new form of existence for the People of God is not founded on a view of time contrary to our understanding of reality, but on the confrontation with the God who subjects time to the establishment of his rule (see pp. 80-84).[2])

---

[1]) "Anmerkungen zur theologischen Auffassung des Zeitproblems", *ZThK* 51 (1954), pp. 377-384.
[2]) "Heilserfahrung und Zeitverständnis im Alten Testament", *ThZ* 12 (1956), pp. 113-125.

14. *Boman*. Thorleif Boman interprets the Greek-European view
of time on the basis of motion (*cf.* von Orelli, above, pp. 2 f.) according to Aristotle. To this, however, he contrasts the Hebrew concept,
where "time is identical with its content". On the basis of the lunar
phases and the alteration between light and darkness, warmth and
cold, he concludes that time is represented by a structure of rhythms.
A longer period is thought of as a continued rhythm. Considering
the Hebrew psychologically, Boman does not arrive at a "corporate
personality" (see pp. 74 f.), but at an individual, identical only with
himself, who lives in the world of his own experiences. He therefore
lives primarily in time, but for this reason differences in time are
of little importance. This is also true of God. For him, too, the qualitative difference in events is of greater importance. Except for a
passing reference to *'ēth* as "psychological time, time as content",
Boman treats it only in view of Ecc 3:1-8, which he interprets as
reflecting the rhythms of opposites in the inner life (see pp. 118-120).
He further recognizes simultaneity "when the psychological content
of two times are identical" (*cf.* Pedersen and Marsh above, pp. 4, 8).
Finally, history for the Hebrews is described as a movement toward
a goal set by God; and because it is movement, even the past is
alive.[1])

Boman's linguistic shortcomings are pointed out in the main by
Barr, as well as his procedure of contrasting Hebrew language with
Greek philosophical thought.[2]) The peculiar idea of rhythm is suspect
anyway, for the manner of expressing natural changes in contrasts is
common in European languages as well as in Hebrew. It is also an
inconsistency for Boman, after distinguishing the Hebrew view of
time from the Greek, which is supposedly based on movement
toward a goal, as if it were independent of the time concept.

15. *Knight*. George Knight speaks of "a series of 'times', *'ēth*
or "moments'" (*cf.* Cullmann and Eichrodt above, pp. 9, 10), that
constitute the divine plan in history moving toward its End. However, he identifies only the five most significant events in Israel's
history as God's "moments", although *'ēth* is not peculiarly used in
reference to these occasions in distinction from others. He identifies
time in the Hebrew concept with its substance (*cf.* Pederson above,

---

[1]) *Das hebräische Denken im Vergleich mit dem griechischen*, 3rd ed., Göttingen:
1959, pp. 105 f., 113-121, 127 f., 148.

[2]) *The Semantics of Biblical Language*, pp. 46-79.

p. 4), *e.g.*: "The 'Day of the Lord' was thus a term full of 'substance', and was not just a mere calendar date. . . . It referred to a fulness of *time* when God would act once again within history . . ." [1])

16. *von Rad*. On the basis that Israel's faith was based on the historical facts of Yahweh's activity, Gerhard von Rad emphasizes the early creeds that recapitulate the salvation history, and concludes: "Reden wir von bekenntnishafter Art, so heißt das, daß das spätere Israel in den Geschichtszeugnissen des Hexateuch etwas für das Gottesvolk Typisches gesehen hat und daß das Erzählte jeder späteren Generation durch eine verborgene Gleichzeitigkeit aktuell geblieben ist." [2]) It would rather appear that a creed of historical facts is characterized by the singular character of incomparable events (not at all typical), and by the continuity of the presence of God (not of the events). These aspects appear inconsequent in von Rad's otherwise historically-oriented presentation.

He also speaks of the Hebrew's life in the rhythm of nature (*cf.* Boman above, p. 11) and of cultic festivals (see Pidoux above p. 9). Yet, Israel was to have historicized the nature festivals, which would seem to repudiate the rhythmic character. On the other hand, Yahweh's historical acts were seen to be absolute so that they were realized in the presence of the worshipping congregation. Thus it was only the festival time that was "filled time" in the full sense of the word.[3]) However, a conception that involves the participation in past events must fail to recognize either the firm place of the events in history or that of the participants in the present, which is not an historical view of time. The Hebrews left the events in the past where they were and only remembered them (*zkr*—Ex 13:3; Dt 7:18, *etc.*); it was the person of God that was present both in the past and present (*cf.* Gen 28:13; Ex 3:6; Dt 26:7-10; Isa 48:16; see pp. 85 f.).

The significance of the role of God is not overlooked by von Rad when he states, "Geschichte gab es also für Israel nur, sofern und so weit Gott mit ihm gegangen ist." In fact, he finally admits the "anti-

---

[1]) *A Christian Theology of the Old Testament*, Richmond: 1959, pp. 201-212, 314 f.

[2]) *Theologie des Alten Testaments*, I, 3rd ed., München: 1961, pp. 112, 124, 127, 131. *Cf.* his idea of "subjektiver Vergegenwärtigung" in Deut., p. 225, n. 79; see below, pp. 74 f.

[3]) *Theologie des Alten Testaments*, II, München: 1960, pp. 115-117; see below, p. 109 (n. 2). *Cf.* Artur Weiser: "Psalm 77", *ThLZ* 72 (1947), col. 138: ". . . für die Kultgemeinde mit der Gegenwart Gottes zugleich ist auch die ganze Geschichte seiner Heilstaten . . . unmittelbar gegenwärtig gedacht und real erlebt . . ."

historical" character of cultic simultaneity, although he does not abandon it alongside the historical view. Further, the prophets were to have "eschatologized" the historical thought. However, von Rad relates their message to a significant new event and not to the End-situation. As for the role of *'ēth*, its use is generalized as indicating that "alles Geschehen hat seine bestimmte zeitliche Ordnung". On the basis of Ecc 3 and the plural form (Ezek 12:17; Ps 31:16; Job 24:1), it is concluded: "das Menschenleben setzt sich aus einer Abfolge vieler Zeiten zusammen."[1]) However, no hint of a sequence is implied in these passages.

17. *Jocz.* J. Jocz is impressed by the Biblical emphasis on occurrences and acts to the detriment of dates and duration. "This specifically biblical concept of time . . . we call the prophetic Now"—the conjunction between past and present. Further, "the conjunctive Now is at the same time the Now of decision"—the "Kierkegaardian Instant"—as well as the "Now of renewal" of life. These "Nows" constitute time in the Biblical sense, that is, vertically measured in the realm of faith. Thus time is "the dimension in which God performs His mighty acts."[2]) This inconsequential statement is the result of supposedly discovering a peculiar concept of time after eliminating the chronological aspect. The identification of three "Nows" may be significant for a portrayal of Israel's faith that experiences the urgency and pregnancy of the present situation. But this peculiarity of the experience reflects upon the encounter with God and not upon a different concept of time. Such a "Now" may be applied to any situation that is decisive and vital (*cf.* pp. 109 f.).

18. *Muilenburg.* The discussion of the "Biblical View of Time" by James Muilenburg runs in a similar vein. In contrast to the Greeks' supposed cyclical view of time, Israel grasped time "in terms of purpose, will, and decision". Thus Israel always experienced Yahweh's activity "in the concrete context of time". He borrows Robinson's etymological explanation of *'ēth* as "occurrence" (see p. 6) —concrete and "identical with substance"—and concludes that "the Old Testament has no way of distinguishing between chronological and concrete or 'realistic' time."[3]) It might be asked whether the Greek idea of decisive time had nothing to do with their view of time,

---

[1]) *Theologie des Alten Testaments*, II, pp. 139 f., 119-123, 126-131.
[2]) *The Spiritual History of Israel*, London: 1961, pp. 220-228.
[3]) *HTR* 54 (1961), pp. 229-236.

whether other peoples experienced the intervention of their gods apart from the concrete context of time, and whether the distinction between chronological and realistic time is to be based on certain meanings of words or on the textual context—that is, if it is to be maintained that chronological time in Hebrew thought was not concrete or realistic.

Muilenburg also emphasizes the urgency of the decisive situation (*cf.* Jocz above); the demand of Yahweh's Day indicates that Biblical time is comprehended by immediacy and quality, not by extent or measurements. However, his observation that the sacred history is understood in terms of the succession of generations implies a comprehension of time in the sense of extension and even quantitative measurement. He further sees the present experience of past events in the cultic celebration (*cf.* Pidoux and von Rad above, pp. 9, 12), which, however, he also describes as a mere recollection that actually evidences a movement toward the future.[1]) Thus his representation of the historical factor of time remains unclarified.

19. *Barr*. James Barr has applied his semantic principles (see below, p. 19) in a detailed criticism of attempts to treat the Biblical concept of time on a linguistic basis. In opposition to Marsh (above, p. 8), he shows that the oft-made distinction between καιρός and χρόνος is false, for καιρός has been used in post-classical Greek— and particularly in the LXX and NT—for "time" in general in contrast to the specialized classical designation for "opportune time."[2]) The similar method employed by Cullmann in distinguishing between the "moment" of καιρός and the "period" of αἰών in the NT in order to characterize the two components of salvation history is likewise criticized.[3]) Delling, too, is taken to task for assigning the meaning of "moment" to ʿēth and of "periods" to *yāmîm*, instead of deriving the meanings of a word from its usage (see p. 6).[4]) He also attacks the antiquated methods of von Orelli (see above, pp. 2-4), particularly as they still produce such conclusions in modern study of Hebrew as the lack of a general word for time that corresponds to χρόνος (see p. 8), the correspondence of ʿēth to καιρός (see pp. 5, 7, 8), reference to "period" by *leʿōlāmîm* (see pp. 17 f.), the significance of the peculiar verbal system for the idea of time (see pp. 8, 15 f.),

---

[1]) *Ibid.*, pp. 237-239, 243-246.
[2]) *Biblical Words for Time*, pp. 20-46; see below, pp. 151-154.
[3]) *Ibid.*, pp. 47-81; see below, p. 154.
[4]) *Ibid.*, pp. 55-58.

and the concrete character expressed by the words for time (see pp. 13, 16).[1])

In his own brief discussion of the Biblical words for time, Barr notices no particular differences between them and comparable words in modern languages, considering that words normally have several uses. In conclusion, he points out that "the important thing for the Bible lies not in the idea of time but in the use made of the historical sequence for the presentation of an encounter with God", for the view of time is not the foundation for the basic Biblical assertions. Doubting the possibility of arriving at "a solid 'biblical view'", he assigns the task of developing a Christian doctrine of time to philosophical theology.[2])

20. *Sekine.* Masao Sekine takes up the distinction between chronological and "realistic" time (see Marsh, p. 8), handling it strongly from the psychological standpoint. He distinguishes "die am äußeren Objekt orientierte, äußerlich meßbare, äußere Zeit und die am Subjekt orientierte, innerlich gelebte, innere Zeit". The characteristic of the Hebrew understanding of time is that it often combines the two views. Thus an expression as "on that day" indicates a temporal setting "der zwar konkret mit dem Geschehen zusammenhängt, aber im gewissen Sinne schon gegenüber dem Geschehen selbst verselbständigt ist." Besides *yōm*, *'ēth* also frequently indicates the temporal setting in which an event occurs, particularly as "in that time". This combination of "inner" and "outer" time may best be seen in the "filled time" of cultic present realization that raises the past occurrence to a present experience (see Pidoux and von Rad, pp. 9, 12) and that even means a suspension of time. In view of the prophetic and apocalyptic eschatology, time is seen in the OT from God's standpoint, but, in contrast to Vollborn (see above p. 8), God is a reality who always works within time and space.[3])

Sekine then supports his argument with linguistic considerations. He corresponds "inner" time to the verbal function of the mood as psychological category, "outer" time to the function of the aspect as logical category, and denies the Hebrew verb the function of indicating the tempus. Thus the expression of relative temporal gradation is very inexact. For example, the references of "at that time" in Dt

[1]) *Ibid.*, pp. 82-96.
[2]) *Ibid.*, pp. 116-126, 144, 149, 157.
[3]) *Op. cit.*, pp. 67-74.

1-10 (see Marsh, p. 8) demonstrate that the period from the Exodus to the entrance into Canaan was seen as a unity.[1]) Attention may be directed to the fact that the modern Western temperament uses the words "day" and "time", as well as "occasion", to refer to the temporal setting in which an event occurs, so that this is scarcely a phenomenon peculiar to Hebrew psychology. Supporting the argument with the function of the verbs could only be valid if Hebrew had no other means for indicating the tempus in a sentence. The investigation should be extended to considerations of adverbs, particles, and word order.

21. *Wildberger.* Hans Wildberger presumes that it was the prophets who formed the OT understanding of history. In searching for a representative term for history, he chooses not *'ittīm* ("decisive moments"), but *debārīm* as an annalistic row of occurrences (1 Kgs 11:41; 14:19, *etc.*), because "Geschichte ist erst ein Komplex von Ereignissen, die in ihrem Zusammenhang als sinnvoll verstanden sind."[2]) Basic to this view is Yahweh's work, which is particularly emphasized in Isaiah (*'sh, p'l, y'ts*), who is concerned with Yahweh's work as a whole: History is his work according to his plan. It was not till later that Israel began to understand the salvation history as a succession of Yahweh's works. Although God remains the Lord of history, his plan is formed in the encounter with man, so that man's decision receives great significance in this responsibility before God. Wildberger also denies that Isa. gives evidence of a real eschatological expectancy. In fact, the prophets do not eschatologize the new object of their proclamation, for it is immediate—they speak of the end for Israel as Yahweh's intervening judgment, not the end of an epoch or the end of time. This is a healthy shift of emphasis in the historical activity of God from the accidence of its temporal aspect to the essence of its content as effective divine encounter with man.

22. *Ebeling.* Gerhard Ebeling attempts to localize the essence of the historical encounter in the spoken word. He appears to reason in a circle, beginning with the structure of the Hebrew language with its supposed indefinite sense of the dominance of the structure of real events (*cf.* Ecc 3:1 ff.). Thus time is always concrete. This he combines with the OT idea that time has a beginning and an end, conclud-

---

[1]) *Ibid.*, pp. 75 f., 80 f.
[2]) "Jesajas Verständnis der Geschichte", *SVT* 9, 1963, pp. 83-89, 98, 103, 108, 112-115; *cf.*, below, pp. 108-110.

ing that time is always eschatological in character, pressing on to its end. Therefore, since every time is qualified by the eschatological moment, it becomes a time of decision. From this position, Ebeling makes the jump from the category of time to that of personal encounter. The decision of faith, confronted by the presence of God, leaves the past and future up to him, the Lord of time. Thus the End and eternity are dissolved into conversation with God: "Ewigkeit, theologisch verstanden, ist das Zur-Sprache-Kommen des Zeitverständnisses Jesu im Evangelium".[1]) This line of reasoning does more than overcome the problems of eschatology and eternity—it also overcomes the fact of man's historical existence. The question is whether God's confronting word affects the finitude of time or the confronted man.

Excurse 1

The Concept of Eternity

The subject of eternity in the OT had been thoroughly discussed by Conrad von Orelli, who described it as "motion into the unforeseeable"—time that "loses itself in the infinite". The basic principle of motion provides the means of putting unlimited time into expression.[2]) Johannes Pedersen thought of eternity as the concentration of history,[3]) and Hermann Sasse limited it primarily to the "hidden, distant time ... in the distant, unsurveyable past or future"—a wholly relative concept, with the idea of an eternal duration being expressed by the plural *'ōlāmīm* and by *mē'ōlām le'ōlām*.[4]) This last phrase is identified by H. Wheeler Robinson as a standard form of doxology, "from the most ancient time to the remotest future", which expresses the transcendence of God above temporal limitations.[5]) This basic reference to what lies in the remote distance is distinguished by Gerhard Delling from αἰών, which is concerned primarily with a continuing line.[6]) John Marsh ignores these distinctions and interprets *'ōlām* consistently as "eternity, everlasting."[7])

---

[1]) "Zeit und Wort", *Zeit und Geschichte* (Dankesgabe an Rudolf Bultmann zum 80. Geburtstag), Tübingen: 1964, pp. 346-352. The goal at which Ebeling is aiming is obviously the same that Bultmann reached in his religio-historical study, *Geschichte und Eschatologie* (Tübingen: 1958); see esp. p. 180.

[2]) *Op. cit.*, pp. 89, 99 f.

[3]) *Op. cit.*, p. 491.

[4]) "αἰών", *TWNT*, I, 1933, pp. 199 f.

[5]) *Op. cit.*, pp. 114 f.

[6]) *Das Zeitverständnis des Neuen Testaments*, p. 49.

[7]) "Time, Season", pp. 265 f.

However, Werner Vollborn defines the various relevant terms as periods of time that disappear beyond what is perceivable,[1]) and Otto Eißfeldt characterizes them as "duration, permanence", especially referring to the person of God as the "Eternal."[2])

A seemingly decisive word to the subject has been spoken by Ernst Jenni in his thorough study of *ʿōlām*. Avoiding a clear-cut conclusion from the etymological investigation, he was able to support his thesis of "most distant time" as the basic meaning throughout the witness of Ugaritic, Canaanite and Aramaic dialects, as well as Biblical Hebrew. The doxological formula *mēʿōlām ʿad-ʿōlām* only appears once in the OT as eternity without beginning and end (Ps 90:2), and the plural is only extensive, not an expression for "eternity".[3]) The term was first especially employed for "ecclesiastical" language by Deutero-Isaiah with respect to history as the world of God and his activity (40:8, 27 f.; 51:6, 8; 53:3, 13). Then, apocalyptic appropriated it as an attribute of the world beyond (Dan 12:2). The meaning of the Greek κόσμος is first given to it in Tobit (3:2; 13:18) and Jubilees (5:25; 10:17; 25:23). Special mention is made of the occurrences in Ecclesiastes, where *leʿōlāmīm* in 1:10 indicates "long temporal duration" under influence from αἰών. Such duration is also meant by *hāʿōlām* in 3:11 in distinction to *ʿēth* in the sense of καιρός for "moment of time". Finally, *bēth-ʿōlamō* in 12:5 represents the influence from Egypt witnessed in Punic grave inscriptions, signifying the "irrevocable end."[4])

Although the occasional reference to the idea of eternity may well have had its Hebrew origin in the historical concept of Dt.-Isa., the convincing repudiation of all Greek influence in Ecc. by Oswald Loretz [5]) leads to caution in this point. It is quite possible that the Hebrew thinker Koheleth deliberately employs the term unconventionally as an independent substantive according to the basic meaning that had never been lost in the adverbial and construct expressions. With this consideration, 1:10 may be rendered, "it has already belonged to distant times that have been before us", and 3:11, "also, the distant time he has put into their heart". The latter is indeed a contrast to *ʿēth* ("everything he has made beautiful on its occasion"),

---

[1]) *Op. cit.*, pp. 117-134.
[2]) *Ewigkeit im Alten Testament*, Berlin: 1947, pp. 26-30.
[3]) "Das Wort ʿōlām im Alten Testament", *ZAW* 64 (NF 23, 1952), pp. 199-247.
[4]) *Ibid.*, *ZAW* 65 (NF 24, 1953), pp. 15-19, 24-28, 32-34.
[5]) *Op. cit.*, p. 56.

in the sense of what is perceivable but not attainable by man in contrast to what belongs to the range of his immediate experience (see p. 126). The construct expressions provide analogies that indicate not simply the furthest removed distance thinkable,[1]) but rather an absolute quality that can best be rendered "permanence"; thus: "permanent covenant" (Gen 9:16), "permanent possession" (48:4), "permanent slave" (Dt 15:17), "his permanent house" (Ecc 12:5). The only reason to withhold this concept of permanence from Biblical Hebrew is the attempt to establish a unified picture of a certain word as if it could be restricted to a single concept.

C. THE PROCEDURE OF THE STUDY

The foregoing review of the problem of time in OT study reveals, on the one hand, the wide differences in the many attempts at clarification and, on the other hand, many weaknesses in these attempts. The need for a sound exegetical study of the material has been pointed out in Part A. Yet, the warning voiced by James Barr (see p. 15) calls for caution, for the question is raised whether this is at all possible.

However, Barr himself offers encouragement by having pointed out poor linguistic methods and inconsistencies in earlier investigations. He has been chided by Sekine for cutting through the positive connection between thought and language,[2]) and by Cullmann for implying that every use of lexicography be dispensed with in Biblical theology.[3]) However, Barr has only tried to confront theology with principles of method that have long been accepted by philologists. He therefore attacks the use of etymology for semantics, the confusing of words with concepts, the corresponding of grammatical and thought forms, and the failure to recognize the sentence as the "real bearer of the theological statement". He thus exposes the errors in method made by Boman in his distinction between Hebrew and Greek thought based on the characteristics of the verb system and by various contributors to TWNT in identifying words with theological concepts.[4]) It is therefore hoped that an avoidance of these pitfalls may indeed lead to positive results.

---

[1]) So Jenni, *op. cit.*, *ZAW* 64, p. 229.
[2]) *Op. cit.*, p. 74.
[3]) *Op. cit.*, p. 27.
[4]) *The Semantics of Biblical Language*, pp. 43, 51-80, 107, 206-265.

With this in view, this study of a certain word is begun in the realization that it alone does not represent an entire concept. In fact, it may represent a variety of meanings, uses and even aspects of various concepts. Its meaning is to be derived from its contextual use alone and not at all from its etymology. A consideration of the etymology will not, therefore, be presented at the outset, but only at the end of the study in the interest of the history of the word itself (Excurse 2). Because the purpose of the investigation is not simply a word study but a clarification of the concept of time, other temporal words are to be taken into consideration extensively in comparison and contrast to each other. Yet, *ʿēth* provides a good foundation for the study of the general concept, for it is a frequently employed temporal word that may usually be translated "time".

Therefore, the primary task of this investigation is to provide a clarification for the use of *ʿēth* in the OT. In constant comparison with other temporal expressions, this study may at least offer some considerations toward understanding the OT concept of time. To enable a practical grasp of the 297 instances of *ʿēth*, it is necessary to treat them systematically according to fundamental differences in usage. This basic part of the study is therefore primarily exegetical in nature, treating the cases individually according to their function in the context (Chs. II-IV). In order to take the wider environment of the OT into consideration, the investigation is extended to the usage in other extant Hebrew texts of the OT period or shortly thereafter, as well as to the LXX as its first translation that was of great significance for the NT (Ch. V).

CHAPTER TWO

THE BASIC USE OF *'ETH*: A DEFINITE OCCASION IN THE NATURAL AND SOCIAL ORDERS

Many instances of *'ēth* in the earlier literature of the Old Testament are concerned with occasions that belong to a definite order of earthly life. Whether referring to situations in nature or in human society, they are connected with regular or appointed events. It is the temporal occasion for such an established event that is expressed by the word *'ēth*.

A. An Occasion in the Order of Nature

1. *Time of Day or Year*

One of the earliest instances of *'ēth* in the OT indicates the temporal occasion of evening. In the "Story of the Succession to David's Throne", *le'ēth hā'ereb* (2 Sam 11:2) gives the temporal setting for the scene of David's first experience with Bathsheba: "And it was at the time of evening, and David arose from his couch . . ." The temporal occasion for the narrated event belongs to the natural order of time; the occasion of evening is a regulated event according to a higher order. Now, *'ereb* is ordinarily used in similar fashion without *'ēth*. Its earliest instance may well be in the "Blessing of Jacob" with the form *lā'ereb* (Gen 49:27). The more usual form, *bā'ereb*, appears in 2 Sam 11:13: ". . . and he (Uriah) went forth in the evening to sleep on his couch . . ." Whereas both the longer and shorter forms indicate the regulated occasion of evening, *le'ēth hā'ereb* at the beginning of the sentence is used in anticipation of an event of special significance. One might be tempted to render "Now it was just at evening, when . . .", as if the emphasis indicated by the addition of *'ēth* to the expression would mean the exact moment of the occasion. However, evening is temporally not a moment, but a period of time. In contrast to morning with the increasing intensity of the sun's heat and to mid-day with the solar heat at its highest, evening is the third period of daylight when the heat of the day gradually recedes.[1]) The particular emphasis in the expression is

---

[1]) *Cf*. Pedersen, *op. cit.*, p. 489. Mention may also be made here of U. Cassuto's observation (*A Commentary on the Book of Genesis*, I—*From Adam to Noah, Genesis I-VI 8*, Jerusalem: 1961, pp. 29 f.) that there were two methods of reckoning the

not on the moment of the occasion but on the fact of its occurrence. This is also the case when the same form appears in Gen 8:11, followed by the exclamation *wehinnēh*, and in Gen 24:11, where the peculiarity is a significant coincidence of occasions. The other instances in Isa 17:14 and Zech 14:7, as well as the similar phrase *beʿēth tsohorāyim* in Jer 20:16, refer to unique occasions that interrupt the normal order of life, *e.g.*, in the last instance: "an alarm at the time of noon" (see below, pp. 78, 86).

It may be argued from instances in later literature that *ʿēth* may indicate an exact moment. The expression in Jos 8:29, *ʿad-ʿēth hāʿāreb*, is used in parallel to *ūkebō' hashshemesh*: "And the King of Ai he hung upon the tree until the time of evening; and at the setting of the sun Joshua commanded, and they took his corpse down from the tree." For the same kind of situation in 10:26 f., the use is reversed with *ʿad-hāʿāreb* and *leʿēth bō' hashshemesh*. This is also the case in a different setting in 2 Chr 18:34. Although the time required for the sun to set in Palestine is much more like a moment than the period of evening, the preposition *ke* never refers to exactitude of a temporal nature. It rather indicates approximation and in a temporal situation is characteristically vague; it is best rendered with "about". Thus the parallel expressions in Jos 8:29 and 10:26 f. do not refer to the moment of evening or sunset, but to the approximate time of day. The emphasis on the peculiarity of the occasion refers to the Deuteronomic provision for removing a hanged criminal's body from the hanging tree before sunset (21:23). The expressions in 2 Chr 18:34 emphasize the singular circumstance attending the death of Ahab of Israel. The same may be said for a reference to the spring of the year in 1 Chr 20:1 with *leʿēth teshūbath hashshānāh*: "at the occasion of the turn of the year", which was the season for the kings to go campaigning.

It is striking that *ʿēth* occurs in the expression of a regular time of day or year only at the crucial turning-point: at evening or sunset, which was the end of one day and the beginning of the next; at mid-day, when the sun reached its zenith before commencing its descent; and at the turn of the year. It may seem that a precise point

---

day in the OT. In civil life, the day began in the morning according to the general practice in Canaan. But the religious practice of reckoning the day's beginning in the evening came from nomadic tradition and was retained for festivals, the Sabbath, and ritual observances and laws. Thus, the provision for the removal of a hanged body in the evening (Dt 21:23), *i.e.*, before the beginning of a new day, is a religious law (see Jos 8:29).

of time is indicated in these instances. But it is actually the *conjunction of two occasions* that is stressed; it is the peculiar event where the one situation is joined to the next. In each case, *'ēth* indicates the definite occasion for a regular event in the order of nature, which may also be used for a situation of special significance.

2. *Time of Natural Event*

a. Augmentation of the Temporal Reference

A problem expression is *kā'ēth chayyāh* of Gen 18:10, 14. Commentators, translators and lexicographers have as a rule understood the phrase as referring to the time when the year renews itself, that is, the respective time in the following year or in the spring. But there is nothing that suggests "year", and the root *chyh* is used nowhere else in the OT with reference to the renewal of life for "time" in any form or for a season of year, in contrast to men or animals. It is possible to imagine that the expression may have been borrowed from mythological thought, *e.g.*, the portrayal of the revival of vegetation in the spring in the Egyptian myth of Osiris, or in the autumn in the Mesopotamian myth of Tammuz and Ishtar and in the Canaanite myth of Baal and Anat.[1] But this proposition is best rejected for lack of evidence. Rather than using this expression for referring to spring or the renewal of the year, Hebrew employs *lithshūbath hashshānāh*: "at the turn of the year", 2 Sam 11:1 (see 1 Chr 20:1, above), or the singular expression *bā' shānāh*: "(when) the year came", 2 Kgs 13:20.

Objection to the usual rendering was already raised by Ehrlich, and later by other commentators.[2] Although his identification of the moment of speaking as the *terminus a quo* is doubtful, his point is well taken that the object of temporal consequence can only be the time from conception to birth, that is, the nine months of pregnancy. His proposition should also be appropriate that the reference is to the birth at the end of the period of pregnancy. Skinner refers *chayyāh* to a woman in pregnancy by appropriating a usage from Late Hebrew, "according to the time of a pregnant woman", while Montgomery and Snaith apply it to the period of pregnancy itself.

---

[1] See E. O. James: *Myth and Reality in the Ancient Near East*, London: 1958 pp. 41, 45, 50 f., 54, 58 f.

[2] Ehrlich: *Randglossen zur hebräischen Bibel*, I, Leipzig: 1908, p. 72; John Skinner: *Genesis*, 2nd ed., *ICC*, 1, 1930, p. 301; James A. Montgomery: *The Books of Kings*, *ICC*, 11-12, 1951, p. 369; Eduard König: *Die Genesis*, Gütersloh: 1919, p. 506.

In order to clarify this expression, it will be well to compare it with *kāʿēth māchār*, which appears in early texts, *e.g.*, in the "Story of David's Ascendancy", 1 Sam 20:12. Here, a conjunction is connected to a noun with the definite article and is followed by a noun without an article (see pp. 34-40 for a thorough treatment of *ke* and its temporal use). This is clearly a case of apposition. Such would also be true in Gen 18:10, 14, if *chayyāh* may be a noun for "life". It is so used as a poetic form for the usual plural *chayyīm*, *e.g.*, Ps 78:50, and sometimes as a parallel to *nephesh*, *e.g.*, Job 33:18. It may also appear in this sense in prose, as in Ezek 7:13 (*bis*). But the most relevant expression is *chayyath yādēk* in Isa 57:10: "you found the life of your hand (= your life-strength)". The formation of the noun is the same as *chawwāh*, "destruction" (Job 6:2), from *chwh*, "fall" (37:6).[1])

It is often the case in Hebrew that a static verb may carry an active connotation.[2]) For instance, *hyh* may sometimes mean "to become", Gen 12:10; 2 Kgs 2:21 (*cf.* the Niphal forms, as in Jdg 19:30; 1 Kgs 1:27—"occur", or "bring to pass"). Thus it may analogically be possible that *chayyāh* does not simply mean "life" but rather "coming to life". This sense would also fit very well into the text in Isa 57:10, where the renewal of vitality is meant: "Through the greatness of your way you became tired; you did not say, 'I give up!' You found (= received) the coming-to-life (= revival) of your strength; therefore you were not weak." Thus, in further analogy to *kāʿēth māchār*, "as at this time—tomorrow" (see p. 35),[3]) Gen 18:10 may be given: "I will surely return to you as on this occasion—(the) coming-to-life, and behold, your wife Sarah shall have a son!" It is therefore unnecessary to change the reading from an apposition to a genitive construction with *keʿēth*, as suggested by Ehrlich and Skinner.[4]) But, as Ehrlich further explained, the expression refers to the particular occasion of birth at the end of the natural period of pregnancy, that is, to the "coming-to-life".

---

[1]) *Cf.* G. Bergsträsser: *Wilhelm Gesenius' hebräische Grammatik*, I, 29th ed., Leipzig: 1918, § 24b.

[2]) See Carl Heinz Ratschow: *Werden und Wirken*, BZAW 70, Berlin: 1941, pp. 7-9; Thorleif Boman, *op. cit.*, pp. 18-37.

[3]) Eduard König (*Historisch-comparative Syntax der hebräischen Sprache*, Leipzig: 1897, § 387e), with respect to *kāʿēth chayyāh*, refers to § 299a concerning the demonstrative article of connection for temporal expressions, as, *e.g.*, *hayyōm* and *happaʿam*.

[4]) Skinner, *op. cit.*, and Ehrlich, *op. cit. Cf.* König (*Syntax*, § 387e), who renders, "sowie die(se) Zeit wieder auflebt", treating *chyh* as a verb and indicating the situation. Pedersen (*op. cit.*, p. 488) renders it the same way as König, but understands "time" as a substantial entity, the peculiar qualities of the time (see below, p. 4).

A further difficulty has been the appearance of *lammōʿēd* in Gen 18:14. Having the demonstrative article, it need cause no trouble in itself as a parallel to underline what is emphasized by *ʿēth*. But *kāʿēth chayyāh* occurs again only in 2 Kgs 4:16 f., where Elisha promised the Shunammite woman that she would bear a son. The unique expression was evidently applied in this case through the influence of the transmission of the promise to Abraham and Sarah. But in both instances in 4:16 f., the enlarged phrase *lammōʿēd hazzeh* is placed directly before *kāʿēth chayyāh*, so that it is obviously not merely a parallel but also a clarification for an expression that had since dropped out of normal speech: "At this appointed time, as on this occasion—the coming-to-life, you shall embrace a son!"

Other instances of *ʿēth* as an augmentation of the temporal reference for a natural event occur in texts generally dated in the Exile or later. The only exception is *beʿēth yachēm hatstsōʾn* in Gen 31:10: "And it was at the occasion of the breeding of the flock, and I lifted up my eyes and I saw in the dream..." [1]) Emphasis is placed here upon the peculiarity of the experience by augmenting the temporal reference to a regular natural occurrence. The same is the case in reference to the proper time of menstruation (Lev 15:25), the situation of old age (1 Kgs 11:4; 15:23; Ps 71:9), the regular season of harvest (Jer 50:16), and the normal time for the spring rain (Zech 10:1).

That *ʿēth* in these cases is an addition can clearly be seen by a comparison with similar expressions where it is lacking. Earlier expressions for the temporal occasion of harvest appear as *baqqātsīr*, Ex 34:21, *bīmē kātzīr*, Gen 30:14; Jdg 15:1; 2 Sam 21:9, or *laqqātsīr*, Am 4:7. The prepositions express the temporal situation—"during, in, at"— and *yāmīm* refers to the temporal period of harvest. The probably later form *beyōm kātsīr* in Prov 25:13 seems to be comparable to *beʿēth kātsīr*. But *yōm* here implies nothing further than the temporal aspect and, like *yāmīm*, indicates therefore the season of harvest as a period of time. In contrast, Jer 50:16 refers to the time of harvest to indicate the untimely fall of Babylon, for its destruction is to come as if at the agriculturally crucial times of sowing and reaping. Thus the addition of *ʿēth* indicates not simply the temporality of the natural

---

[1]) This is assigned to the source "E" by Heinrich Holzinger (*Genesis, KHCAT*, 1, Freiburg i. B.: 1898, p. xxvi), Skinner (*op. cit.*, p. 395) and Cuthbert A. Simpson ("The Book of Genesis", "Exegesis", *IB*, I, 1952, p. 710), but to "J" by Otto Procksch (*Die Genesis, KAT*, I, 3rd ed., Leipzig: 1924, p. 185).

season, but also its peculiarity as an occurrence at a regularly set time and therefore vulnerable to a planned attack.

In distinction to the relatively early expression *lizqunāyw* in Gen 21:2, 7, there is no comparable expression to *leʿēth ziqnāthō* (1 Kgs 11:4; 15:23). Since both phrases indicate merely the situation of old age as such, and since *ziqnāh* appears in the later poetry of Ps 71:9 and, in the form *ʿad-ziqnāh*, in Isa 46:4 and Ps 71:18 only together with a parallel expression, it seems that *ziqnāh* was an archaic word for later writers so that it was always modified or supported by a further expression when reference was made to the temporal aspect. Thus *ʿēth* in this respect would carry the connotation of a natural, normal occasion.

The reference to menstruation has other forms of temporal expression in the "Code of Ceremonial Purity": *kīmē niddāthāhh*, Lev 12:2; 15:25b, *keniddāthāhh*, 12:5, and *beniddāthāhh*, 15:19, 20, 33. All of these instances refer to nothing more than the duration of the menstruation, but *belōʾ ʿeth-niddāthāhh* (Lev 15:25) is used as the particularly normal occasion for menstruation in distinction to the event of an issue of blood at an abnormal time.

While there is no other temporal use of *malqōsh* to compare with Zech 10:1, nor of *mātār* and *yōreh*, the expression *beyōm haggeshem* occurs in Ezek 1:28. It may be parenthetically noted that the only occurrences of *yōreh* appear in parallel with *malqōsh* and in connection with *beʿittō* (Dt 11:14; Jer 5:24, see p. 27), and that a predicate use of *ʿēth* with *geshem* appears in the late text Ezra 10:13 (see pp. 4, 27). Whereas the expression with *yōm* in Ezek 1:28 refers merely to the appearance of the rainbow on a rainy day, the use of *ʿēth* in Zech 10:1 emphasizes the occasion as a natural event of regulated occurrence: "Ask from Yahweh rain in the season of the spring rain" (*cf.* the instances of *beʿittō*, below).

b. Direct Reference to the Occasion

Instead of augmenting the temporal reference for the purpose of drawing attention to the peculiarity of the occasion, *ʿēth* may also indicate the occasion itself. In Hos 2:11, *beʿittō* signifies the normal temporal occasion for the ripening of grain: "I well take (back) my grain in its season (= on its occasion)." The expression *bemōʿadō* follows: ". . . and my wine at its appointed time" (see p. 28). This parallel indicates emphasis upon the established character of the natural order as it is upheld—or, as in this case, broken—by the provision of God (*cf.* the parallels in Gen 18:14, p. 21). This same usage later appears repeatedly with respect to rain (Lev 26:4; Dt 11:14; 28:12; Jer 5:24; Ezek 34:26) in divine promises of natural blessings, as well as in reference to God's regulation of the appearance of day and night (Jer 33:20) and of the star constellations (*mazzārōth*, Job 38:32), to the bearing of fruit (Ps 1:3), and to the divine provision of food for all creatures (Ps 104:27; 145:15). Similar use is made concerning the arrival of migratory birds (in parallel with *mōʿadeyhā*, Jer 8:7, see below) and the giving birth of mountain goats and hinds (Job 39:1, 2). [1]

The same sense appears in a predicate construction in Hos 13:13, where the noun is used in place of a temporal conjunction: *kī-ʿēth* [2]) *lōʾ-yāʿamōd*: "The pangs of childbirth come for him; he is not a wise son: when it is time, he does not present himself at the breach of children." Two predicate constructions also occur in Ezek 16:8 to signify the normal occasion of human maturity, *wehinnēh ʿittēk ʿēth dodīym*: "and behold, it was your time, the occasion of loving".

The phrase in Ezra 10:13 has been used by Pedersen to identify time with substance (see above, p. 4). However, it should rather be rendered "the season is that of rain", which indicates only a close relationship between the aspects of time and event. This is not even peculiar to the Hebrew language, for usage in European languages often refers to events according to their "substance", as "good time", "Feierabend", *etc.*

Similar application finds expression in reference to the season of harvest in general (Jer 51:33b) [3]) and of the harvest of grain and wine in particular (Ps 4:8), and to the occasion of the singing of birds in the spring (Cant 2:12). These instances reflect the idea that the normal events of nature are definitely established in relation to the temporal occasion of their occurrence.

---

[1]) The omission of *ʿēth* from 39:1 as an anticipated gloss from v. 2 by Paul Volz (*Weisheit, SAT*, 3:2, Göttingen: 1911, p. 80) and George Buchanan Gray (ed., Samuel Rolles Driver: *The Book of Job, ICC*, 15, 1921, p. 314) is unnecessary, considering the other uses of this sense in poetry and the very frequent practice of poetic repetition; *cf.* Georg Fohrer: *Das Buch Hiob, KAT*, 16, Gütersloh: 1963, p. 511.

[2]) Karl Marti (*Das Dodekapropheton, KHCAT*, 13, Tübingen: 1904, p. 99), Ernst Sellin (*Das Zwölfprophetenbuch, KAT*, 12, Leipzig: 1922, p. 103), and Theodore H. Robinson (with Friedrich Horst: *Die Zwölf Kleinen Propheten, HAT*, I:14, 1938, p. 50) have emended the text to *kāʿēth*.

[3]) Wilhelm Rudolph (*Jeremia*, 2nd ed., *HAT*, I: 12, 1958, p. 287) deletes *ʿēth* with the versions. But the MT makes good sense as it is, both literally as the normal season of harvest and figuratively as the divinely caused occasion for the downfall of Babylon.

The only word that suggests similar application is *mōʿēd*, as already mentioned above (Hos 2:11; Jer 8:7). These instances are in texts of the Late Monarchy, whereas the earlier appearances of *mōʿēd* refer to appointed occasions for activities or feasts determined by man or God: Gen 18:14; Ex 23:15; 34:18; Jdg 20:38; 1 Sam 9:24; 13:11; 2 Sam 20:5. The emphasis is actually placed upon the character of a particular occasion as a definite appointment. For instance, the instance in Jer 8:7 should simply be rendered: "Even the heron in the heavens knows her appointments." That temporality and regularity are implied in the case in Hos 2:11 is a result of the preceding *ʿēth*. Thus the two words supplement each other in parallel, *ʿēth* stressing the aspect of regular temporality and *mōʿēd* the aspect of established appointment.

Whether augmenting the temporal reference to a natural occasion or directly referring to the occasion itself, *ʿēth* emphasizes its qualitative significance as a normal, regular cocurrence.

B. An Occasion in the Order of Social Life

1. *An Appropriate Activity*

Occasions for appropriate activity according to the social order of human life also provide cause to employ *ʿēth* in the temporal reference. The earliest instance appears in the "Story of the Succession to David's Throne" in 2 Sam 11:1, *wahyī lithshūbath hashshānāh leʿēth tsēʾth hammelāʾkīm*. This "occasion of the going forth of the kings" in their military campaigns came in the spring ("at the turn of the year") after the rains.[1] This use of *ʿēth*, which is repeated in 1 Chr 20:1 (see p. 23), refers to an activity that was performed according to custom at a certain time of year. The same usage appears in respect to the customary time of day for the women to draw their water (Gen 24:11) and for the flocks to be gathered (Gen 29:7). In the last case, *ʿēth* stands as the nominative predicate for the appropriate occasion itself: "It is not the occasion of gathering the flock!" The same construction is used figuratively in Jer 51:33 in indicating the customary occasion for stamping out the grain.

The normal time for eating is signified by *ʿēth* in Ruth 2:14 and, with the abbreviated form *bāʿēth*, in Ecc 10:17. In the latter instance, the sense demands a translation such as: "your princes eat at the

---

[1] See George B. Caird: "The First and Second Books of Samuel", "Exegesis", *IB*, II, 1953, p. 1097.

proper occasion". This case stresses the fact that *'ēth* in such a context may imply the aspect of customary propriety. With the grammatical construction of the occasions of divine natural blessings and in the sense of Ecc 10:17, one instance refers to the appropriate situation for putting a certain expression: *wedābār be'ittō mah-tōb,* "and a word on its occasion—how good!" (Prov 15:23). The similar expression in 25:11, *dābār dābur 'al-'āphnāyw,* is probably concerned with the appropriateness of the sense and not of the time for a certain expression: "a word spoken according to its parallels".[1])

A comparable temporal expression from a relatively early text occurs in the festival provisions of the Code of the Covenant, where the Feast of Ingathering is to be held *betsē'th hashānāh be'āspekā 'eth-ma'aseykā min-hassādeh:* "at the going forth (= end) of the year, at your gathering your produce from the field" (Ex 23:16). The same use appears in Lev 23:39 and Dt 16:13. With their respective expressions for the beginning and end of the year, 2 Sam 11:1 (see above, p. 23) and Ex 23:16 seem to be good parallels for temporal reference to a customary activity. But whereas that in the latter passage is no more than an ordinary temporal reference for the activity, that in the former case is placed in a prominent position at the beginning of the opening sentence of a story. Here, the addition of *'ēth* serves to add emphasis to the temporal reference as a form of speech that introduces a story by establishing the temporal setting. Other temporal references to the regular occasion for eating do occur with *'ēth,* namely in Ps 104:27 and 145:15 (see above, p. 27), where the reference is to divine provision, although apparently on the occasion of the need of all creatures.

2. *An Appointed Situation*

Situations in the human social order of life that are determined not merely by the rule of custom but by definite appointment or regulation may also be designated by *'ēth.* The earliest instance is concerned with the appointed occasion for the giving of Saul's daughter Merab in marriage to David: *be'ēth tēth 'eth-mērab,* 1 Sam 18:19. In the same context, the indication that the appointed occasion for betrothal had

---

[1]) Light may be shed on the case by Sira 50:27—*mwsr shkl wmwshl 'wphnym.* The original is *mōshel,* "image", which in rhetoric would mean "simile". As the Hebrew simile is built of parallel lines, *'wphnym* could well have this special sense here: "the simile of parallels". Word parallels were found especially beautiful to the understanding Hebrew ear. Of course, it is parallelism in sense which is meant and not poetic meter.

not yet arrived is given with *welō' māle'ū hayyāmīm*: "now, the days were not full" (18:26). This expression occurs in the OT for the passage of a normal period of time: the period of pregnancy (Gen 25:24), Jacob's seven years' service for the hand of Rachel (29:21), the forty days for embalming in Egypt (50:3), the seven days for ordination to the priesthood (Lev 8:33), and the twelve months for beautifying young women in Persia (Est 2:12). The emphasis in these cases is on the normal length or the completion of the particular period, but not specifically on the aspect of an established, appointed occasion.

The established time for the daily evening offering, according to the ordinance in Ex 29:38 f., is indicated with the expression *keʿēth minchath-ʿāreb*, Dan 9:21. This *terminus technicus* of the post-exilic sacrificial terminology appears ordinarily in a temporal sense without *ʿēth*, as *ʿad-leminchath hāʿāreb* in Ezra 9:4 and *ūbeminchath hāʿereb* in 9:5. The enlargement in Dan 9:21 will evidently stress the peculiarity of the situation as the occasion when the "man" Gabriel came to Daniel to announce the seventy weeks of years until the advent of everlasting righteousness (9:24).

Similar uses of *yōm* indicate that it may also refer to a temporal occasion of particular quality, but without necessarily implying the aspect of established appointment. For instance, reference is made to the occasion of a pilgrimage festival to Yahweh (*ūleyōm chag yhwh*) in Hos 9:5b as the occasion for Israel's going on a pilgrimage to Assyria (9:6).[1] That *yōm* does not include the aspect of appointment becomes obvious through the parallel expression *leyōm mōʿēd* in 9:5a, where *mōʿēd* is used for the express purpose of bringing this aspect to attention. Likewise, when "the day of our king" in 7:5 refers to the occasion of the king's birthday or coronation as the occasion for a drunken festival,[2] emphasis is on the aspect of temporal relationship and not on that of appointment. The expression *beyōm*

---

[1] *Cf.* T. H. Robinson, *op. cit.*, p. 34. Artur Weiser (*Das Buch der zwölf Kleinen Propheten*, I, 4th ed., *ATD*, 24, 1953, p. 72) wrongly applies the singular form of *chag* to the so-called annual Yahweh-Festival of the Covenant. *chag* is used strictly for a pilgrimage festival (naturally, to the honor of Yahweh).

[2] *Cf.* William Rainey Harper: *Amos and Hosea, ICC*, 28, 1905, p. 295. The textual changes by T. H. Robinson (*op. cit.*, p. 28) and Weiser (*op. cit.*, p. 61) prove to be unnecessary when it is considered that the Hifil of *chlh* may carry an intransitive connotation ("become weak"; see Bergsträsser, *op. cit.*, II, 1929, § 19d), and that *yōm* may be used poetically as a temporal reference ("on the day of") without a preposition (see Ezek 28:18).

zebach yhwh is used figuratively in Zeph 1:8 in reference to the occasion of Yahweh's general punishment *(yōm yhwh*, 1:7; see p. 94). The frequent uses of *yōm* in this context all emphasize the content of the event (see esp. 1:14-16), while the aspect of definite appointment is stressed by other means, as with *qārōb* in 1:7, 14.

Appointed occasions for eating and drinking once each day are designated in Ezk 4:10 f. by *mēʿēth ʿad-ʿēth* (*i.e.*, "between the definite time of one day and that of the next"), and for the week's service of the gate keepers in 1 Chr 9:25 by *mēʿēth ʾel-ʿēth*. The former case refers to an ordinance by God and not by man, but the regulated mealtimes characterize it as a conditioned activity of the social sphere of life. The plural form is employed by the Chronicler for appointed occasions (*leʿittīm mezummānīm*) for the summoning of the Jews involved in mixed marriages (Ezra 10:14), and for the regular provision of wood for the temple (Neh 10:35; 13:31; *cf.* p. 77). A similar expression in 1 Kgs 5:7 concerns the monthly supplies for Solomon's court provided by his twelve governors (*ʾīysh chādeshō*), but without expressly indicating the appointed aspect of the time of responsibility.

Specific designation of appointment may be made by *mōʿēd* as the time appointed for Amasa to summon the men of Judah (2 Sam 20:5) and the time set for Saul to wait for word from Samuel (1 Sam 13:11). It indicates primarily the aspect of appointment and, if at all, only secondarily the temporal aspect of the situation. This is made clear not only by the local and qualitative meanings of the word for an appointed place or celebration, but also by an early occurrence in 1 Sam 20:35. Here, *lemōʿēd dāwid* ("for the appointment of David") indicates the bare fact of appointment (see above, pp. 26-28). Werner Vollborn assumes that *mōʿēd* means basically an established moment of time, which as an established time came to be used for the time of a festival and of an assembly, and then for the assembly itself or place of assembly.[1] But he fails to devote attention to the earliest occurrences of *mōʿēd*, where it is not the time of appointment that is indicated. In fact, in Jdg 20:38, which is most likely the earliest appearance of *mōʿēd*, it means an appointed *signal*. The consideration of the earliest instances shows that the probable basic meaning was purely and simply "appointment", which could be applied to an act (Jdg 20:38), a meeting (1 Sam 20:35), a special occasion (9:24), or a regular appearance (Jer 8:7), and that secondary meanings arose

---

[1] *Op. cit.*, pp. 56-63.

later according to emphasis on the temporal, local or qualitative aspects of the particular situation.[1])

The distinctive connotation of ʿēth refers not simply to the temporal aspect of a qualitative occasion as *yōm*, nor to the aspect of appointment as *mōʿēd*, but to the peculiar qualitative aspects of a specific occasion as being both temporal and appointed.

Summary

1. Most evident is the factor that permits the grouping of the mentioned instances of ʿēth together in this chapter, namely *the factor of a definite occasion as being subject to a higher order*. Reference is made to a regular time of day or year, to the normally expected occasion for a natural event, or to the customary or appointed occasion for human activity. Whether ʿēth is added to the temporal reference or designates the occasion itself, it indicates a qualitative aspect of the occasion as a definite, established occurrence.

2. Some cases may as well be assigned to another category, since a living language does not let itself be easily subjected to superimposed mechanical innovations. This would especially hold true for the category of relationship to be discussed in Chapter III. This fact of double possibility demonstrates how ʿēth may embody more than one side of the matter simultaneously. It also indicates already how greatly the application is bound to the relationship of occasions.

3. ʿēth shows indications in the early instances of references *to the relationship or to some qualitative aspect of the occasion*, e.g., in respect to the occasion of the breeding of sheep (Gen 31:10), of betrothal (1 Sam 18:19), of the campaigning of kings (2 Sam 11:1), of evening (11:2), of the ripening of grain (Hos 2:11), and of birth (13:13). This usage reflects the manner of thought that springs from the events of the everyday life of the average inhabitant of the Canaanite hills and plains in the late second Millennium before Christ. This is the usage that may be expected in the popular speech of the day, without being influenced by a particular philosophy or theology of the thinkers and believers. As popular speech, it is not only to be regarded as the earliest known usage, but also as a usage that may be expected in all periods of the spoken Hebrew whose literary testimony is the Old Testament.

---

[1]) Delling (*Das Zeitverständnis des Neuen Testaments*, p. 52) holds essentially the same opinion in identifying the original meaning as "Verabredung".

In contrast, some late cases are designations of the occasion itself, in particular the appointed occasions of Ezek 4:10 f.; 1 Chr 9:25; Ezra 10:14; Neh 10:35 and 13:31, and some are additions to chronologically temporal references, as in Jos 10:27; 1 Chr 20:1 and Dan 9:21. It apparently became possible in later practice to objectivize *ʿēth* from a means of reference to an object of consideration.

4. *ʿēth does not always refer to the temporal aspect of an occasion* and, even when it stands in the temporal reference, it often is not primarily related to the temporality *but to a certain quality or peculiarity*. This is especially borne out in comparison to the use of other expressions in similar situations. The temporality of evening or sunset may be expressed by a preposition without *ʿēth* (Jos 8:29; 2 Sam 11:13), as well as the occasion of old age (Gen 21:2), harvest (Ex 23:16; 34:21), menstruation (Lev 15:19), and the evening sacrifice (Ezra 9:5). Likewise, *yōm* may be added to the expression in place of *ʿēth* in reference to the harvest season (Gen 30:14), menstruation (Lev 12:2), the arrival of an appointed time (1 Sam 18:26), the rainy season (Ezek 1:28), and the occasion for a festival (Hos 9:5). Furthermore, *mōʿēd* may indicate an appointed temporal occasion, as in Jdg 20:38; 1 Sam 9:24; Jer 8:7 and Hos 2:11. These examples illustrate that the "temporal" prepositions refer only to the aspect of relationship which, according to the context, may be temporal; that *yōm* may refer to the temporality as well as imply that an occasion possesses some peculiar quality whose closer identification is left to the context; and that *mōʿēd* properly refers to a certain quality and only incidentally to the temporal aspect. Thus *ʿēth* emerges through contrast as an expression for the quality of a higher order and for indicating the temporal aspect of a particular occasion. Its uniqueness lies in the combination of these two aspects.

5. It appears that the proper basic direction in meaning is toward *a qualitative clarification or modification of the temporal element*. In fact, it is primarily a reference to the specific occasion itself as such. What is of primary importance is the *occasion*—the occasion with a peculiar quality or singular circumstances, *the occasion as a regular occurrence, as an established event, as a customary activity, as an appointed situation*.

CHAPTER THREE

THE USE OF ʿ*ETH* WITH AN OCCASION OF SINGULAR CHARACTER

In comparison with the occasions which are related to a higher order, ʿ*ēth* is used more frequently for occasions that do not reflect a normal, regulated aspect. They are rather characterized by the uniqueness of the time and manner of their occurrence as a singular event.

A. The Relationship of Singular Occasions

The temporal relationship of occasions to each other is commonly indicated in Hebrew by joining sentences with the simple conjunction *we, way* in the form of consecutive statements, instead of using temporal conjunctions or more definite temporal references,[1] *e.g.*, Jdg 13:10 f., "And the woman hurried and ran and told her husband, ... And Manoah rose and went after his wife, and he came to the man and said to him ...; and he said, 'I am'." Temporal relationship may be indicated more precisely in earlier texts through conjunctions, such as: *kīy* (Jdg 13:17), *'im* (6:3), *terem* (Gen 19:4); through adverbs, *e.g.*: *'āz* (Jdg 8:3), *ʿattāh* (6:13); and through prepositions, *e.g.*: *ʿad* (Num 23:24), *le* (Ex 16:1). The adverbial prepositional constructions *beʿēth*, *keʿēth* and *leʿēth* also belong to this category of temporal expressions.

1. *Comparison*

Most of the instances of ʿ*ēth* that primarily indicate the temporal relationship of occasions do this in a direct manner which may be paraphrased simply with "when". But one group, which is notably well represented in earlier passages, is concerned with the aspect of comparison in particular. This group may be easily identified by the singular construction *kāʿēth*. Although this form occurs some nineteen times, it is nearly always a troublesome object for commentators and translators, who usually emend it or simply render it as "now".

---

[1] See E. Kautzsch: *Wilhelm Gesenius' Hebräische Grammatik*, 28th ed., Leipzig: 1909, § 164a, b; Carl Brockelmann: *Hebräische Syntax*, Neukirchen: 1956, § 163c.

However, *kāʿēth* can scarcely be expected to mean "now",[1]) as if it were nothing more than a substitute for *ʿattāh*, and to alter it to *kī ʿattā* [2]) simply seems to be a means of escape from grappling with the fact of the word as it stands. The possibility for this abbreviated consonantal spelling of *ʿattāh* (Ezek 23:43; Ps 74:6) is a doubtful choice in favor of *ʿēth*, and will be discussed below (pp. 81, 83). The only use that enjoys wide agreement is the complex construction *kāʿēth māchār*, commonly translated according to the *hapax legomenon* in a late text (*māchār kāʿēth hazzoʾth*, Jos 11:6) as "tomorrow at this time". This appears to be a weak attempt at solution for lack of a better expression.

A consideration of this disputed form must begin with a clarification of the so-called preposition *ke*, which occurs in only four other instances with *ʿēth* in another form (1 Sam 4:20; Ezek 16:57; Dan 9:21; 2 Chr 21:19; pp. 30, 38, 51). This is properly nothing more than the common particle of comparison, and not a preposition.[3]) In the systematization of Hebrew, it is better classified as a conjunction or adverb in the manner of "as" in English, or "wie" in German, *etc.*[4]) Properly understood, it compares one sentence thought to another, although the second member is ordinarily reduced to a phrase or word, *e.g.*: "He came to us as a messenger" for "He came to us as a messenger comes", which expresses the manner of the

---

[1]) So Ludwig Koehler (with Walter Baumgartner: *Lexicon in Veteris Testamenti Libros*, Leiden: 1958) and Frants Buhl (*Wilhelm Gesenius' Hebräisches und aramäisches Handwörterbuch über das Alte Testament*, 17th ed., Leipzig: 1915) and Ernst Bertheau (*Das Buch der Richter und Ruth, KEHAT*, 6, 2nd ed., Leipzig: 1883, p. 218) to Jdg 13:23. To the contrary, see Karl Budde (*Das Buch der Richter, KHCAT*, 7, Freiburg i.B.: 1897, p. 97) to Jdg 13:23.

[2]) So George Buchanan Gray (*Numbers, ICC*, 4, 1912, p. 356) to Num 23:23; Budde (*op. cit.*, pp. 97, 142) and Hugo Gressmann (*Die Anfänge Israels, SAT*, 1:2, Göttingen: 1914, pp. 238, 268) to Jdg 13:23; 21:22; Vincenz Zapletal (*Das Buch der Richter, EHAT*, 7:1, Münster: 1923, p. 304) to 21:22; Harry Torczyner (ed.: *The Lachish Letters (Lachish* I), London: 1938, p. 107) to Isa 8:23.

[3]) Against Kautzsch (*op. cit.*, § 102, but *cf.* § 118s), Eduard König (*Hebräisches und aramäisches Wörterbuch zum Alten Testament*, 7th ed., Leipzig: 1936, p. 109; *Historisch-kritisches Lehrgebäude der hebräischen Sprache*, II, Leipzig: 1895, pp. 280-284), and Brockelmann (*op. cit.*, § 109). Buhl (*op. cit.*, p. 329) calls it a "Vergleichungswort". *Cf.* Koehler, *op. cit.*, pp. 417 f.

[4]) So Hans Bauer and Pontus Leander: *Historische Grammatik der hebräischen Sprache des Alten Testaments*, I, Tübingen: 1922, § 82. *Cf. The Oxford English Dictionary*, I, Oxford: 1933, pp. 477 f.; Jacob and Wilhelm Grimm: *Deutsches Wörterbuch*, Leipzig, I, 1854, pp. 247-250, 254, 257; XIV, 1960, pp. 1448, 1470, 1474, 1491.

action, as if to say: "His manner of coming was as the coming of a messenger." Thus in Hebrew, *weʾohabāyw ketsēʾth hashshemesh bigeburāthō* (Jdg 5:31) may be rendered: ". . . and may his friends be as is the rising of the sun in its strength."

When used in a temporal sense, *ke* indicates the approximation of a temporal reference,[1]) which is really nothing else than applying the comparative function to the category of time rather than of manner. Thus, Jdg 18:10, literally "as (at the time of) your arriving (*keboʾakem*), you will come to an unsuspecting people", may be given "about (the time of) your arriving", or even "when you arrive". The temporal aspect does not actually reside in the particle *ke* itself, but in an assimilated temporal preposition, according to Eduard König's shrewd observation.[2]) This assimilated preposition, contrary to the apparent temporal use of *ke*, is most likely *be*, which appears frequently in the earliest texts in this sense (*e.g.*, Jdg 5:4). A few examples where the assimilation was not accomplished are still extant, although only with adverbs: *kebāriʾshonāh* (Jdg 20:32) and *kebattechillāh* (Isa 1:26). Therefore, *ke* is in every case to be regarded as a particle of comparison ("as") or of temporal approximation ("about").

One peculiar aspect of the construction *kāʿēth* is the employment of the *qamets*. This could be a retention of the original vowel which is normally reduced to a *shewa*.[3]) However, considering the expression as a temporal reference, the *qamets* is more likely the demonstrative article,[4]) as with *hayyōm* (1 Sam 4:3), *hallayelāh* (19:11), *hashshānāh* (2 Kgs 19:29), and *happaʿam* (Jdg 15:3). By comparison, *kāʿēth* may then be literally rendered "as at this time". C. F. Keil and August Dillmann render it "according to the time" in Num 23:23,[5]) but their application of it for "the right time" hardly fits into the context. It is the act of God upon Israel that occurs at the right time, and not necessarily the reaction to it.

---

[1]) Brockelmann, *op. cit.*, § 109b.

[2]) *Syntax*, § 319b ff.; see Koehler, *op. cit.*, p. 417; against Kautzsch, *op. cit.*, § 118s, n. 4. *Cf.* also the form in a spatial category: *kebachatsiy maʿanāh*, "about half a furrough", 1 Sam 14:14. For *ke* with the prep. *be*, see Jdg 20:32; 1 Kgs 13:6; Isa 1:26 *bis*; Jer 33:7, 11.

[3]) See Bauer and Leander, *op. cit.*, §§ 81f-y, 82p-v; Kautzsch, *op. cit.*, § 102d-i.

[4]) See König, *Syntax*, § 299a; Brockelmann, *op. cit.*, § 21a; see Procksch, *op. cit.*, p. 120.

[5]) C. F. Keil: *Leviticus, Numeri, Deuteronomium*, 2nd ed., BCAT, I:2, 1870, p. 332; August Dillmann: *Die Bücher Numeri, Deuteronomium und Josua*, 2nd ed., KEHAT, 13, 1886, p. 154.

The foregoing chapter has shown that *'ēth* properly refers to an occasion as such rather than to a "time". Very much in this sense, Keil has paraphrased the occurrence in Jdg 21:22 with "in this case".[1]) Among the instances discussed in Ch. II, many could also be classified in the category of the relationship of occasions, *e.g.*, it was at the occasion of the breeding of sheep that Jacob received a divine direction in a dream (Gen 31:10, p. 25).

When the instances of *kā'ēth* without further modification are examined, it is likewise evident that the relationship of occasions is meant, and not a reference of purely temporal character. Balaam's oracle compares the occasion of Israel's exodus from Egypt with the present situation of Balak (Num 23:23); Manoah's wife contrasts the announcements of the angel of Yahweh with the theoretical possibility of Yahweh causing their death (Jdg 13:23); it is pointed out to the men of Shiloh that they would have encountered guilt if they themselves had given their daughters to the Benjaminites (21:22); and Isaiah contrasts the humiliation of Galilee by Tiglath-pileser with the occasion of its impending glorification (8:23). All of these cases retain the comparative aspect of *ke*. The comparison is made between the present situation and either a theoretical occasion in a subjunctive sense ("as on this occasion", Jdg 13:23, 21:22), or a past historical occasion ("as on that occasion", Num 23:23; Isa 8:23; see pp. 51, 56).

Since the situation in Isa 8:23 is a contrast instead of a comparison, the *we* introducing the second member of the sentence carries the connotation of "but", so that this may be combined in translation with *kā'ēth* and rendered: "Whereas on that occasion the former humiliated the land of Zebulon and the land of Naphtali, the latter shall glorify the Way of the Sea...." The masculine adjectives *hāri'shōn* and *ha'acharōn* are often translated as modifying *'ēth*, which, however, is hardly possible immediately following a feminine noun.[2]) They therefore evidently refer to certain persons or events. This is

---

[1]) *Josua, Richter und Ruth*, 2nd ed., *BCAT*, II:1, 1874, p. 376.

[2]) See the thorough, convincing argument by Torczyner (*op. cit.*, pp. 106 f.; the further exception of Ezra 10:14 is identified as a copyist's error (apparently also Neh 10:35) in view of *be'ittīym mezummānōth* in Neh 13:31; see p. 31). This is against most commentators, who translate, "as the former time...", so the latter (time)...", *e.g.*: Heinrich Ewald: *Die Propheten des Alten Bundes*, I, Stuttgart: 1840, p. 225; Karl Marti: *Das Buch Jesaja*, *KHCAT*, 10, Tübingen: 1900, p. 91; George Buchanan Gray: *The Book of Isaiah 1-39*, *ICC*, 21, 1912, p. 161; Otto Kaiser: *Das Buch Jesaja, 1-12*, 2nd ed., *ATD*, 17, Göttingen: 1963, p. 97.

appropriate for the meaning of ʿēth as a definite occasion, and not as a general reference to the period of the past.[1]) One further occurrence of kāʿēth without modification appears in Job 39:18, but indicates a simple temporal relationship and not a comparison (see p. 41).

The unique expression kemō ʿēth occurs in Ezek 16:57, where the aspect of the comparison of occasions is very obvious. A direct comparison is made between the occasions of the revealing of Jerusalem's wickedness and the disgrace of the Syrians. In fact, the full emphasis is placed on the aspect of objective comparison so that ʿēth in this case does not refer to the temporal aspect at all. Most commentators have emended the text rather freely. The basic difficulty is removed by simply connecting verses 56 and 57 to make one sentence, so that a predicate need not be conjured up for v. 57.[2]) ʿēth usually becomes ʿattā,[3]) and kemō is lengthened to kāmōhā with the explanation that it does not appear without a suffix in prose.[4]) However, it does occur in at least two other instances in prose, namely Gen 19:15, ūkemō hashshachar ʿālāh ("and as the dawn rose"), and Neh 9:11, kemō ʾeben ("as a stone"). This clears the way for a rejection of the conjectures and a literal reading of Ezek 16:56 f.: "Was not Sodom your sister a byword in your mouth in the day of your pride, before your wickedness was revealed as on the occasion of the disgrace of the daughters of Syria and of all her neighbors, of the daughters of the Philistines—those round about who despise you?"

A further related instance occurs in the early "Story of the Ark of the Covenant" in 1 Sam 4:20, where the wife of Phineas was about to die after giving birth to Ichabod: ūkeʿēth mūthāhh. Because she did not die right away at the moment under consideration but remained alive long enough to receive the word that she had borne a son and to give him a name, it is evident that the comparative particle ke is used for temporal approximation: "And it was about the occasion of her dying, and the attending women said to her, 'Fear not, for you have borne a son!'"

---

[1]) So Wilhelm Gesenius: *Der Prophet Jesaja*, I, Leipzig: 1821, p. 349; Kaiser, *op. cit.*

[2]) See, *e.g.*, Ewald, *op. cit.*, II, 1841, p. 273; Georg Fohrer: *Ezechiel, HAT*, I:13, 1955, p. 91; Herbert G. May: "The Book of Ezekiel", "Exegesis", *IB*, VI, 1956, p. 150; Walter Zimmerli: *Ezechiel, BKAT*, 13, 1956-1961, p. 341.

[3]) So BH, Ewald, *op. cit.*, Fohrer, *op. cit.*, May, *op. cit.*, Zimmerli, *op. cit.*

[4]) So BH, Fohrer, *op. cit.*, May, *op. cit.* To the contrary, see Brockelmann, *op. cit.*, § 163b; *cf.* also § 109e.

Turning now to the phrase *kā'ēth māchār* (*cf.* above, pp. 24 f., 34 f.), the fuller form in Jos 11:6 hardly seems to be a natural parallel. Instead, this late form is evidently not derived from the spoken language, but is a post-exilic clarification of an expression from the time of the early monarchy which had since fallen into disuse and was no longer clearly understood. The original form does occur in exilic texts (Ex 9:18; 2 Kgs 7:1, 18), apparently as a literary retention of the earlier spoken practice. That this retention is very imaginable may be explained by the nature of the use of the formula, for it always appears in connection with an oath. Because of the solemnity of its characteristic application, it would be easily retained in memory, even when its original meaning is forgotten and when it is even altered to conform to the misunderstood interpretation in Jos 11:6 "tomorrow, about this time".

For strengthening an oath, promise or grave statement, the formula *chay yhwh* is frequently used, as in Gideon's promise that he would have spared Zebah and Zalmunna if they had spared his brothers (Jdg 8:19), Saul's oath to execute the man who had violated his curse (1 Sam 14:39), and David's emphasis to Jonathan on the gravity of the situation of his being hunted by Saul (20:3). Whether the formula is to be understood as a genitive construction in the sense of "by the life of Yahweh",[1] or as a predicated adjective in the sense of "as Yahweh lives",[2] it is basically a form of comparison that establishes the truth of the statement on the basis of the existence of Yahweh. This aspect of comparison appears in a more obvious manner in other oaths, *e.g.*, "So (*koh*) may God do to me and so (*wekoh*) may he intensify, if I taste bread or anything at all before sunset" (2 Sam 3:35). Actually, the first member of this comparison is lacking,[3] which could be imagined in the form: "As God had done to . . ., so may he do to me." But the formula *chay yhwh* in the other oaths serves as the first member of the comparison, *e.g.*: "However, (as) Yahweh lives and your soul lives (*wechēy naphshekā*; or: according to the life of Yahweh and the life of your soul), surely it is as a step between me and between death" (1 Sam 20:3). The first fact substantiates the second.

---

[1] So Pedersen, *op. cit.*, III-IV, 1940, p. 450; Brockelmann, *op. cit.*, § 170c.

[2] So Buhl, *op. cit.*, Koehler, *op. cit.*, *ad loc.*, Bauer and Leander, *op. cit.*, § 17w, and Kautzsch, *op. cit.*, § 149a.

[3] See Brockelmann, *op. cit.*

This aspect of comparison in oaths corresponds to the use of *kāʿēth*, where, as explained above, the *ke* properly retains its comparative connotation in the sense of "as on this occasion". It may thus be concluded that the formula *kāʿēth māchār*, with *māchār* as temporal accusative and apposition to *ʿēth*, is to be rendered "as on this occasion—tomorrow" or, in better keeping with the situation of an oath, "according to this situation—tomorrow". The intention is a substantiation of the fact of the intended action the next day on the basis of the fact of the present situation as if to say, "as surely as the fact of the present situation, so surely will be the fact of the situation tomorrow". This is therefore not merely a reference to the time for the promised activity, but is also an intensification of the temporal reference that serves to emphasize the reality of the intended action. An appropriate example is offered in 1 Kgs 19:2 by Jezebel's warning to Elijah: "So (*koh*) may the Gods do (to me)[1]) and so (*wekoh*) may they intensify: surely, according to this situation—tomorrow (*kiy-kāʿēth māchār*), I will make your soul as the soul of one of them!" This formula also occurs in the same sense in the early passages 1 Sam 9:16; 20:12; [2]) 1 Kgs 20:6 and 2 Kgs 10:6. The same interpretation may be applied to the formula *kāʿēth chayyāh* (see pp. 23-25).

A similar expression that is also used in an emphatic statement is *beyōm māchār* in Gen 30:33, "on the day of tomorrow". However, it is not used comparatively but rather figuratively for "in the future". This is in sharp contrast to the use of *ʿēth*, to indicate a definite occasion.

2. *Direct Relationship*

The use of *ʿēth* in a prepositional construction is ordinarily an indication that it is employed for the purpose of relating two occasions to each other. Although many of these instances carry another emphasis besides, as the indication of an ordered, historical or interruptive event, some cases have no other emphases than that of simple relationship.

---

[1]) Probably insert *līy* with 24 MSS and the versions.

[2]) Contrary to BH and Samuel Rolles Driver (*The Books of Samuel*, 2nd ed., Oxford: 1913, pp. 161, 164), who omit *hashshelishīyth* as a gloss to *kāʿēth māchār*, it may well be rendered according to the context: "according to this situation—the day after tomorrow". The same applies to *ʿad hāʿereb hashshelishīyth* in 20:5—"until the third evening".

The earliest instances of this group occurs in the novelette of Judah's affair with Tamar in Gen 38:27, when she was giving birth: "And it was at the occasion of her giving birth (be'ēth lidtāhh), and behold, twins were in her womb!" A similar use is employed by the Chronicler for emphasizing a dependent relationship between simultaneously occurring events, as in 2 Chr 29:27—"and on the occasion (when) the burnt offering began (ūbe'ēth hēchēl hā'ōlām), the song of Yahweh began . . ." (so also 20:22). The grammatical construction is that of a subordinate clause where the relative pronoun is replaced by the temporal reference, or where a connecting we is omitted, in contrast to Gen 38:27, above.[1]) This use of be'ēth with a finite verb is of later grammatical usage. Taking the place of 'asher as a temporal conjunction, it may simply be paraphrased "when".

The same applies to kā'ēth in Job 39:18, which obviously does not refer to a comparison of situations but to a relationship as is also the case with ke'ēth in Dan 9:21 (p. 30). Various conjectures are made to Job 39:18, e.g., Bernhard Duhm and S. R. Driver emend the reading to ke'ēth.[2]) Yet, the verse may be read according to the MT with good sense: "On the occasion (when) it beats on high (=into the air), it laughs at the horse and at its rider." [3]) The reference is to the relationship of the ostrich's sudden burst into flight and of the resultant embarrassment of its out-distanced pursuer. Thus 'ēth does not indicate "at the very moment in which", as Georg Fohrer suggests.[4]) The use of the qamets in this case is not the article, but is due to the fact that, contrary to the usual secondary accentuation of 'ēth when it modifies a verb (cf. Dt 32:35), kā'ēth receives one of the three full accents in its half of the verse.[5])

Comparable expressions of temporal relationship occur normally without 'ēth, e.g., in Gen 38:28—"and it was at her giving birth (wayhīy belidtāhh), and one put forth a hand", and in v. 29—"And

---

[1]) Cf. Wilhelm Rudolph: Chronikbücher, HAT, 1:21, 1955, p. 296, and Brockelmann, op. cit., § 176a.

[2]) Bernhard Duhm: Das Buch Hiob, KHCAT, 16, Freiburg i. B.: 1897, p. 191; Driver, Job, p. 319.

[3]) See Heinrich Ewald: Die poetischen Bücher des Alten Bundes, III—Das Buch Job, Göttingen: 1836, p. 230; Franz Delitzsch: Das Buch Iob, BCAT, IV: 2, 1864, p. 511; Gray (with Driver), Job, p. 344; Artur Weiser: Das Buch Hiob, 4th ed., ATD, 13, 1963, p. 240.

[4]) Op. cit., p. 490.

[5]) Cf. Bauer and Leander, op. cit., §§ 82v, 9e'; Buhl, op. cit., p. 329.

it was as he was drawing back (*wayhiy kemēshiyb*) his hand, and behold, his brother came out." It is not because of the use of ʿ*ēth* in v. 27 that it indicates the very moment of occurrence, for the instances in the following verses refer to such a situation to a greater degree. Neither is ʿ*ēth* employed simply to mark the occasion as one of peculiar significance, considering the accompanying *hinnēh*, for this exclamation also occurs in v. 29. Rather, it is commonly the case in Hebrew that the occurrence of simultaneous or temporally closely related events is not indicated by any special expression, but simply by the conjunction *we* or the construction of a preposition with an infinitive or participle.[1] The latter case especially implies simultaneity, for the on-going action indicated by the participle [2] is then interrupted.

In contrast, the use of ʿ*ēth* in v. 27 draws attention to the situation as a whole, uniting the temporal and objective aspects in the idea of the specific occasion filled with content. It is neither the very moment of occurrence nor the simultaneity of two events that is indicated, but purely and simply—yet with emphasis—the situation of the occasion as such, as in this case, the occasion of the birth of the twins Perez and Zerah with its attending circumstances. The introduction of a sentence with *wayhī* or *wehāyāh* already draws attention to the fact of the particular occasion with peculiar quality, as the literal translation conveys: "and it was (will be) . . .". This sense is lost in smoother translations, as "and it came to pass" or simply "when". The sense may properly be paraphrased for v. 28: "It was on the occasion of her giving birth that one put forth a hand." Although this figure of speech, which enjoys a very high frequency of application, implies a particular occasion, this fact is not thereby expressly stated, as is the case with the employment of ʿ*ēth*, which designates the occasion itself. The result of these considerations is, that the significance of ʿ*ēth* may not be limited to a specific temporal moment, as has widely been assumed,[3] but may be applied to a situation of more or less undefined duration. The distinction made is not in favor of a point of time in contrast to a period of time, but for a specific occasion of peculiar quality

---

[1] *Cf.* Brockelmann, *op. cit.*, §§ 163c, 135a; Kautzsch, *op. cit.*, §§ 154, 164a, 114e.

[2] See Kautzsch, *op. cit.*, § 116a.

[3] See esp. Delling, "χαιρός", pp. 459 f., and *Das Zeitverständnis des Neuen Testaments*, p. 49; Vollborn, *op. cit.*, pp. 6 ff.; Knight, *op. cit.*, pp. 201 ff.; Ebeling, *op. cit.*, pp. 346 ff. (see below, pp. 5, 7, 11, 16).

and content in contrast to an occasion whose content is defined only according to a certain aspect or not at all.

This distinction is further illustrated by other indications of the relationship of occasions in using prepositions and conjunctions (see p. 29), *e.g.*: "when (*kīy*) I do them evil" (Jdg 15:3); "when (*ka'asher*) there is distress for you" (11:7); "and as (*ūkemō*) the dawn rose" (Gen 19:15); "and it was as Gideon was hearing (*wayhī kishmoa' gide'ōn*) the interpretation of the dream" (Jdg 7:15); "and it was at his arriving" (*wayhī bebō'ō*) (3:27); "upon his knowing (*leda'tō*) to reject the evil" (Isa 7:15). Only the relationship of the occasions is basically indicated without any particular emphasis upon the situation as an occasion of peculiar content. In this sense, each case could just as well be rendered as a temporal clause with "when".

One late instance of '*ēth* refers to a specific occasion of indefinite circumstances, insofar as it was an event that was repeated whenever the particular situation arose: "And it was on an occasion (when) (*wayhī be'ēth*) he had the chest brought to the king's office by the Levites . . ., and the king's secretary would come . . ." (2 Chr 24:11). According to the context, it may be rendered "on every occasion when" or "whenever".[1]) That the emphasis made by '*ēth* in this case can hardly be construed to be placed upon an occasion of peculiar quality and content is quite obvious. This is a characteristic that appears in a few instances in late texts, and is probably due to an objectivization of the term and a consequent loss of its peculiar content. Thus it could be reduced to an artificial and redundant addition to a temporal reference (see 1 Chr 20:1; 2 Chr 18:34; 21:19, pp. 22, 51). Thus *be'ēth* is used in 2 Chr 24:11 as an ordinary temporal conjunction, in the same way as others in the same sense, *e.g.*: "and it was as often as (*wayhī middēy*) their coming forth, David was successful" (1 Sam 18:30); "and it was at the 'becoming' (*wehāyāh biheyōth*) of God's spirit unto Saul" (16:23); "and it was when (*wehāyāh kīy*) the fugitives of Ephraim would say" (Jdg 12:5). Each case may be given with "whenever".

Very similar in sense to "whenever" is the use of a group of fifteen instances of the formula *bekol-'ēth*. All of them appear in comparatively late literature, although the occurrences in Ps 10:5 and 34:2 may well come from the later monarchical period. The meaning "occasion" for '*ēth* passes admirably into these contexts: "his ways

---

[1]) *Cf.* Rudolph, *Chronikbücher*, p. 274, "so oft".

prosper on every occasion" (10:5); [1]) "I shall bless Yahweh on every
occasion" (34:2). In both cases the reference is to the repetition of the
experience or activity whenever the appropriate situation for it arises.
Thus the formula does not properly mean "always" or "at all times",
as is commonly translated (note the singular), nor "continually" or
"every hour",[2]) nor "in every single moment of time".[3]) The rendering offered here may be applied equally well to the other occurrences
in Ex 18:22, 26; Lev: 16:2; Ps 62:9,[4]) 106:3; 119:20; Job 27:10;[5])
Prov 5:19; 6:14; 8:30; 17:17; Ecc 9:8. The instance in Est 5:13 is
enlarged with ʾasher and is "degraded" to fulfil the purpose of a
temporal conjunction in the sense of "whenever", "on every occasion
when I see Mordecai" (see 2 Chr 24:11, p. 43). In one late instance,
ʿeth is added to a formula with yōm, "for on the occasion of every day
(kiy leʿeth-yōm beyōm) they were coming unto David" (1 Chr 12:23).
This is likewise an example of artificial augmentation, reducing ʿeth
to an enlargement of the temporal preposition. The connection of
the two temporal expressions is a contradiction in itself, with the
indefiniteness of yōm beyōm nullifying the specific connotation of

---

[1]) Read with Q, derākāyw; see Samson Raphael Hirsch (Die Psalmen, Frankfurt
a. M.: 1924, p. 57) and Hans-Joachim Kraus (Psalmen, BKAT, 15:1, 2, 1960,
p. 75) for the reading of yāchīylū against the conjectures of W. Stärk (Lyrik, SAT,
3:1, 1911, p. 154) and Charles Augustus Briggs (with Emilie Grace Briggs: The
Book of Psalms, I, 4th imprint, ICC, 16:1, 1927, p. 86).

[2]) So Kurt Galling (with Max Haller: Die fünf Megilloth, HAT, 1:18, 1940,
p. 82) to Ecc 9:8.

[3]) So the interpretation of Hirsch (op. cit., p. 187) to Ps 34:2 in explaining his
rendering, "in jeder Zeitlage".

[4]) Whether or not the "lonesome" ʿām should be omitted or altered to ʿammīy
may possibly be open to question (so Bernhard Bonkamp: Die Psalmen nach dem
hebräischen Grundtext, Freiburg i. B.: 1949, p. 292, and William R. Taylor (with
W. Stuart McCullough): "The Book of Psalms", "Exegesis", IB, IV, 1955, p.
1323). But the conjectures to change it and ʿeth to ʿittōth (Stärk, op. cit., p. 222)
or to ʿittēykem (so Bernhard Duhm: Die Psalmen, 2nd ed., KHCAT, 14, Tübingen:
1922, p. 241) are poor attempts out of the difficulty. The widely acclaimed solution
of Hermann Hupfeld and Wilhelm Nowack (Die Psalmen, II, 3rd ed., Gotha:
1888, p. 101) to read kol-ʿadath ʿam according to the LXX (accepted by, e.g.,
BH, Briggs, op. cit., p. 71; Kraus, op. cit., p. 436; Artur Weiser: Die Psalmen,
II, 5th ed., ATD, 14, 1959, p. 303), or the proposal bekol-ʿadath by Franz Wutz
(Die Psalmen, München: 1925, p. 155) and Heinrich Herkenne (Das Buch der
Psalmen, HSAT, 5:2, 1936, p. 213), is unnecessary, for there the problem is only
with ʿām and not with bekol-ʿeth. However, this singular appearance of ʿām does
not rule out the possibility of its use here in the vocative, and it fills out the meter
of the verse to 3 + 3 + 3.

[5]) See Fohrer (Hiob, p. 386) against the conjectures by Duhm (Hiob, p. 133)
and Gustav Hölscher (Das Buch Hiob, HAT, 1:17, 1937, p. 64).

ēth, so that the phrase means in effect nothing more than "day by day".[1])

Similar *yōm*-formulas are used in the same way to denote the repetition of a daily action: *debar-yōm beyōmō*, Ex 16:4; *yōm yōm*, Gen 39:10; Prov 8:30; *yōm wāyōm*, Est 3:4; *leyōm beyōm*, 2 Chr 24:11; *miyyōm-'el-yōm*, 1 Chr 16:23. Since all of these formulas appear only in late texts, they are obviously variations of an attempt to indicate repetition.[2]) These expressions with *yōm* never lose the implication of occurrence upon a *day*, which *bekol-'ēth* as such never means. Furthermore, whereas the latter always indicates definite occasions in a situation of relationship without further reference to temporality, the other expressions are indefinite in referring to the occasion itself but not to its temporality that recurs on each day.

The same distinction applies to other comparable formulas with *yōm* that appear in somewhat earlier passages: "a God who reprimands every day (*bekol-yōm*)" (Ps 7:12); and "Saul was hostile to David all the days (*kol-hayyāmīm*)" (1 Sam 18:29). The latter formula actually designates an indefinite period of time, according to the indistinct use of the extensive plural,[3]) which cannot properly be applied to *ēth* in this indefinite sense. But both *bekol-yōm* and *bekol-'ēth* may well be temporal counterparts to the spatial formula *bekol-mākōm*, "in every place (= everywhere)", which first appears in the period of the Late Monarchy in Am 8:3. These formulas may be compared to each other as figures of speech that refer to an occurrence that takes place, respectively, on a certain day, on a certain occasion, or in a certain place repeatedly.

The formula *kol-yemēy* may be compared to the use of *ēth* in Est 5:13 (p. 44) indicating temporal relationship to the full length of a certain period of time: "and they stayed with him all the days of David's being in the stronghold" (1 Sam 22:4); "all the days when (*'asher*) the leprosy is on him he is unclean" (Lev 13:46); "all the days of discharge is her uncleanness" (15:25b). In contrast, *ēth* properly refers to a definite occasion with the stress on the occasion as such, even though it be repeated. This occasion may possibly continue over a period of time, but this aspect may only be discerned from the nature of the situation, and not according to the inherent meaning of *ēth* (*cf.* 15:25a, p. 25, and Gen 38:27, p. 41).

---

[1]) So Rudolph, *loc. cit.*, p. 106; see also 2 Chr 30:21.

[2]) *Cf.* Kautzsch, *op. cit.*, § 123c.

[3]) *Ibid.*, § 124b.

Although most of the remaining instances of the uses of ʿēth with singular occasions will be discussed below under the more closely defined historical and intervening aspects, a few may preferably be handled in the context of simple relationship. In Isa 18:7, a relationship is made between the sending of messengers to Ethiopia (v. 2) and the bringing of gifts to Yahweh: "On that occasion (bāʿēth hahīʾ) a gift will be brought to Yahweh of Hosts." [1]) Another passage is probably identified justifiably by virtually all commentators as a later addition: [2]) "Therefore the prudent will keep silent in that situation" (baʿēth hahīʾ, Am 5:13a). This serves to relate the occasion of injustice to the appropriate reaction of the prudent. Both instances of ʿēth relate the respective occasions objectively as well as temporally.

Direct relationship to a present situation is indicated by a similar form in Est 4:14a: "For if you really do keep silent in this situation (bāʿēth hazzoʾth) . . .". That this occasion was one of peculiar content is clearly shown by the context, for it was Esther's "time for decision" —it was the crucial situation which offered her the opportunity to save her people at the risk of losing her own life. This is the only obvious instance where ʿēth is used for a "decisive time", which is the connotation frequently given to it as its basic meaning.[3]) That this is the case here is merely coincidental, for ʿēth cannot be pressed into signifying anything more than a singular occasion of peculiar content. Moreover, it cannot refer to a "moment" of decision, for Esther requests three days' time to make her decision, which would have been impossible if Mordecai had meant a single moment of time with his employment of ʿēth.

---

[1]) The whole verse is omitted as a gloss by Marti (*Jesaja*, p. 149), Bernhard Duhm (*Das Buch Jesaia*, 3rd ed., *GHAT*, 3:1, 1914, p. 115), Gray (*Isaiah*, p. 309), and Edward J. Kissane (*The Book of Isaiah*, Dublin: 1960, p. 200); *cf*. R. B. Y. Scott ("The Book of Isaiah, Chapters 1-39", "Exegesis", *IB*, V, 1956, p. 278). But objection should only be raised to the last phrase (7bβ) with its obviously post-exilic terminology. The rest of the verse may well be given the meter 3 + 3, 2 + 2, 3 + 3, and be regarded as a fitting conclusion to the prophecy in both thought and style.

[2]) So Hugo Gressmann: *Die älteste Geschichtsschreibung und Prophetie Israels*, *SAT*, 2:1, 1910, p. 329; Otto Procksch: *Die kleinen prophetischen Schriften vor dem Exil*, *EAT*, 3, 1910, p. 81; T. H. Robinson, *op. cit.*, p. 91; Robert H. Pfeiffer: *Introduction to the Old Testament*, 5th ed., London: 1941, p. 583; Weiser, *Kleine Propheten*, p. 167.

[3]) So Delling, "καιρός", p. 459; Vollborn, *op. cit.*, pp. 6 ff.; Marsh, "Time, Season", p. 259; Eichrodt, "Heilserfahrung und Zeitverständnis im Alten Testament", p. 117 (see below, pp. 5, 7-10).

Many other expressions may be employed for referring to the temporal relationship of occasions, *e.g.*: "here is the day (*hinnēh hayyōm*) (of) which Yahweh spoke to you" (1 Sam 24:5); "for yet today (*kehayyōm*) you will meet him" (9:13); [1] "Sell me your birthright yet today (*kayyōm*)" (Gen 25:31); ". . . to rise up upon me, to lie in wait, as at this day? (*kayyōm*)" (1 Sam 22:13); "I see him, but not now (*welo' 'attāh*)" (Num 24:17); "And it was on that day (= the same day, *bayyōm hahū*), and Isaac's servants came" (Gen 26:32); "and he attained in that year (*bashshānāh hahiwh*) to a hundredfold" (26:12); "If you are not saving your life tonight (*hallayelā*)" (1 Sam 19:11); "and please strengthen me yet this time (*happa'am hazzeh*)" (Jdg 16:28).

These examples substantiate again in the case of simple relationship the conclusions that have been previously drawn. The above expressions are employed in order to emphasize the significance of the situation by drawing special attention to the aspect of temporal relationship. In distinction to the comparable use of *'ēth*, their actual reference is to a certain temporal situation and not to the particular occasion itself. This applies as well to *pa'am*, which does not mean "this occasion", but rather indicates a contrasting relationship between a past situation and the present one.

B. An Occasion of Singular Historical Character

One of the most interesting usages of *'ēth* is that in historical relationship. It exhibits several modes of employment, but, together with a comparison of other temporal expressions, it opens the way to a fundamental appreciation of the structure of the Hebrew historical consciousness. This becomes apparent in the realization of the phenomena of the historical causal relationship of events and of historical reality in the interrelationship of the past, present and future *tempora*.

1. *The Relationship of Occasions in a Complex Situation*

The earliest instances of *'ēth* with respect to the aspect of historical relationship appear within the course of a narrative for the purpose

---

[1]) *'attem* is read here for MT *'othō*. See Brockelmann (*op. cit.*, § 109b) for the excellent translation of the troublesome *kehayyōm*, which is usually rendered simply "now", and which renders unnecessary Torczyner's attempt at a solution in favor of the Babylonian *kiām = keyom* (*op. cit.*, pp. 108-111). The same translation may also be made of *kayyōm* in the following quotation; the difference is not in the meaning (so Kautzsch, *op. cit.*, § 35n), but in the exceptional retention of the consonantal article (*cf.* Kautzsch, *ibid.*).

of indicating the temporal relationship of certain events. The Israelites' blocking of the Moabites' way of escape at the Jordan is related
to the resultant massacre: "And they smote Moab on that occasion
(bāʿēth hahīyʾ), about 10,000 men" (Jdg 3:29). The respective formula
is used with an "ulterior motive". It serves the purpose of connecting
occasions that are basically identical in fact. In effect, it helps draw
attention to another aspect of the same occasion, so that it could as
well be rendered "on the same occasion". This illustrates further
the reference of ʿēth to a specific occasion as such.

The same usage occurs further in narrating a characteristically
many-sided climactic event, namely, when Jephthah's Gileadites
slaughtered the Ephraimites at the Jordan (12:6), and when the
Israelites dispersed upon bringing the affair with the Benjaminites to a
conclusion (21:24). It is also employed to describe the complex
situation of making a truce with the Benjaminites and handing over
the virgins of Jabesh-Gilead to them (21:14). The same usage appears
further in later texts in Dt 2:34; 3:4, 8, 12; 1 Kgs 8:65; 2 Chr 7:8;
13:18; 35:17. In regard to Dt 3:12, it is evident that 12a, with its
object at the beginning, is the logical continuation of vv. 8 and 10
(considering the interpolations of vv. 9 and 11), and not the introduction to 12b. As in 2:34; 3:4, 8, bāʿēth hahīwʾ in 12a appears in a
summarizing statement, which repeats 8a because of the lengthy
intervening clause. It thus draws a solid line at the end of the conquest
of Heshbon and Bashan, 2:16-3:11, before attention turns to the
subsequent apportionment of the land, 3:12b-17, and the charge to
the affected two and one-half tribes, 3:18-22.

One aspect of the use of ʿēth in these instances is of essential significance. The indicated relationship of the events to each other is of
causal character. In Jdg 3:29, the result of Ehud's crafty murder of
Eglon and of the taking of the Jordan fords was the slaughter of
10,000 Moabites. The outcome of the situation had a certain cause,
and the relationship between the causative event and the effected result
was indicated by bāʿēth hahīyʾ. All the other passages reflect the same
idea, that of representing the principle of historical causal relationship.

A second manner of expressing the historical relationship appears
in Jdg 4:4: "And Deborah . . . was judging Israel at that time."
In this case, it is not a further aspect of a complex climactic situation
that is indicated, but of a complex situation at the introduction of a
story. The usage helps to "set the stage" for the narration by temporally connecting the position of Deborah with the oppression by

Jabin and Sisera. Thus the expression may well be rendered "in the same situation". The same may be said for the usage in Num 22:4, where it is reported that Balak was king of Moab at the time of the Israelites' encampment in the plains of Moab at Shittim (22:1; 25:1), as well as for Isa 20:2, where the verse interrupts the train of thought to relate a previous occurrence which is necessary for the understanding of the principal event in vv. 3-6. These statements are sometimes thought to be later glosses for clarification.[1]) However, it is very obvious that Jdg 4:4 is an integral part of the story [2]) and not an addition, for it is presumed by v. 5 as well as at the beginning of the narration of the event proper in v. 6. Isa 20:2 could be a late parenthesis, but is not a contradiction to the temporal reference of v. 1,[3]) for it refers back to this reference in an indefinite way of indicating the general occasion.[4]) Significant here is the fact that the reference of *ʿēth* is so indefinite as to allow for a time span of three years (v. 3), which underlines the earlier observation that it refers to the occasion as such and not primarily to the temporal moment of the occasion.

As for the circumstances in Num 22:2-5, difficulty arises because of the appearance of two subjects on the one side, namely Moab in vv. 3, 4a and Balak in vv. 2, 4b. This has led to a dissection of the text into the sources J and E. The incisions are performed differently by the various commentators, so that clarity is impossible.[5]) Whether v. 3 contains a redundancy or represents an emphasis upon an aspect of the situation through a parallel construction, the passage need cause no further textual difficulty. It merely represents the several actors in a scene that is narrated in typical Hebrew fashion by jumping from actor to actor,[6]) and not strictly systematically as the Western

---

[1]) So Budde, *op. cit.*, p. 35, to Jdg 4:4; Dillmann (*Numeri*, p. 137) and Gray (*Numbers*, p. 324) to Num 22:4b; and Marti (*Jesaja*, p. 159) and Duhm (*Jesaja*, p. 123) to Isa 20:2.

[2]) *Cf.* Zapletal, *op. cit.*, p. 56.

[3]) So Hans Schmidt: *Die grossen Propheten*, *SAT*, 2:2, 1915, p. 86.

[4]) So Franz Delitzsch: *Biblischer Commentar über das Buch Jesaia*, 3rd ed., *BCAT*, III:1, 1879, p. 253; Otto Procksch: *Jesaia I*, *KAT*, 9, 1930, p. 257; Eduard König: *Das Buch Jesaja*, Gütersloh: 1926, p. 208; and *Syntax*, § 340i; Kautzsch, *op. cit.*, § 164a, b.

[5]) *Cf.* Gressmann (*Die Anfänge Israels*, pp. 52 f.), Heinrich Holzinger (*Numeri*, *KHCAT*, 4, Tübingen: 1903, pp. xvi f.), Dillmann (*loc. cit.*), and John Marsh ("The Book of Numbers", "Exegesis", *IB*, II, 1953, pp. 137, 248-261).

[6]) For examples of this style of abruptly alternating subjects and inserting explanatory observations in older narratives, see Num 22:22; Jdg 3:17; 4:11; 11:37b; 16:9, 12, 27, 1 Sam 4:12-22; 5:11 f.; 13:2-4; 14:1-6.

philologist would have it. Thus the sequence goes from Balak's evaluation of Israel's success (2) to the reaction by the Moabites (3) and their frightened warning to the accompanying elders of the beduine Midianites (4a), to the notice that Balak was king of Moab (4b), and to the sending of messengers to Balaam (5). This sequence does not at all prove to be illogical for story-telling, for it portrays observation (2-4a) and resultant action (5). It must be clear that it is Balak, and not the Moabites, who takes the decisive initative (5), for it was he who carefully evaluated the situation (2), whereas his people were driven to despair (3-4a). Thus the subject for v. 5 is to be found in 4b, which is then not a later editorial gloss but an identification of Balak where this is most appropriate, namely where he takes the initiative for action.

Having established this fact, it is evident that the use of *bāʿēth hahīyʾ* in 4b sets up a causative relationship between a certain condition and the ensuing event. The same may be said for Jdg 4:4, where the statement that Deborah was a prophetess and "judge" in Israel serves as the causative factor for her initiative in v. 6 to instigate the attack on Sisera. Likewise, it was Yahweh's command to Isaiah in 20:2 that was the causal factor for the resultant symbolical act and its interpretation (vv. 3-6).

The historical situation may also be complicated by observations inserted into the midst of the story as in Jdg 14:4: "And at that time, Philistines were ruling in Israel." The same is true for 1 Chr 21:29 and 2 Chr 30:3. Although it may be disputed whether or not Jdg 14:4b is an editorial gloss,[1] it is probable that the instances in Dt 10:8 and Jos 6:26 are additions or explanatory interpolations. Other cases involve the use of the expression within a story to connect occasions that are objectively and temporally related to each other, as the revolt of Libnah at the occasion of Edom's rebellion (2 Kgs 8:22=2 Chr 21:10). This also applies to 2 Kgs 16:6; 18:16 and 2 Chr 16:10. An historical causal relationship is indicated in Jdg 14:4b, as *bāʿēth hahīyʾ* relates the causal situation of the Philistines' domination to the resultant event of Yahweh's use of Samson against the Philistines. The same applies to Dt 10:8. But in 2 Kgs 8:22, it identifies the revolt of Libnah as the result of the revolt of Edom. This latter relationship also appears in Jos 6:26; 2 Kgs 16:6; 18:16; 2 Chr 16:10; 21:10.

---

[1] Budde (*op. cit.*, p. 99) and Gressmann (*loc. cit.*, p. 239) count it as an addition, but Zapletal (*op. cit.*, p. 216) considers it to be original.

Reference to the complex situation of historical occasions occurs a few times in later texts in other constructions. In Neh 13:21, reference is made to the occasion at the beginning of a certain period of time as the causal event in an historical relationship: "From (after) that occasion (*min-hā'ēth hahī'*), they did not come (any more) on the Sabbath." The same use is applied with an infinitive in Dan 12:11: "and from (after) the occasion (*ūmē'ēth*) of the removal of the continual offering . . ." Likewise, reference may be made to the occasion at the end of a certain period of time as the resultant event in a causal relationship (*'ad-hā'ēth hahīy'*) in Neh 6:1—"Also until that occasion, I had not set up doors in the gates", and Dan 12:1c—"which has not been since the origin of a nation until that occasion" (see pp. 111 f.). Such a period may even be expressly designated chronologically: "and about the occasion of the coming forth of the end for the days of two years (*ūke'ēth tsēth haqqēts leyāmīym shenayim*), his bowels came forth because of his sickness" (2 Chr 21:19; see pp. 35, 43).

It may now be noted that the use of *'ēth* in the instances cited in this section never indicates merely the temporal relationship of occasions, but always implies the causal relationship of historical circumstances.

Special mention may be made in this context of some instances handled above in another connection where the aspect of historical causal relationship plays an active part. The formula *kā'ēth* (pp. 34-40), whereas it basically indicates a contrast between the present situation and a hypothetical probability in Jdg 13:23; 21:22, denotes an historical comparison in other cases. In Num 23:23, the Exodus of Israel from Egypt (v. 22) is compared to the present hostile confrontation with the Moabites. Yahweh's deliverance on the former occasion is made the causal factor for predicting a similar result in the situation with the forces of Balak (v. 24). The former conquest of Galilee, Gilead and Sharon by Tiglath-pileser is contrasted with the occasion of its future restoration in Isa 8:23; the causal factor in this historical relationship is reversed into a contrasting factor. In Ezek 16:57, the Jerusalemites are blamed for not learning a lesson from the fate of the Syrians, Philistines and other neighboring peoples; their "disgrace" was the causal factor which should have revealed the eventual result of the Jerusalemites' "wickedness". The same sense is evident in the exclusive use of *kā'ēth māchār* with oaths; the fact of the present situation is the causal factor substantiating the promised or threatened action of the morrow. The related expression *kā'ēth chayyāh* (see pp. 23-25), which is also used in specially emphasized promises, likewise compares the reality of the present situation as the causal factor that ensures the promised result on the future occasion.

2. 'ēth, yōm, 'āz and Historical Causal Relationship

It will be helpful now to compare the discussed use of 'ēth with the similar use of the expressions *yōm* and *'āz* when referring to a complex relationship of historical occasions. This comparison is limited to these two words because no others lend themselves to this category.

In contrast to 'ēth, the other two temporal expressions appear already in ancient poetry in connection with historical events. In the Song of Deborah, reference is made to events "in the days of Shamgar" and "in the days of Jael" (Jdg 5:6). But the attempt is not made here to establish the historicity of the particular events by means of such a temporal reference. The fact of the reality of the occurrence is much rather taken for granted; it is proclaimed and simply reported, and therefore requires no substantiation. The temporal references do not direct attention to an historical situation as such, but to the principal actors; they indicate the meaningful, specific situation of Shamgar and Jael without further reflection about the relationship of the situation within an historical context. The word *yāmīym* lends itself very well to such a use, for it is nearly always very indefinite in character. It is the favorite term in the OT for indicating an undefined passage or extension of time, *e.g.*, length of life (Ex 20:12), a continuing condition (1 Sam 18:29), the duration of a situation (22:4), an indefinite interlude (Jdg 11:4), and an indefinite period (1 Kgs 17:15; *cf.* 1 Sam 29:3—*zeh yāmīym 'ō-zeh shānīm*—"one or two years"). Thus *yāmīym* does not indicate a period of time that has been pressed into a moment, as Delling suggested (p. 6).

The early use of *'āz* is similar. It is usually rendered "then" or "at that time". But in Jdg 5:11, 13, 19, 22, and in the Blessing of Jacob, Gen 49:4, it merely indicates the simple sequence of events without any hint of relationship to an historical setting.

Considering that 'ēth is frequently used in narratives in conscious reference to historical occasions, it is noteworthy that it does not appear in the ancient poetic traditions in the corresponding temporal references. The character of early Hebrew poetry is, in respect to historical events, filled with the proclamation of the content of the particular occasion without reflection over the questions of historicity, substantiation or application. Therefore, the temporal references are correspondingly few and vague. Their characteristic use in representing the temporal perspectives is to intensify the effect to the event, and not to emphasize the historical perspective. In addition to the various ancient blessings, curses, lists and sayings, special attention may be given to the Song of Lamech, Gen 4:23 f.; the Song of Miriam, Ex 15:21; the Amalek Oath, 17:16; the Well Song, Num 21:17 f.; the Mocking Song of Sihon, 21:27-30; the Oracles of Balaam, 24:3-9, 15-24; the Song of the Long Day, Jos 10:12 f.; Samson's Jawbone Song, Jdg 15:16; the Song of David's Successes, 1 Sam 18:7; David's Lament over Saul and Jonathan, 2 Sam 1:19-27; David's Lament over Abner, 3:33 f.; Sheba's Rally-Cry, 20:1 (*cf.* 1 Kgs 12:18); and Solomon's Temple Dedication, 1 Kgs 8:12 f. Nowhere is there a temporal reference to an occasion in the historical perspective. The only possible exceptions occur in the last of Balaam's oracles, where *'attāh* indicates the present situation (Num 24:17), but only as a means of contrast to an impending event in the indistinct future; *'acharīyth* in v. 20 refers to the end of Amalek as such without indication of historical relationship. Special reference is not made to the first two of Balaam's oracles, Num 23:7-10, 17-24, because weighty arguments have been brought to bear in favor of their composition during the later period of the monarchy.[1]

It was probably not until the time of Solomon that the principle of historical causal relationship made its first appearance in Hebrew literature. At this time, the hero tales of the Judges attained literary form. But this was a lone exception until later in the monarchy, when Isaiah (*cf.* 8:23, pp. 37, 51) and the editors of the narrative traditions were at work. It then came into more frequent usage in the Deuteronomistic work and still later in that of the Chronicler. It has been ably demonstrated by Henri Frankfort that early man with his mythopoetic thought-forms recognized the relationship of cause and effect, but as a personal relationship of wills and not in the sense of our

---

[1] So Sigmund Mowinckel: "Der Ursprung der Bilᶜamsage", *ZAW* 48 (NF 7, 1930), pp. 262-271; Leonhard Rost, ed., Ernst Sellin: *Einleitung in das Alte Testament*, 9th ed., Heidelberg: 1959, pp. 48 f.; Artur Weiser: *Einleitung in das Alte Testament*, 5th ed., Göttingen: 1963, p. 109. But Dillmann (*loc. cit.*), Gray (*loc. cit.*, p. xxxii), Gressmann (*loc. cit.*, p. 67), and Marsh (*loc. cit.*, p. 248) generally hold that all of the oracles predate the narrative sources considerably. In contrast, Holzinger (*loc. cit.*, 115-124) gives all the oracles a much later date than the narrative.

modern "view of an impersonal, mechanical and lawlike functioning of causality".[1]) The basic difference between the conceptions of causality in the Near Eastern cultures and that of the Hebrews lay in the identification of the personal causative will; the Egyptians, Babylonians and Canaanites found it in nature, the Hebrews found it in the autonomous will of a transcendent God.[2]) This essential difference in identifying the cause of events enabled the Hebrews to arrive at a basically different evaluation of the events themselves and of their relationship to each other. While the other ancients found the cause of event in the never-changing, ever-repeating cycle of nature, the Hebrews found it in God's independent, unpredictable will; that is, God's will could only be predicted through special revelation or on the basis of former experience. For, as William Irwin has pointed out, "the objectives of the Hebrew philosophers of history were to discover principles which determine the course of events so that these might serve as guides for their contemporary world." Over against the chaotic attempts of man they postulated the will of God as the supreme force in events: "Through the strange interplay of human freedom and divine sovereignty which the Hebrew thinkers affirmed, he was molding human life to his own will." [3]) Thus it was Yahweh who instigated Deborah (Jdg 4:4 f.), Samson (14:4) and Isaiah (20:2) into action in order to accomplish his purposes. In the same way, the result of human action was also attributed to his guidance, as in Ehud's victory over the Moabites (Jdg 3:28 f.) and the provision of wives for the surviving Benjaminites (21:3, 14, 24).

It is true that the beginnings of recognizing causal relationship in an historical situation may be found in ancient Babylonian thought. Like the Egyptians, the Babylonians identified the causative will of events in the forces of nature and evaluated them by trying to discern their character, which was given corresponding personification in a god. In contrast to the orderly process of nature in Egypt, the forces of nature in Mesopotamia were highly unpredictable, leading to a corresponding explanation of events. The cause of political or historical events was attributed to the discussions of the council of the gods; but they were so arbitrary that no further explanation could be

---

[1]) *Kingship and the Gods*, Chicago: 1948, p. 15; *cf.* also pp. 16-20.
[2]) "The Emancipation of Thought from Myth", *IAAM*, pp. 363-373; see also William A. Irwin: "The Hebrews", *IAAM*, pp. 224, 230-234, 244.
[3]) *Ibid.*, p. 323.

given nor was required.[1]) Thus each event received an independent explanation. But the Hebrews studied the events themselves more closely and sought out the causes that prompted the particular actions of God.

It is apparent that the Hebrews did not develop a terminology for their historical consciousness, as we modern Westerns might have expected—a terminology that would include specific expressions for "event", "time" and "history". The word *'ēth* was often used in reference to historical event. But in its basic connotation as "definite occasion", it had already found application for non-historical usage, and furthermore lacked a definite indication of the temporal aspect. Other expressions also had disadvantages, implying only the aspects of temporality and relationship, as *'āz*. The very frequently used *yōm* never escaped the implication of a particular day as such, lacking specific indication of the occasion itself. *mōʿēd* meant a specific appointed occasion, but without clear reference to the temporal aspect.

Corresponding to the appropriateness of using indefinite temporal expressions as *yāmiym* and *'az* in contexts where the historical consciousness is not apparent, their inadequacy for definite historical events is quite evident. Like the equivalent expression in Jdg 5:6 (p. 51), *biymēy shā'ūl* in 1 Sam 17:12 offers only an indefinite reference to the historical situation of Jesse's old age. "In the days of Abraham" in Gen 26:1, 15, 18, serves primarily in a comparison with a similar event in Isaac's time without presuming any further degree of accuracy or relationship. The general statement in 1 Sam 14:52 with "all the days of Saul", is not in the form of a summarizing notice with causal relationship, but rather appears as an incidental remark for an indefinite period. Similar indication of an indefinite duration is made in 22:4 by "all the days of David's being in the stronghold".

The evidently earliest use of *'ad hayyōm hazzeh*, "until this day", is presented in 1 Sam 29:3, where Achish employs it as a means to emphasize the faultless integrity of David without implying a radically literal application to the historical situation (so also 12:2; 29:6, 8). The more frequent use of this expression indicates the continuation of a certain condition up to the present time, such as the

---

[1]) See Irwin, *op. cit.*, p. 322, and Thorkild Jacobsen: "Mesopotamia", *IAAM*, pp. 127, 168, 192, 195 f. Thus, the Babylonians actually did not have a cyclical view of time. As Loretz has shown (*op. cit.*, p. 251), for them "war die Zeit etwas, das nie mehr zurückkehrte".

possession of Ziklag by Judah in 27:6. Although this might be considered the result of an historical occasion, the actual emphasis of *yōm* is laid on the aspect of the continuing duration of the particular condition and not, as *ʿad haʿēth hahīyʾ* in Dan 12:1c, Neh 6:1 (p. 51), on the definite occasion at the end of a period. This difference can be made even more clear by the example in Gen 19:37—"He is the father of Moab to this day" (*ʿad-hayyōm* with the demonstrative article; so also v. 38).

In apparent similarity to the use of *kāʿēth* in Num 23:23 (pp. 37, 51), reference is made in Jdg 19:30 to the historical event of the exodus from Egypt and to the present situation: "Such as this has not occurred or been seen from the day (*lemayyōm*) of the coming up of the Israelites from the Land of Egypt to this day!" In Num 23:23, the causal factor of the deliverance from Egypt (v. 22) is compared to the prospect of deliverance for Israel in the present confrontation (v. 24); the Exodus is put into a causal historical relationship with the present situation. In contrast, its relationship in Jdg 19:30 to the present simply presumes to encompass the entire period of the existence of the Israelite nation. The mention of the two "days" is not a comparison of expressly related occasions, but an indication of a certain temporal duration for the primary purpose of stressing the uniqueness of the tragedy at Gibeah. The same may be said of the extreme behaviour of Mephibosheth throughout David's absence from Jerusalem: ". . . from the day (*lemin-hayyōm*) of the going of the king until the day (*ʿad-hayyōm*) when he came in peace" (2 Sam 19:25). Indication of the beginning of a continuing situation, such as the "penetration" of David by Yahweh's spirit in 1 Sam 16:13, *mēhayyōm hahūʾ wāmāʿlāh* ("from that day and beyond"), is likewise an emphasis on the persevering aspect of the condition. In this respect, the grammatical construction makes no difference. The meaning of the usage with *yōm* is essentially the same whether it is used with a demonstrative adjective or infinitive, as in the cases above, or whether it is connected directly with a finite verb, as in 2 Sam 7:6, or with a temporal conjunction, as with *ʾasher* in v. 11.

Of frequent occurrence in the early Hebrew narratives is *bayyōm hahūʾ*, a comparable expression to *bāʿēth hahīyʾ*. Where the latter normally appears in narratives in an historical causal relationship, some early instances of the former indicate only the occurrence of events "on the same day", as in the Story of the Ark of the Covenant: "And a man of Benjamin ran from the ranks and came to Shiloh on

that day" (1 Sam 4:12; *cf.* also 14:37; 21:8; 31:6; 2 Sam 5:8; 11:12).
It is striking that this otherwise frequently occurring expression is
used so sparingly in the stories of the Judges and in the narratives
attributed to the Yahwist (including Otto Eissfeldt's "L"-source).
In Judges, it appears in the sense of "on the same day" in 20:21, 26,
and in an historical relationship only in statements that very probably
belong to the later framework, as 3:30; 4:23; 6:32, the only
possible exceptions being 20:35, 46. The Yahwist employs the expression only three times, twice in the non-historical sense of "on the
same day" (Gen 26:32; 30:35), and once in an historical relationship
(Ex 32:28). This strongly indicates that at least some of the early
Hebrew narrators felt the inadequacy of *bayyōm hahūʾ* in referring to
a situation of historical relationship, and therefore often preferred
bāʿēth hahīʾ.

Evidence of differing authorship is readily seen in the early narratives about the Ark, David, and Samuel and Saul, where *bāʿēth hahīʾ*
is totally lacking while *bayyōm hahūʾ* occurs some 24 times in an
historical relationship and but six times without historical significance,
as cited above. For example, the relationship of occasions in a complex
situation is indicated in 1 Sam 6:15, where the cart with the Ark
came to Beth-shemesh and sacrifices were offered to Yahweh (so
also 6: 16; 12:18; 14:24; 18:2; 20:26; 22:22; 2 Sam 6:9; 19:3a, b, 4).
The relationship may be represented in an inserted notice, as the
mention of the presence of the Ark with the Israelites when they were
encamped against the Philistines at Michmash (1 Sam 14:18), or in
a summary statement, as the report of the number of priests whom
Doeg the Edomite killed, 22:18 (so also 9:24; 10:9; 14:23, 31; 2 Sam
2:17; 3:37; 18:7 f.; 23:10, as well as Ex 32:28; Jdg 20:35, 46).

The form *bayyāmīym hahēm* also appears in early texts to relate a
parenthetical notice to the context; thus mention is made of the esteem
given to the counsel of Ahithophel "in those days", 2 Sam 16:23,
and to the mighty Nephilim, Gen 6:4. The expression is obviously
very vague in its reference, not indicating a specific occasion but a
general situation or period. This also applies to the repeated formulas
in Jdg 17: 6; 18: 1a; 19:1a, and 21:25, which are commonly held
by commentators to be editorial glosses, probably from the Late
Monarchy.[1])

---

[1]) So Ernst Bertheau: *Das Buch der Richter und Ruth*, 2nd ed., *KEHAT*, 6,
1883, pp. 238 f.; George Foot Moore: *Judges*, *ICC*, 7, 1895; Gressmann, *loc. cit.*,
pp. 258, 263, 269; C. F. Burney: *The Book of Judges*, 2nd ed., London: 1920, pp.

As in the instances of ʿēth discussed above, the principle of historical causal relationship also finds expression in these cases. For example, the sacrifices to Yahweh in 1 Sam 6:15 were the result caused by the coming of the Ark to Beth-shemesh; the Israelites' repossession of the Ark enabled Saul to call for it in 14:18; Saul's order to Doeg in 22:18 resulted in the death of 85 priests. Although these instances are clearly used to indicate the historical relationship and the significance of the particular occasion, their inadequacy to fulfil the demands of the intended idea is also apparent, for the basic connotation of yōm remains in every case, that it has to do with a certain day. When applied to the relationship of events "on that day", it never loses the primary meaning that the events occurred on the same day. In none of these early cases is the expression employed where the events could have transpired on different days. It is thus evident that yōm, in its application to historical situations in the early narrative literature, is always conditioned by the limitations of its inherent temporal meaning. It cannot do full justice to the idea of historical causal relationship because it fails to indicate specifically the necessary reference to the relevant occasion as such. This weakness was especially realized by the narrators and editors who either used it sparingly or rejected it occasionally in favor of ʿēth.

Similar use is made of ʾāz with the relationship of occasions in a complex situation. A double observation is made in 2 Sam 23:14 to explain the positions of David and the Philistine garrison when three of David's thirty mighty men came to him at the Cave of Adullam. The same explanatory notice is made in the Story of Solomon in 1 Kgs 9:24; 11:7, and by the Yahwist in Gen 4:26; 12:6. Causal relationship is also frequently indicated in a more literal sense; the first instance appears in Jdg 5:8—"One chooses new gods, then there is fighting in the gates." [1]) The same indication of the resultant situation is made in 8:3; 13:21; 1 Sam 6:3; 20:12; 2 Sam 2:27; 19:7; Ex 4:26. However, it is clear that this word primarily indicates only the fact of simple temporal relationship, as has been discussed above with respect to the simple sequence of events (see to Jdg 5:11,

---

410 f.; Jacob M. Myers: "The Book of Judges", "Exegesis", *IB*, II, 1953, p. 801; Hans Wilhelm Hertzberg: *Die Bücher Josua, Richter, Ruth*, 2nd ed., *ATD*, 9, 1959, p. 254.

[1]) *lāchem* is likely a denominative from *lchm*, "to fight", and is modified in apposition by the adjectival position of *sheʿārīym*, so that the rendering "gate-fighting" would be appropriate (see König, *Syntax*, § 306a; Kautzsch, *op. cit.*, § 131 c; Brockelmann, *op. cit.*, § 62g).

etc., p. 52). Whether in a supplementary observation or in a causal context, it therefore never "outgrows" this basic reference to the bare relationship without closer definition; as far as direct reference to the occasion as such, it remains in the sphere of indistinct approximation.

The result of the discussion in this section is that the idea of causal relationship between historical events made an appearance in early Hebrew narrative literature through the expressions *ʿēth*, *yōm* and, to a lesser extent, *ʾāz*. This idea was an innovation in the thought of the Near Eastern cultures which had always found the cause for event in the forces of nature or in the wills of the nature gods, without trying to postulate an historical causal relationship between the events themselves. But the Hebrew narrators either encountered some difficulty in finding the appropriate words to give adequate expression to their idea, or else the concept was not so fully developed so as to demand more precise formulation. *ʾāz* could indicate result, but properly referred only to an approximate relationship without direct indication of the occasion itself. More adaptable was *yōm*, which was indeed employed in this sense with the most frequency. Although it could indicate a close temporal relationship, its temporal reference was limited in applicability and lacked a definite reference to the specific occasion. Most appropriate for the desired occasion seems to have been *ʿēth*, for it unquestionably gave direct reference to the definite occasion as such, even though it was found lacking to a certain degree with respect to a specific temporal reference.

3. *The Relationship of Occasions in the Historical Setting*

In comparison to the above uses of *bāʿēth hahīʾ* (*resp. bāʿēth hahīwʾ*) and related expressions where reference is made to a complex situation, employment may also be made to introduce a story or indicate relationship to a former event. The parenthetical narrative of Judah and Tamar is introduced by this expression: "And it was about that time, and Judah went down from his brothers" (Gen 38:1). The translation "about" is used because it is obviously meant to be a loose connection to the preceding section of the Story of Joseph for the purpose of establishing a temporal relationship in the manner of historical relevance. Thus the semblance of an historical setting is given to the story. The same may be said of 1 Kgs 14:1 introducing the story of Abijah's fatal sickness, as well as of the later passages Gen 21:22; Jos 5:2; 1 Kgs 11:29; 2 Kgs 20:12 (= Isa

39:1); 24:10; 2 Chr 28:16. A temporal sequence of events is indicated in some later texts, as in Jos 11:10, where, after having defeated and pursued the united forces of the Canaanites (vv. 7-9), Joshua takes advantage of the occasion to destroy Hazor (10 f.). The same may be said of the uses in v. 21, Est 8:9; Dan 12:1a, d (see p. 112), Ezra 8:34;[1]) 1 Chr 21:28; 2 Chr 16:7.

Relationship to the historical setting may also be made by referring to a past occasion: "And why did you not take (them) in that time?" (Jdg 11:26). This passage presents a very significant use of ʿēth. It is employed as a direct reference to shālosh mēʾōth shānāh (v. 26a), i.e., to the chronological period of 300 years. Thus, ʿēth does not always refer to a "moment" (cf. Delling, p. 5), but may also mean a period or extension of time. It seems probable that Jephthah's verbal defense against the Ammonites (vv. 12-28) belongs either to the original narrative or to an old source because of its portrayal of Yahweh and Chemosh as national gods on a comparative level.[2]) Even if it is argued that the cited chronological reference be a later interpolation [3]) as a closer definition of ʿēth, the latter's character is not changed in the least. In comparison to the use in Gen 38:28 (p. 42), where it refers to an entire situation without restriction of temporal duration, it here, regardless of the questions whether the chronological number is meant to be approximate [4]) or exact or if it is a gloss, refers unquestionably to a certain historical period of time. Nevertheless, ʿēth retains its usual connotation of indicating a singular occasion of peculiar quality, for it is employed for the purpose of signifying the occasion when the Ammonites had the opportunity to take back the land between the Arnon and the Jabbok.

Since the formula bāʿēth hahiwʾ is a favorite expression in Deuteronomy (see pp. 64-66), occurring fifteen times, it would not be

---

[1]) BH and Wilhelm Rudolph (*Esra und Nehemia samt 3. Esra, HAT,* 1:20, 1949, p. 84) advocate joining the *bāʿēth hahīʾ* at the end of v. 34 to the beginning of 35 because of an asyndeton. But the supposed asyndeton is not so obvious, for the initiatory *habbāʾiym* in 35 is an accepted use of the participle as subject (see Kautzsch *op. cit.,* § 116d; König, *Syntax,* §§ 235b, 241i-k; Brockelmann, *op. cit.,* § 44c), and the *bāʿēth hahīʾ* makes just as good sense at the end of 34 (see also below to Dan 11:6, p. 77).

[2]) So Samuel Oettli: *Das Deuteronomium und die Bücher Josua und Richter, KKHS,* München: 1893, p. 268; Gressmann, *loc. cit.,* p. 230; Burney, *op. cit.,* p. 300.

[3]) Burney (*op. cit.,* p. 304) assigns the expression to Rp; *cf.* Moore (*op. cit.,* pp. 297 f.).

[4]) So Zapletal (*op. cit.,* p. 180) and Myers (*Judges,* p. 768) against Moore (*op. cit.,* p. 297, n.).

surprising if it were employed elsewhere by the Deuteronomic editors in their work of compiling historical narratives. The instance in 1 Kgs 8:65 is included in a passage commonly attributed to D (8:14-66) [1]) as the summarizing statement concerning the significant occasion of the dedication of the Temple by Solomon. As for the related instances in Jdg 3:29; 12:6; 21:14, 24, they show similarity in form, but this is not too obvious and the verses are closely related to their contexts; further, no commentators assign them to D.

With respect to other instances, the opinion was defended above (pp. 48-50), that Jdg 4:4 belongs to the narrative proper and probably 11:26 as well. The doubtful case of 14:4 is not given to D, but it appears that Dt 10:8 stems from the hand of a second Deuteronomic editor,[2]) as well as Jos 5:2, which reports Yahweh's command to Joshua to circumcise the Israelites.[3]) Although used for the sequence of events, Jos 11:10 and 21 refer to occasions of conquest in the same way as Dt 2:34; 3:4, 8, 12, so that they likewise may be attributed to Deuteronomic redaction.[4]) While the case in 1 Kgs 11:29 probably belongs to the narrative as a connective between a description of the situation (vv. 26-28) and the first reported event concerning Jeroboam (29 ff.), further evidence of editorial addition may be seen in the use of *bā'ēth hahīy'* as a "loose connection" in 1 Kgs 14:1; 2 Kgs 8:22; 16:6; 20:12; 24:10.[5]) It thus appears that the formula could well have been used by D for connecting or introducing stories. Even if all these instances are assigned to D, this usage was also known to other editors, namely the editor of JE (Gen 21:22; 38:1), the compiler of Judges, and especially the Chronicler (Ezra 8:34; Neh 4:16; 1 Chr 21:28, 29; 2 Chr 7:8; 13:18; 16:7, 10; 21:10; 28:16; 30:3; 35:17).

For the purposes of this work, it is basically of secondary importance to which editors specific instances may with good probability be

---

[1]) So Rudolf Kittel: *Die Bücher der Könige, GHAT,* I:5, 1900, pp. 60, 82; Martin Noth: *Überlieferungsgeschichtliche Studien,* 2nd ed., Tübingen: 1957, p. 104.

[2]) *Cf.* Samuel Rolles Driver: *Deuteronomy, ICC,* 5, 1895, p. 121; Gerhard von Rad: *Das fünfte Buch Mose. Deuteronomium, ATD,* 8, 1964, p. 56.

[3]) So Dillmann, *Josua,* p. 458; Noth, *op. cit.,* p. 42.

[4]) So Carl Steuernagel: *Das Buch Josua,* 2nd ed., *GHAT,* I:3:2, 1923, p. 193; *cf.* Hertzberg, *op. cit.,* p. 69.

[5]) So Immanuel Benzinger (*Die Bücher der Könige, KHCAT,* 9, Freiburg i. B.: 1899, p. 94) and Kittel (*Könige,* pp. 116-119) to 1 Kgs 14:1; Benzinger (*op. cit.,* p. 147), Kittel (*loc. cit.,* p. 225) and Noth (*op. cit.,* p. 77) to 2 Kgs 8:22; Noth (*op. cit.,* p. 76) to 16:6; 18:16 (pp. 76 f.) and 20:12 (p. 139); and Kittel (*loc. cit.,* pp. 307f.) and Noth (*op. cit.,* p. 78) to 24:10.

assigned.[1]) Of primary importance is the fact that the expression under consideration was employed as a formula for expressly indicating the historical relationship between occasions that were likewise considered historical. Because it is a connective formula without a definite temporal reference, many commentators have characterized *bāʿēth hahīyʾ* as being indefinite.[2]) Indeed, it offers only approximation in a temporal sense. However, it undoubtedly refers to a very definite, specific occasion and may therefore be of historical significance.

Attention may now be directed to other temporal expressions that relate to occasions in an historical setting. A reference to the historical setting at the beginning of a story is made in 1 Sam 28:1 by *bayyāmīym hahēm*, to relate David's sojourn in Gath to the preparations of the Philistines to attack Israel. It is obviously a vague expression that serves no further purpose than to indicate the fact of some temporal relationship between the two situations; there is no evidence of definiteness, of a specific occasion, or of causal relationship. The same case appears in Jdg 18:1b, which connects the two parts of the story of Micah and the Danites.

A reference to the general historical setting is also made at the beginning of the Yahwistic opus with the phrase, "on the day of Yahweh-God's making earth and heavens" (Gen 2:4b). Despite the semblance of some repetition and the opinion of most commentators, the construction of vv. 4f. indicates that the division between the accounts of the Creation and of Paradise is to be made between vv. 3 and 4 and not between 4a and 4b. [3]) It is obvious that the first

---

[1]) Procksch (*Jesaia*, p. 468) remarks that the expression occurs too frequently in the OT to be able to presume any particular source on the basis of its appearance.

[2]) So Procksch (*loc. cit.*, pp. 207, 308), von Rad (*loc. cit.*, p. 57), Martin Noth (*Das Buch Josua, HAT*, 1:7, 1938, p. 69), Gressmann (*loc. cit.*, pp. 239, 249), Benzinger (*op. cit.*, p. 94), Kittel (*loc. cit.*, p. 117), Montgomery (*op. cit.*, p. 270), C. F. Keil (*Die Bücher der Könige*, 2nd ed., *BCAT*, II:3, 1876, p. 383), Delitzsch (*Jesaia*, p. 253), Dillmann (*Jesaia*, p. 183), Marti (*Jesaja*, p. 159), Kissane (*op. cit.*, p. 412), and Rudolph (*Chronikbücher*, p. 291). Alfons Schulz (*Das Buch der Richter und das Buch Ruth, HSAT*, 2:4, 1926, p. 31) seems to have at least captured the sense of *bāʿēth hahīyʾ* in Jdg 4:4, where he defines its purpose "zur Kennzeichnung einer Handlung".

[3]) So Friedrich Tuch: *Commentar über die Genesis*, 2nd ed., Verlag der Buchhandlung des Waisenhauses, Halle: 1871, p. 28; Cassuto, *op. cit.*, p. 97; and Karlheinz Rabast: *Die Genesis*, Berlin: 1951, p. 74. Dillmann (*Genesis*, p. 38), Julius Wellhausen (*Die Composition des Hexateuchs und der historischen Bücher des Alten Testaments*, 3rd ed., Berlin: 1899, pp. 2 f.,) Procksch (*Genesis*, p. 451), and R. de Vaux (*La Genèse, SBtf*, 1, 1953, p. 43) regard 2:4a as the concluding statement to the first account. Hermann Gunkel (*Genesis*, 3rd ed., *GHAT*, I:1, 1910, p. 101) and Budde ("Ellä toledoth", *ZAW* 34 (1914), pp. 245 f.) transplant it

report reaches a satisfactory conclusion in v. 3. Instead of a repetition of content in 4, it is chiastic, synthetic parallelism that carries the thought further from the fact of the Creation to the person of the Creator. In style, sense and form, 4b is the logical continuation of 4a, upon which it also depends for a subject, being separated from 5 syntactically, but connected to it logically, by a *waw*. Thus the expression "on the day of making" repeats essentially *behibbāre'ām* in 4a, "in (= when) their being created" (*cf.* 5:1). Contrary to the cases dealt with in the previous section, *yōm* in this case does not necessarily refer to a particular day as such, but rather to the temporal relationship of the particular event (*cf.* Num 3:1; 7:84; 2 Sam 22:1). It is evident that the temporal aspect of the situation is not closely defined. Nevertheless, the primary emphasis is laid upon the temporal aspect itself and not, for example, upon the situation. This indication of an indefinite temporal relationship may be compared with the use of the plural form, as in the formula *bayyāmīym hahēm*, (p. 62). The use in v. 4b simply reflects the attempt of the writer to place the Paradise account in a temporal "historical" setting. Since 4a, and all other occurrences of the phrase in similar wording (*'ēlleh tōledōth*) at the beginning of a section (5:1; 6:9; 10:1; 11:10, 27; 25:12, 19; 36:1, 9; 37:2; Num 3:1; Ruth 4:18), is ordinarily attributed to P, it might possibly be considered whether the entire verse comes from his pen or from that of an editor as a connection between the two accounts. However, v. 5 demands an opening temporal reference according to the general practice in the OT.

Reference may also be made by *yōm* to a definite event in the past, as in 2 Sam 21:12—"... on the day of the Philistines' slaying of Saul on Gilboa". Although it literally denotes that two events simply occurred on the same day, it does give the events a temporal relationship and place them in an historical setting. This limited historical

before 1:1 as the original introduction. Hermann L. Strack (*Die Genesis*, 2nd ed., *KKHS*, A:I, München: 1905, p. 10) also assigns it to P, but as a connection to the following. Blame for the puzzling half-verse is placed on an editor or interpolator by Holzinger (*Genesis*, pp. 15 f.), Skinner (*op. cit.*, p. 41), König (*Genesis*, p. 194), and Simpson (*op. cit.*, p. 490). Despite some thorough arguments to the contrary, esp. by K. Budde ("Wortlaut und Werden der ersten Schöpfungsgeschichte", *ZAW* 35 (1915), pp. 67 f.; *Die Biblische Urgeschichte (Gen. 1-12, 5)*, Giessen: 1883, p. 489, n. 1; *Die biblische Paradiesgeschichte*, Giessen: 1932, p. 5), the most convincing explanation has been offered by Cassuto, who demonstrated that the division of the verse results in "a syntactic construction that defies the rules of Hebrew grammar and composition" (*op. cit.*). He also points to its chiastic parallel structure and the occurrence of *behibbāre'ām* in Ezek 28:13, 15, in the context of a "Paradise tradition" (*op. cit.*, pp. 98 f.).

reference is also seen in 19:20; 2 Kgs 2:8, 37, 42. The last two cases refer to a future possibility in the sense of "on the very day that . . .". This is a causal relationship, but in the objective and not in the historical sense. Similar use is made with the short form *bayyōm* with the demonstrative article in Jdg 13:10 when Manaoh's wife wished to identify "the man who came on that day to me". A general use of the plural *yāmiym* is used in reference to the forty-year length of David's reign, 1 Kgs 2:11, further illustrating its adaptability to a "time" that properly requires a more exact definition.

A narrative may also be introduced by *ʾāz*, as that of Solomon's wise decision in 1 Kgs 3:16. This is obviously nothing else than a very loose temporal connection with the foregoing, as if to say, "about that time". It illustrates again the Hebrew style of ordinarily introducing a narrative with a temporal reference, however general. The form *mēʾāz*, which later appears more frequently in the prophets, occurs in 2 Sam 15:34 as a most general reference to a former temporal situation in contrast to the present (*ʿattāh*).

Thus the uses of *yōm* and *ʾāz* for historical references in narratives do not carry much further connotation than indication of the temporal relationship, which may often be of a very general nature. In comparison, the formula *bāʿēth hahiyʾ*, which may also be employed for a more general historical reference (Gen 38:1, *etc.*) indicates a special occasion, and thus is an appropriate reference to the historical character of a significant situation (1 Kgs 11:29; Jos 11:10, *etc.*).

4. *Deuteronomy*: *Substantiation of Occasions as Historical Reality*

a. Historical Use of *ʿēth*

Among the frequent instances of *bāʿēth hahiwʾ* in the introductory discourses of Deuteronomy, ten may be grouped together according to a certain peculiarity. For instance, the case in 1:9 ("And I said to you on that occasion, saying . . ."), serves as a connecting link between the subject matter of vv. 6-8 and that of 9-17. The formula may also be used in a concluding remark to a section, as in v. 18, or within a section in respect to a significant action, as in v. 16 with Moses' charge to the appointed judges. In fact, all of these ten instances are concerned with certain occasions where a special announcement (1:9; 5:5; 10:1), command (1:16, 18; 3:18, 21; 4:14) or petition (3:23; 9:20) is made, usually by Moses, but sometimes by Yahweh (4:14; 10:1). It is striking that this formula is used repeatedly in a unique way in these chapters in connection with Moses and Yahweh,

besides further instances in 2:34; 3:4, 8, 12; 10:8 (p. 63). It is generally agreed that Dt 1-4 (or 1:6-4:40) and 5-11 are two introductions
to the Deuteronomic Code, 12-26 (28),[1]) which expressly present Moses as the proclaimer of the divine revelation (1:1, 3, 5; 4:44 f.; 5:1,
with subsequent use of the 1st pers. sing. in reference to Moses).[2])
Thus the program of Deut. as proclamation of the divine will for the
social, political and cultic life of the people [3]) resorts to the authority
of Israel's great leader and founder of its religion, who has been
characterized as the "super-prophet", "prototype for all successors"
and "unequaled model", through whom alone Yahweh spoke to
Israel.[4])

If this is the Deuteronomic argument for support and authority that
is established in the two introductions, then it is significant that the
formula $b\bar{a}{}^{\varsigma}\bar{e}th$ $hah\bar{\imath}w$ occurs here 15 times and nowhere else in the
book. In fact, the special use defined above which appears 10 times
in this context is used nowhere else in the OT at all, with the possible
exception of an accidental similarity in Neh 4:16, where Nehemiah
gives an order to the men to remain overnight in Jerusalem. It is
therefore obvious that this particular formula, which is only used here
with such frequency, was a favorite expression of the author(s) of Dt
1-11, and that it was very likely employed for a special purpose. This
purpose is particularly revealed in the cases where Moses is portrayed
as the mediator between Yahweh and the people: he appoints and
charges judges over the tribes (1:9, 16, 18); he delivers the commands
of Yahweh to the people (3:18, and concerning the Decalogue:
5:5) and Joshua (3:21); he intercedes for himself (3:23) and for
Aaron (9:20); and he receives commands from Yahweh (4:14, 10:1).
The formula is therefore one means of stressing the fact of Moses'

---

[1]) 1:6-4:40 is usually handled as an addition by Rd, as by Dillmann (*Deuteronomium*, p. 229), Driver (*Deuteronomy*, pp. lxvii, lxxii) and König (*Das Deuteronomium*, *KAT*, 3, Leipzig: 1917, p. 48), and chs. 5-11 as an introduction by D
(see Driver, *loc. cit.*, p. 65; von Rad, *loc. cit.*, p. 16). But Otto Eissfeldt (*Einleitung
in das Alte Testament*, 3rd ed. (Neue Theologische Grundrisse), Tübingen: 1964,
264 f.) considers both introductions the work of Rd (*cf.* Rost, *op. cit.*, p. 71),
while Martin Noth (*Überlieferungsgeschichte des Pentateuch*, 2nd ed., Stuttgart: 1948,
pp. 14-16) regards Dt 1-3 as the beginning of the Deuteronomic history which
incorporated 4:44-30:20 (so Weiser, *Einleitung*, p. 123).

[2]) *Cf.* Otto Procksch: *Theologie des Alten Testaments*, Gütersloh: 1950, p. 78;
Walter Eichrodt: *Theologie des Alten Testaments*, I, 5th ed., p. 190.

[3]) See Eichrodt, *loc. cit.*, p. 291.

[4]) So Albert Gelin: "Moses im Alten Testament", *Moses in Schrift und Überlieferung*, Düsseldorf: 1963, pp. 47, 49; see von Rad: *Theologie des Alten Testaments*,
I, pp. 292 f.

mediatorship and of the authority of the Deuteronomic pronouncements, sometimes in key passages. Thus 'ēth does not merely indicate
the temporal relationship of certain occasions, but is employed as a
means of emphasis for underlining the truth of a statement—in
effect, *for substantiating the fact of the reality of a certain occurrence*. It is
used to support the historicity of specific occasions.

b. Use of 'āz, shānāh, mō'ēd

In connection with the use of 'ēth in Deut., a consideration of the
use of other expressions likewise yields very striking results. 'āz
occurs only once, in 4:41, where it loosely connects a short account
of the designation of cities of refuge in Transjordan to the conclusion
of Moses' first admonitory address, 4:1-40. The form *bashshānāh
hahīw'* in 14:28 may be mentioned, although it merely has to do with
the bringing of the three-year tithe "in the same year".

mō'ēd has little more to offer. It refers only to the appointed seventh
year as the set occasion for the reading of the Law in 31:10. In 16:6,
it denotes "the set time of your coming forth from Egypt". This is,
however, not strictly an historical reference, but, preceded by "in
the evening, about sunset", it refers to the set time for the Passover
sacrifice which was at the same time of day as the beginning of the
Exodus. It thus exhibits a case of cultic terminology for an established
time being employed for the occasion of an historical event, and does
not present a natural use of *mō'ēd* in the historical sense. To the
contrary, Pedersen has connected *mō'ēd* in an essential way to historical
events. He reasons from the doubtful conclusion that the Israelite
conception of time is characterized by "not so much the distances
as the substance and contents of the events", because the decisive
factors in dividing the day into periods "are the different peculiar-
ities of the sun which leave their different impress upon everything".
Therefore, "each continuity of time, e.g. a month, is a sum of expansion
of life, merged into a unity, and this is concentrated in certain days,
chiefly in the first day. Out of these festal days (*mō'ēdh*) the events
develop." [1]) Obviously proceeding more by speculation than on
evidence, he ends up by actually reversing the effect of the festivals,
which were characterized and impressed by the events.[2]) For, as has

---

[1]) *Op. cit.*, I-II, pp. 489 f.

[2]) *Cf.* Pidoux (*op. cit.*, p. 123), who, although without referring to *mō'ēd*, also
speaks of a "concentrated time" of the cult in relation to historical events: "La
notion du temps concentré expliquerait que certaines périodes histoires, comme
celle de Moïse, aient subile 'gonflement' qu'on observe dans Amos, par exemple.

been shown, *mōʿēd* is not characterized by any natural tendency to be related to an event of historical significance; this can only occur in a secondary fashion, as in 2 Sam 24:15 (pp. 88 f.).

c. Use of *yōm*

Of the exactly 100 instances of other temporal expressions that may be compared with the usage of *ʿēth* in the historical sense, *yōm* alone holds title to 96. Yet, many instances of *yōm* in a definite, chronological sense where it is used literally, or in indefinite reference to a temporal period, including 4:32a, where it indicates the whole of the past ("For ask now concerning former days which were before you"), are irrelevant to the subject at hand. For the relevant cases, the frequent use of the simple expression *hayyōm* is fairly normative. Occurring 58 times in Deut., it appears three times in the accounting or recounting of events (Dt 1-3; 32:48-34:12), 46 times in the admonitory addresses (4-11; 27-32:47), and nine times in the body of statutes (12-26). In seven cases it is used for occasions where God (Yahweh) is the agent, in 49 where he appears in indirect relationship, and in but two where he is not affected. This pattern is easily explained according to the material presented. Referring properly to the present situation, *hayyōm* naturally occurs seldom in the contexts that deal with past events. In all three cases it occurs in quoted addresses from past occasions: 1:10, 39; 2:18. In the body of statutes it likewise appears on rare occasions, for such temporal references are not ordinarily relevant to the nature of the subject. In this respect it appears in a short, parenthetical admonitory passage (13:19; 15:5, 15; 19:9), in the quotation of a proposed address in a certain future situation (20:3; 26:3b), in a comparative reference to the present situation (12:8), or in the concluding verses to the section where the present is particularly emphasized (26:17 f.).

It is precisely such emphasis on the present situation that characterizes the 46 cases in the admonitory addresses and, in fact, these addresses themselves. Here, *hayyōm* is employed in reference to a certain significant condition of the present (*e.g.*, "But you who have held fast to Yahweh your God are all alive today"; 4:4; also 5:3;

Il est possible que cette notion du temps concentré ou temps cultique nous donne le secret de la place qu'occupent certains événements du passé d'Israël que les motifs de la création ou de l'Exode, par exemple, se retrouverait dans les tableaux de l'avenir et dans ceux de la fin des temps." The cult may foster the tradition of certain events, but it is not the place from which the events develop (see below, p. 9).

29:9, 14a, b; 31:2); it refers to a significant activity (*e.g.*, "Hear, Israel, you who are passing over the Jordan today", 9:1; also: 11:26; 29:11 f., 17; 30:15; 31:21, 27); it is used with an oath or solemn warning (*e.g.*, "I make the heavens and the earth witnesses against you today", 4:26; also: 8:19; 30:19), or with a special charge (*e.g.*, "Know today . . . that Yahweh is the God in the heavens above and upon the earth below", 4:39; also: 9:3; 11:2; 30:18); but it is most frequently employed (29 times) with the giving of statutes, usually in the set formula *'asher 'ānokīy metsawwekā hayyōm*, e.g., "And you shall keep his statutes and his commands which I command you today" (4:40, also: 4:8; 5:1; 6:6; 7:11; 8:1, 11; 10:13; 11:8, 13, 27 f., 32; 13:19; 15:5, 15; 19:9; 27:1, 4, 10; 28: 1, 13-15; 30:2, 8, 11, 16; 32:46).

It is thus obvious that *hayyōm* is used with an unusual frequency in Deut. to lay special emphasis upon the present situation as the occasion of the giving of the Law by Moses. This is in keeping with the tenor of the book as a whole and not merely with the admonitory addresses or the introductory or concluding chapters. Even the legal sections—the Code of the Covenant—are presented in the form of an address by Moses to the people of Israel in the present situation. It is only natural that the basic purpose behind the writing of the book should be most apparent in the admonitory sections that build the framework and introduction to the laws.

The purpose of Deut. reflected in the use of *hayyōm* may also be clearly seen in other related expressions. *hayyōm hazzeh* appears as a strengthened form for particularly significant situations, connected either to a divine act, as a promise of protection (2:25) or command (26:16; 32:48), or to a unique experience (5:24; 27:9; *cf.* esp. the last instance: "this day you have become a people for Yahweh your God"). *kayyōm hazzeh* is also a strengthened form, used always in reference to a present situation that is the result of a former divine act (2:30; 4:20, 38; 6:24; 8:18; 10:15; 29:27; *cf.* esp. 8:18—"so that he (Yahweh) may fulfil [1]) his covenant which he swore to your fathers, as at this day"). As usual, *'ad hayyōm hazzeh* indicates a condition that even exists up to the present situation (2:22; 3:14; 10:8b;

---

[1]) That *hāqīym 'eth-berīythō* means specifically "fulfil his covenant" in distinction to usage with verbs as *nthn* and *krth* in the sense of "make", and that this distinction is standard usage in Hebrew independent of the sources, see U. Cassuto: *The Documentary Hypothesis and the Composition of the Pentateuch*, Jerusalem: 1961, pp. 47 f.).

29:3; 34:6), including the unique exception of 11:4, where, in referring to Yahweh's "signs and deeds", he wiped out Egypt's army
at the Reed Sea "until this day". This last is evidently an example of
the carry-over of a special usage into the historical sphere (*cf.* 16:6
with *mō'ēd*, p. 66). Thus a past historical event may be signified as
having effective consequences for the present. This is, in fact, the
whole character of Deut., namely, the identification of the effective
relevance of a certain past historical event for the present situation.

Other expressions refer to either a certain past or future occasion.
Various constructions point back to a past situation for the purpose
of establishing the authority of what is being presented in an admonitory form: *yōm 'asher* (4:10), *beyōm* with verb (4:15), *lemin-
hayyōm 'asher* (4:32a; 9:7), *miyyōm* with verb (9:24), *beyōm haqqāhāl*
(9:10; 10:4; 18:16). As simple temporal references, they relate to
the past event concerning the requirements of the present situation,
as: "For you did not see any form on the day of Yahweh's speaking
to you on Horeb from the midst of the fire; beware, lest you act
corruptly and make for yourselves a sculptured form of any idol"
(4:15 f.). A similar construction, *beyōm 'asher*, is also used in reference
to an occasion seen in the future (27:2).

The future situation may be denoted with particular emphasis
through the formula *be'achariyth hayyāmiym* (4:30; 31:29), literally,
"at the end of the days". Although often translated "in the latter
days", as if it always appeared in the apocalyptic sense of Dan 10:14
(see pp. 112 f.), the phrase actually points to an occasion in the future
which takes place at the end of a certain but indefinitely defined length
of time. This is most clearly seen in Num 24:14—"I shall counsel
you what this people will do to your people at the end of the days."
Balaam is obviously referring to a future event involving Moab and
Israel, and not to the ultimate end of all time. The "end" is precisely
what it says: "the end of the days", that is, according to the indefinite character of *yāmiym*, "the end of some days". The formula is
thus used to put emphasis upon the fact of an event that is sure to
come after a period of time.

This same meaning is intended in Gen 49:1, and there is no reason
why the cases in the prophets cannot reflect the same intention. For
example, the cases in Jer 23:20; 30:24, clearly demonstrate that an
occasion is meant which comes as the fulfilment of the preceding,
intervening time: "At the end of the days, you will understand it
with understanding." The same is certainly the case in Hos 3:5 as

the end of the *yāmīym* in v. 4. Even in Isa 2:2 and Mic 4:1, the eschatological tone does not necessarily refer to the absolute end, for the
loʾ ʿōd of Isa 2:4 and Mic 4:3 implies a continuation, which is expressly
stated in 4:7 with *mēʿattāh weʿad-ʿōlām* — "from now and until
distant time". The usage of *bayyōm hahūʾ* in the contexts (Isa 2:11;
Mic 4:6) further indicates a "day" as such, not the end of all time.
What is meant by the contexts is a transformation of the physical
situation, not of the phenomenon of "time"; the spatial and temporal
dimensions remain. This also holds true for the cases in Jer 48:47;
49:39; Ezek 28:16. Thus the formula *beʾacharīyth hayyāmīym* is
nowhere absolutely eschatological in the temporal sense (except
in Dan 10:14), as is usually presumed,[1] but only with respect to the
content, that is, to the specific situation.

In a special study of the expression, W. Staerk proceeded on the
eschatologically-minded premise that it relates to the advent of the
Messianic kingdom and then explained all instances except Ezek
38:16 as post-exilic.[2] But N. Messel saw that it basically means
nothing more than "finally", "at the end", and is to be compared
with *beʾacharīythāhh*, "at the end of the matter" (Jer 5:31; Prov 25:8),
as if to say, "an dem den Zeiten angehörenden, d.h. mit der Zeit sich
einstellenden, Schluß (der Sache)." [3] The cause of the general misunderstanding of the formula has been traced by Messel [4] to the
translation of the LXX, which simply rendered it literally. Thus it
was adaptable to the late Jewish idea of the absolute end of the present
world age. In every case, the LXX renders it in the same phraseology

---

[1] So König (*Wörterbuch*, p. 13) and Koehler (*op. cit.*, p. 33) for the prophets;
Procksch (*Jesaia*, p. 62) for Isa 2:2; Paul Volz (*Der Prophet Jeremia*, Leipzig:
1922, pp. 235, 276) to Jer 23:20, 30:24; Artur Weiser (*Der Prophet Jeremia*,
25, 15-52, 34, 3rd ed., *ATD*, 21, 1960, p. 410) to 48:47; Alfred Bertholet
(*Hesekiel*, *HAT*, I:13, 1936, p. 133) to Ezek 38:16; T. H. Robinson (*op. cit.*,
p. 16) to Hos 3:5; and Robinson (*ibid.*, p. 140) and Weiser (*Kleine Propheten*, pp.
263 f.) to Mic 4:1. It is generally regarded as simply a term for the future in the
non-prophetical writings, but also by Scott (*op. cit.*, p. 180) and Kaiser (*op. cit.*,
p. 20) for Isa 2:2; Rudolph (*Jeremia*, pp. 141, 262) for Jer 23:20; 48:47; John
Mauchline ("The Book of Hosea", "Exegesis", *IB*, VI, 1956, p. 599) for Hos
3:5; and Roland E. Wolfe ("The Book of Micah", "Exegesis", *IB*, VI, 1956, p.
922) for Mic 4:1. Wolfe considers it a technical term for the end of the Exile.

[2] "Der Gebrauch der Wendung *bʾchryth hymym* im at. Kanon", *ZAW* 11
(1891), pp. 247-253.

[3] *Die Einheitlichkeit der jüdischen Eschatologie*, *BZAW* 30, Giessen: 1915, p. 63;
so also Peter Andreas Munch: *The Expression Bajjom Hāhūʾ*, Oslo: 1936, p.
59, n. 4.

[4] *Op. cit.*

as in Dan 10:14 : ἐπ' ἐσχάτου τῶν ἡμερῶν. Thus, for all other instances, one may apply the rendering, "after a certain time".

It is significant that the expressions most closely related to *bā'ēth hahīy'* occur relatively seldom in Deut., and then in a distinctively different sense. The more general formula *bayyāmīym hahēm* appears only in the body of laws in respect to the particular judge or priest in office in the future situation (17:9; 19:17; 26:3a). The more specific expression *bayyōm hahū'* means simply "on the same day" in 21:23, and appears in the more emphatic sense only in the concluding admonitions, in which section *bā'ēth hahīw'* fails completely. This phenomenon cannot be attributed to a change in style, for each instance of the former expression indicates a different intention than is the case with the latter. Whereas *bā'ēth hahīw'* always relates to an occasion in the past, *bayyōm hahū'* in three instances refers to a future situation (31:17a, b, 18). The other two cases (27:11; 31:22) clearly mean simply "the same day", referring to the same temporal situation in a general sense.

d. Temporal Expressions and Historical Conception

The result of these considerations over the relevant temporal expressions in Deut. reveal a very unified picture throughout. When referring to an occasion of the past as a significant historical event, *bā'ēth hahīw'* is used; but *yōm* is employed in a conjunctive construction when a specific relationship between events is indicated. When special emphasis is to be laid upon the present situation, *hayyōm* is made use of, or *hayyōm hazzeh* and *kayyōm hazzeh* in strengthened forms. *bāyyōm hahū'* may either indicate occurrence in the same situation or, as also *bayyāmīym hahēm* and *be'acharīyth hayyāmīym*, a significant future situation. It is thus evident that the principal temporal expressions in Deut. are always carefully and deliberately employed according to a certain temporal conception. They are not interchanged with each other or with other expressions, which are practically ignored. The scheme is readily seen in the usage of certain expressions for future occasions, in the decisive preference of "on that occasion" over "on that day" to denote the historical character of past events, and in the oft-repeated mention of the present situation.

It is clear that there is a very definite historical conception in Deut. that is more emphatically expressed than in any other pre-apocalyptic writing. The usual interpretation of historical events according to the rule of divine activity seen in the narrative literature is greatly surpassed. The author interprets the whole scope of the history of Israel according to the *tempora* of past, present and future. He projects himself into a certain past situation, speaking of it as the present, of his actual present situation as the future, and of certain preliminary events as having occurred in the past. But he doesn't simply assign events to their respective category. The major center of attention focuses on the present in order to emphasize the continuing validity of the statutes. But the past and future events are not thereby pushed into the background, as is usually the case when propagating ethical codes. The very authority for the code is based upon the fact of certain events of the past, and its positive and negative consequences determine the course of future events.In this way, both present and future events are formed by the past.[1]) Likewise, both past and future events are not simply left to their historical position, but are valued as having relevance for the present situation. This does not mean that the temporal and historical nature of past and future events is nullified. To the contrary, they are seen precisely in the full effect of their historicity, that is, in the scheme of causal relationship that characterizes the interrelationship of historical events. The present situation is the actual, existential experience of "today", which has been determined by the concrete fact of the past occasion (ʿēth), and which itself determines the outcome of the future (beʾachariyth hayyā-miym).

e. "Realistic Time" and Chronological Order

John Marsh, who likes to find evidence in the OT of the historical moment filled with significance that bursts out of God's eternity into worldly temporality, interprets ʿēth with the so-called καιρός-concept of the NT. Noting that the theologically significant events pertaining to the Exodus complex (the emancipation from Egypt, the desert wandering, the Sinai covenant and the conquest of Canaan)

---

[1]) Thus a unique relationship appears between the concerns of Deut. and those of prophecy and esp. of apocalyptic, as R. H. Charles (*Religious Development Between The Old and The New Testaments*, London: 1914, pp. 22-24) demonstrated, *e.g.*: "Whereas prophecy incidentally dealt with the past and devoted itself to the present and the future as rising organically out of the past, apocalyptic, though its interests lie chiefly in the future as containing the solution of the problems of the past and present, took within its purview things past, present, and things to come." The similarity is even more striking when it is realized that all three bodies of literature were primarily concerned with ethics and the survival of the Israelite people (*cf.* Charles, *ibid.*, p. 32).

are not presented in Dt 1-10 in the actual chronological order, he concludes that the "realistic time" of the OT does not appear to the writer as a chronological continuum but as a theological row of events with divine content and independent of chronological succession. All periods of God's acts thus have the same significance and force because of their identity and content. Throughout Israel's history, each one is simply known as "that time". He may thus offer the comforting conclusion that a man may live through faith regardless of his position in the chronological line of time, for he is immediately related to the intervention of the Eternal in time.[1]) James Barr has already effectively repudiated such reasoning with respect to considering the Biblical concept of time as "realistic time" in essentially diametrical opposition to the modern Western concept of "chronological time", and with respect to filling the words *'ēth* and καιρός with a concept borrowed from classical Greek by way of the modern καιρός-philosophy, which has no direct linguistic relationship to the Bible.[2])

As for his interpretation of the formula "at that time", Marsh apparently ignores the fact that it is structurally a temporal reference that relates two occasions to each other. As such, it never indicates "time" *per se* or "a time" without specific temporal relationship. The expression *bā'ēth hahiw'* in Deut. is always used for the purpose of relating a certain occasion to the past, in distinction, *e.g.*, to *hayyōm* for the present and to *bayyāmiym hahēm* for the future. Thus "on that occasion" does not indicate the lack of chronological thought or the existence of the idea that the past event itself is immediately related to, or even realized in, the present situation. To the contrary, the formula actually relates past events to a confirmed position in the past in distinction to the present, admitting only of the continuing effect of their consequences.

If the events are not always arranged in strict chronological order, it does not necessarily follow that a chronological concept of time was lacking or that conflicting traditions were employed. It would rather demonstrate that the events and their relationship to each

---

[1]) *The Fulness of Time*, pp. 28, 35 ff., 47 ff., 64 f.; see above, pp. 8 f. He also calls attention to erroneous sequence in Ps 114:1-3; Isa 63:11-14. For the same reason, Sekine (*op. cit.*, p. 80; see above, pp. 15 f.) concludes: "Das Deuteronomium sieht also die Zeit zwischen dem Auszug aus Ägypten und dem Einzug in Kanaan als eine Einheit und nennt sie 'jene Zeit'."

[2]) *Biblical Words for Time*, pp. 22 ff.

other were more highly valued than the purely secondary details of chronological date and exact sequence. Barr has also sufficiently emphasized the OT capacity for chronological thought, as also Eichrodt has done before him, so that further discussion of the topic here would be superfluous.[1]) The numerous genealogies, repeated emphasis on the sequence of generations, and the two great historical complexes of Genesis to 2 Kings and Chronicles should be able to speak for themselves.

f. "Present Actualization" and Corporate Relationship

The strongest indications for a present actualization of, or an immediate relationship to, past events in Deut. are offered by the presentation of Moses' account to the people of events that happened to the previous generation as if they themselves had experienced them. Furthermore, Moses even explicitly says that the people before him were present in the former time of their fathers, *e.g.*: "Not with our fathers did Yahweh make this covenant, but with us, we who now today are all alive" (5:3). Significant is the change in this case to the first person plural; Moses identifies himself with this generation in the same solidarity as he had with the previous one.

The important factor to be recognized is that of "corporate personality", the sense of family and community that surpasses the limits of generations, the sharing by the sons in the experiences of the fathers. This phenomenon was first pointed out by Johannes Pedersen who, however, drew misleading conclusions regarding a relevant view of time, when he said that "the differences in point of time are not decisive".[2]) Such a statement might imply that the Hebrews did not appreciate differences between the *tempora* of past, present and future, and that they experienced an actualization of the past and future in the present in the same way as the cultic rituals of the nature religions. To the contrary, the Hebrew appreciation for chronology and the historical *tempora* has been adequately demon-

---

[1]) Barr, *ibid.*; pp. 26 ff.; *cf.* Eichrodt; "Heilserfahrung und Zeitverständnis im Alten Testament", pp. 113 ff.; see above, p. 10.

[2]) *Op. cit.*, I-II, pp. 276-278. Pedersen himself actually goes too far on the basis of this single phenomenon, identifying "this law of community" as "the basis of the Israelite conception of history" (pp. 277 f.). H. W. Robinson ("The Hebrew Conception of Corporate Personality", *BZAW* 66, 1936, p. 49) was the first to employ the term for the designation, deriving it from the definition of English law for a corporation: "a body corporate legally authorized to act as a single individual; . . . an artificial person . . . having the capacity of perpetual succession."

strated above and elsewhere. The so-called "present actualization"
of past events does not belong to the temporal category of perception,
but to the recognition of corporate relationship. No Israelite could
have an experience relationship to the Flood, *e.g.*, for his people was
not yet in existence "at that time". As Gerhard von Rad has said, the
Deuteronomist was urging a subjective present actualization
("subjektive Vergegenwärtigung").[1] For the purposes here, the same
basic standpoint was presented in criticism of Oscar Cullmann's
view of salvation history (*Heilsgeschichte*) by Franz Hesse, namely
that the category of time is not sufficient to denote the essence of
this history, for the different temporal stages correspond to two forms
of human existence that are actually differentiated through the realization of faith in Christ or the lack of it. This is therefore not essentially a category of time but one of experience.[2] So also, the interest
of the Deuteronomist in the present actualization of the giving of the
Law on the basis of past events and for the purpose of preventing
future national disaster does not rest upon a peculiar sense of time,
but on an acute sense of the needs of the specific situation.

g. Causal Relationship and Historical Substantiation

We find in Deuteronomy the only example of a carefully thought
out historical conception according to the principle of causal relationship which has been successfully applied to a particular existential
situation. This is a piece of genuine history, for it places the events
into a causal temporal relationship to one another. "History" is not
simply an event that appears as such, nor the interpretation of events,
but the demonstration of causal relationship between the events,
particularly by means of a logical conception.[3] In this light, the
special role given in Deut. to *'ēth* may be better appreciated, for it
has been singled out because of its characteristic indication of a definite occasion for the purpose of referring to the definite events of the
past upon whose actual occurrence the whole Deuteronomic argument
rests.

It may now be concluded that the formula *bā'ēth hahīy'* was generally known and accessible to the OT historiographers in order to

---

[1] *Theologie des Alten Testaments*, I, p. 225, n. 79.

[2] "Zur Frage der Wertung und der Geltung alttestamentlicher Texte", *Fest-schrift, Friedrich Baumgärtel zum 70. Geburtstag*, Erlangen: 1959, pp. 90 f.

[3] *Cf.* Wildberger, *op. cit.*, p. 83.

indicate a further aspect of a complex situation, to relate occasions objectively and temporally, whether approximately simultaneous or in sequence, and to introduce or connect narratives. The Deuteronomist appropriated it for the special use of substantiating the historical fact of certain occurrences. If it could be used for the purposes of substantiation, then it must have been a term that was associated with *real event*. Thus the character of ʿ*ēth* as definite occasion proves itself appropriate for application to the *actual occurrence of historical events* and to emphasis upon this fact.

5. *Objectivization and Generalization of the Historical Reference*

A few variant constructions in late texts give evidence of an employment of ʿ*ēth* for historical occasions which differs basically from the other cases. The construction *ūmēʿēth ʾasher* as a compound temporal conjunction appears in 2 Chr 25:27. Considering the difficulty with the temporal connotation of the phrase, Wilhelm Rudolph changes *mēʿēth* to (*le*)ʿ*ummath*, "corresponding to". [1]) However, when *leʿummath* is used for objective correspondence, it always indicates situations or activities that are of a like nature, *e.g.*, 1 Chr 24:31—"and these also cast lots corresponding to their brothers". But Rudolph's use would apply the expression to a situation that corresponds only according to its appropriateness as a reaction to a "non-corresponding" situation, and not to a situation corresponding in kind. Furthermore, the temporal connotation of *mēʿēth* need not be pressed literally in respect to the intermediate span of fifteen years in verse 25, for ʿ*ēth* does not primarily refer to a point of time or even to the temporal aspect, but to a particular occasion or situation as such, which may in fact be indefinite in length of time (*cf.* Jdg 11:26, p. 60), or even practically devoid of temporal character. Thus the objective sense that fits the context best may be expressed with the MT: "And because of the situation that Amaziah had turned away from (following) after Yahweh . . ."

Constructions in the plural form also occur in the historical sense, as in 1 Chr 15:5 in description of the conditions of a former situation in the prophecy of Azariah: "And in those times (*ūbāʿittīym hāhēm*) there was no peace for him who went out or came in." The same form is used in Dan 11:14 to indicate the sequence of events, but appears in shortened form with the demonstrative article in v. 6 to refer to the

---

[1]) *Chronikbücher*, p. 280.

occasion of temporally coinciding events—"and she will be given (up), she and her attendants and her child and her supporter, in those times (*bāʿittīym*)". The close temporal and objective relationship to the foregoing allow the rendering "in the same times" or "in the same situation" (*cf.* Jdg 3:29 and 4:4, pp. 48 f.). The effect of this employment of the plural for an approximate temporal reference leads to the further result that the indication of a definite occasion (as in Ezra 10:14; Neh 10:35; 13:31; see p. 31) is lost and replaced by an indefinite reference to the general situation. Commentators usually encounter difficulty with the position of the relevant expression in Dan 11:6 at the end of the sentence and transpose it to the beginning of verse 7.[1]) However, the position at the end of the sentence is no singular phenomenon for an historical reference, for it is chosen in seven other cases where the particular occasions are likewise temporally coincident: Num 22:4; Dt 9:20; Jdg 4:4; 11:26, 2 Kgs 8:22; Ezra 8:34 (see p. 60, n. 1), and 2 Chr 16:10.

In this context mention may be made of Dan 11:13 and the remarkable reading: *ūleqēts bāʿittīym shānīym*. Considering the impossibility of a sensible reading with the temporal reference as it stands, and that the similar expression *ūleqēts shānīym* is used in v. 6 in much the same way, it is obvious that *bāʿittīym* has accidentally crept into this verse.[2]) This could well have been a dittography from the following line, where *ūbāʿittīym* appears in v. 14. The other possibility, that *shānīym* be a dittography from v. 6, is improbable according to the context, for "the times" succeed each other (vv. 6, 14) and the "time of the end" does not make its appearance until v. 40.

It is evident from these considerations that, although the formula *bāʿēth hahīyʾ* was the "standard" form for applying *ʿēth* to a situation entailing historical relationship, variant forms were introduced in late texts (see p. 51), including the plural. These are indications of the later practices of adding *ʿēth* superfluously to temporal references, of objectivizing it from a reference to an occasion to the designation of the occasion itself (*cf.* Dan 9:25, pp. 85 f.), or even of emptying it of its proper indication of a definite occasion by generalizing it for application to an indefinite situation.

---

[1]) So BH; Karl Marti: *Das Buch Daniel*, KHCAT, XVIII, Tübingen: 1901, p. 79; Aage Bentzen: *Daniel*, HAT, I:19, 2nd ed., 1952, p. 76; and Norman W. Porteous: *Das Danielbuch*, ATD, 23, 1962., p. 121.

[2]) So Marti, *loc. cit.*, and Bentzen, *op. cit.*, p. 78; *cf.* BH.

C. INTERVENTION BY A SINGLE OCCASION

Apart from the uses of ʿēth in situations of primarily relative or historical occasions, it also occurs quite frequently with respect to singular, non-recurring occasions that are distinguished by a unique intervention into the course of affairs. Secondary differences are more readily discerned when this category is subdivided according to the aspects of experience, activity and event.

1. *An Intervening Experience*

The intervening experiences are usually of a negative character, the earliest instance appearing in Isaiah: The tumultuous nations, roaring in the self-confidence of their might, are about to experience an interrupting surprise: *leʿēth ʿereb wehinnēh ballāhāh beterem boqer ʾēynennū*—"At evening-time, behold, terror! before morning, they are no more!" (17:14) Similar reference to the extraordinary distress situation is also made in Jer 20:16 (see p. 22), and with a resultant plea for help in 2:27 f.; 11:12; 14:8. One case even concerns intercession for the enemy by Jeremiah (15:11): "if I have not made entreaty with you for the enemy on the occasion of evil and in the situation of misery" (*beʿēth rāʿāh ūbeʿēth tsārāh*). The same type of situation appears in the editorial context of Jdg 10:14, in the so-called apocalyptic context of Isa 33:2, in the confident assurance for the righteous in Ps 37:39, and in the public confession in Neh 9:27. Most commentators read *beʿēth rāʿāthām* in Jer 11:14 (*cf.* v. 12), but Keil and Rudolph do well in retaining the reading of the MT, *beʿad*, which gives a very meaningful sense: "because of their misery".[1]

The same expression for a distress situation is used elsewhere for the occasion when the upright will not be ashamed, Ps 37:19 (*beʿēth rāʿāh*), when men are suddenly snared by death, Ecc 9:12b (p. 116), and when King Ahaz became even more faithless to Yahweh, 2 Chr 28:22. A predicate construction is used for the expression in Jer 30:7 concerning the Exiles: "and it is an occasion of distress (*weʿēth tsārāh*) for Jacob." A similar situation is indicated in Ezek 35:5b, where Mount Seir is blamed for its past act of putting Israel to the sword "on the occasion of their calamity"—*beʿēth ʾēydām*.

---

[1] Against BH, S. R. Driver (*The Book of the Prophet Jeremiah*, London: 1906, p. 68) and J. Köberle (*Der Prophet Jeremia*, 2nd ed., *EAT*, 2, Stuttgart: 1925, p. 112), but with C. F. Keil (*Der Prophet Jeremia*, BCAT, III:2, 1872) and Rudolph (*loc. cit.*, p. 70).

Positive experiences may also belong to this category, as the hoped-for "healing" in Jer 8:15 and 14:19, but which only ended in disappointing terror: *le'ēth marpēh wehinnēh be'āthāh*. The plural form may be employed poetically, as *le'ittōth batstsārāh* in Ps 9:10 and 10:1. The modifying word should probably be read *hatstsārāh*, or understood as a prepositional construction, "at situations in the distress".[1])

The distress may also be brought about by divine punishment, as in Jer 8:12—*be'ēth pequddāthām yikkāshelū*—"On the occasion of their punishment, they will stumble." The same situation is also presented in 10:15 and 51:18, and in a predicate construction in 46:21 and 50:27 (see pp. 91 f., 95), as well as in Ps 81:16 (*wiyhiy 'ittām le'ōlām*—"and their occasion would be (=continue) into distant time".) According to *'akniya'* in v. 15 ("humble") and *yekachashū* in 16 ("simulate surrender"), it is really not "fate" [2]) that is meant, but the situation of being subjugated.

The object of concern in Ps 32:6 is similar, but rather of a testing, purifying character: *le'ēth metso' raq*. Because *metso' raq* seems to hang in mid-air, it has been emended to *mātsōq* to read, "at the time of distress".[3]) But S. R. Hirsch is probably right in dividing the verse between the two words and interpreting the infinitive in the sense of "visitation",[4]) as in Gen 44:34, Num 32:23; Ps 119:143, and especially Ex 18:8 and Num 24:14, where reference is made to the distress of the Israelites in Egypt when God answered their plea for help by rescuing them through the water. This is evidently a deliberate use of the motif from the Pentateuch. Thus the pious need have no fear of being swept away permanently in their trouble if they turn to God: "Therefore may every pious one pray to you on the occasion of visitation; only (= even) at the flood of great waters—they shall not attain unto him!"

Intervention by catastrophic experience may also appear in a construction in the form of a temporal conjunction with the finite verb, as concerning the perverse generation in Dt 32:35 (see vv. 5, 20): "Mine are vengeance and retaliation on the occasion (when) their

---

[1]) The change in reading is suggested by BH and Kraus, *op. cit.*, p. 81. *Cf.* Hupfeld and Nowack, *op. cit.*, pp. 188 f., who regard it as the feminine infinitive Piel from *btsr* III.

[2]) So W. M. L. de Wette (*Commentar über die Psalmen*, 5th ed., Heidelberg: 1856), Hirsch (*op. cit.*, p. 66) and W. Stuart McCullough ("The Book of Psalms", "Exegesis", *IB*, IV, 1955).

[3]) So BH and Briggs (*op. cit.*, p. 283).

[4]) *Op. cit.*, p. 177 f.

foot falters (*leʿēth tāmūt raglām*)." The scene is the case of the
"faithless brethren" who are as freshets (Job 6:17): "On the occasion
(when) they shrivel up, they disappear." This context would be the
place to discuss the instance in Ezek 27:34. However, since the usage
is structurally closely related to three others that belong to the following section, it will be treated there with them (p. 83).

Comparatively late texts use the plural form for indicating the
experiences of danger that happen to the unprotected, as in Isa
33:6: *wehāyāh 'emūnath ʿitteykā*—"And he will be the stability of
your situations (= experiences)"; and in Ps 31:16: *beyadekā ʿittothāy*—
"In your hand are my situations (= experiences)." The text of the
former instance is struck out by Karl Marti because of the difficulty
with *'emūnath*.[1]) However, it should be clear that stable support in
the face of troublesome experiences is the meaning demanded by the
contexts. Both cases are concerned with crisis situations or distressful
experiences, for the subject of Isa 33:1-11 is the welfare of Zion in the
face of oppression (see *beʿēth tsārāh* in v. 2, p. 78), and Ps 31 is a petition for protection against enemies (see esp. vv. 8-11, 14, 16b). It is
therefore not meant in the absolute sense of "fate", as is often attributed to the alternate plural form *ʿittōth*,[2]) which is nothing more
than poetic.

In each of these cases, reference is made to the definite occasion for
a significant, intervening experience, without any specific deter-
mination of the temporal aspect.

2. *An Intervening Activity*

Probably the earliest instance of an intervening activity indicated
by *ʿēth* is in 2 Kgs 5:26, when Gehazi interrupted the course of affairs
set by Elisha to request gifts from Naaman; Elisha confronted him
with the accusing question: *haʿēth lāqachath 'eth-hakkeseph*—"Is it the
occasion to take silver?" The grammatical construction of *ʿēth*
preceding the infinitive as the occasion for an action is perfectly in
order, although Rudolf Kittel prefers the reading of the LXX,
καὶ νῦν ἔλαβες ("Nun wohl, du hast das Geld erhalten"), and emends
to *weʿattāh lāqachtā*.[3]) However, the MT reading is practically necessary
for the syntax, for both sentences in v. 26 are preliminary to the

---

[1]) *Psalmen*, p. 238.
[2]) So König (*Psalmen*, p. 287) and Weiser (*Psalmen*, p. 185), but see Buhl (*op. cit.*, p. 573) and Briggs (*op. cit.*, p. 269).
[3]) *Könige*, pp. 203-209; cf. BH, Gressmann (*Die Anfänge Israels*, p. 295).

concluding statement in 27, and if ʿattāh, which has the force of introducing the concluding statement, would already appear in 26, it
would upset the entire context. The same usage appears in Hag 1:4.

A similar uncalled-for action is blamed on the Jerusalemites by
Jeremiah (2:17), who forsook Yahweh beʿēth mōlīykēk baddārek—"on
the occasion of (his) leading you in the way". It may be a moot
question whether these three words are a dittography in the MT
because of their similarity to the first words of v. 18, or whether the
LXX accidentally omitted them for the same reason. Although the
latter possibility seems the more probable because the phrase adds
to the thought by providing a contrast to the act of forsaking and
because three lines in one verse are not unnatural in this context
(see vv. 5, 8a, 10, 22, 23aβ, b, 24a, 25b, 31a), the recent commentators
omit it, following Ewald's example.[1])

The arrival of the definite occasion for an appropriate action is
indicated in Hos 10:12 as the condition for receiving righteousness
—"and (= then) it is the occasion (weʿēth) to seek Yahweh". Many
commentators suggest reading daʿath [2]) in connection with the preceding clause in favor of the meter and probably because they felt an
incongruency between ʿēth and the following ʿad-yābōʾ—"until he
come". But the difficulty clears up as soon as one realizes that ʿēth
can often mean the occasion of an indefinite temporal duration.[3])
Such an occasion for Yahweh to act occurs in Isa 49:8a—beʿēth
rātsōn ʿanīythīykā—"On the occasion of favor (= on a favorable
occasion), I answered you." The same expression appears in a petition
in Ps 69:14. Similar in sense are the confident declarations in 102:14b:
kīy ʿēth lechannenāhh—"surely it is the occasion to have mercy upon
her"; and in 119:126: ʿēth laʿasōth leyhwh—"It is the occasion for
Yahweh to act." The same use is employed in the warning in Jer
51:6: kīy ʿēth neqāmāh hīyʾ leyhwh—"For it is the occasion of vengeance
for Yahweh."

With an impersonal suffix, reference is made in Isa 60:22 to Yahweh's promise to accomplish his purposes at the intended time—"On

---

[1]) Ewald, *Propheten*, II, p. 31; so BH, Rudolph (*Jeremia*, p. 16), Köberle (*op.
cit.*, p. 38), Weiser (*Jeremia*, p. 12); to the contrary, Ferdinand Hitzig (*Der Prophet
Jeremia*, 2nd ed., *KEHAT*, 3, 1866, p. 7) appreciated the fine grammatical touch
in this breviloquent participial construction (see König, *Syntax*, § 412a).

[2]) *E.g.*, Gressmann (*loc. cit.*, p. 372), T. H. Robinson (*op. cit.*, p. 41), and
Hans Walter Wolff (*Hosea*, BKAT, XIV:1, 1961, p. 234); with the MT see
Mauchline (*op. cit.*, p. 677).

[3]) *Cf.* Hitzig, *op. cit.*, ". . . ist noch immer Zeit, bleibt es Zeit, bis er kommt."

its occasion (*beʿittāhh*), I shall hasten it." Against Franz Delitzsch's
remark that a certain moment of time, "καιρός", is meant here,[1])
it must be said that the reference is to the occasion for all the events
of the chapter, which could all scarcely take place in a moment.

Indication of an intervening action in relationship to another
occasion is the case in Jer 11:14—"For I shall not be giving heed
on the occasion of their calling (*beʿēth qārʾām*) to me." A corresponding use appears in Jeremiah's plea for condemnation of his enemies
in 18:23—"at the occasion of your anger (*beʿēth ʾappekā*), act upon
them!" A comparable statement is made in Ps 21:10. Similar expressions also occur in promises of salvation, as in Zeph 3:20a: *ūbāʿēth
qabbetsiy ʾethekem*—"and on the occasion of my gathering you", and
in Mic 5:2: *lākēn yittenēm ʿad-ʿēth yōlēdāh yālādāh*—"Therefore he will
give them (up) until the occasion (when) the one giving birth gives
birth." In the former case, the controversial *qamets* before the *ʿayin*
is justified because the word receives one of the three accents of the
line;[2]) it is not a demonstrative article, as some have taken it to be
in correcting the text to *ūbāʿēth hahiyʾ ʾaqabbēts*.[3]) As for Mic 5:2,
Torczyner was apparently disturbed by the announcement of even a
temporary evil in v. 2a after the promise in v. 1, and so he proposes:
yittēn moʿēd ʿēth—"Therefore he set a date, a time . . .".[4]) But the
"therefore" modifies not just 2aα but the whole half-verse, finding its
counterpart in 2b: "and (= then) the rest of his brothers will return
unto the children of Israel". A comparable sense is meant in Ecc
8:9 with a temporal conjunction construction—"a situation where
(*ʿēth ʾasher*) man lords it over man".[5])

The occasion of threatened punishment is emphasized in Jer
6:15—"on the occasion (when) I punish them (*beʿēth peqadtiym*),
they will stumble." The same sense appears in a predicate construction
in 49:8—*ʿēth peqadtiyw*—"It is the occasion (when) I punish him",

---

[1]) *Jesaia*, p. 584.

[2]) The word has a *tiphcha*, a lesser distinctive accent, corresponding to the
pashta on *bāʿēth hahiyʾ* at the beginning of the line; *cf.* Kautzsch, *op. cit.*, § 15,
Bauer and Leander, *op. cit.*, §§ 9aʾ, 81t.

[3]) So BH, Ernst Ludwig Dietrich (*Die endzeitliche Wiederherstellung bei den
Propheten*, BZAW 40, Giessen: 1925, p. 27, n. 5), Friedrich Horst (with T. H.
Robinson: *Die Zwölf Kleinen Propheten*, HAT, I:14, 1938, p. 194).

[4]) *Op. cit.*, pp. 274-280; *cf.*, Hugo Gressmann: *Der Messias* (Forschungen zur
Religion und Literatur des Alten und Neuen Testaments 43, NF 26), Göttingen:
1929, pp. 248-250.

[5]) *Cf.* H. C. Leupold: *Exposition of Ecclesiastes*, Columbus, Ohio: 1952, pp.
192 f., that *ʿēth* is technically an adverbial accusative; see König, *Syntax*, § 331b.

and in 50:31—*kīy bā' yōmkā 'ēth peqadtīykā*—"For your day has come, the occasion (when) I punish you" (see p. 92).

A small group of four passages remains to be discussed here. The one, Ezek 27:34, properly belongs to the previous section (p. 80). This instance presents a remarkable reading in the MT: *'ēth nishbereth miyyammīym*. The impossibility of this pointing becomes obvious when it is considered that the syntactical structure of the context demands an independent clause with its own predicate. It comes just where the decisive change is made in the context from describing the proud ships of Tyre to announcing their destruction. Thus the participle should be changed to a finite verb: *nishbartt*.[1]) The syntactic situation could also allow the adverb *'attāh* instead of the noun *'ēth*, according to the usage of, *e.g.*, Gen 3:22; 1 Sam 15:3; Isa 5:3, 5; 30:8. However, this usage of *'attāh*, which is the most common, relates the foregoing situation to its continuation in the present in the form of a result or consequence. This is also the case with such passages as Gen 22:12; Ex 18:11, *etc.*, where the order is reversed, the consequence preceding the cause. In contrast, Ezek 27:34 calls attention to a situation completely different from the previous one; there is no place here for a causal or progressive connection in the sense of *'attāh*. The break is absolute; the emphasis is laid upon the uniqueness of the new situation: The magnificent ships of Tyre are wrecked! The proper stress is therefore laid not so much on the temporal "now" as on the specific factor of the new occasion. It may thus be readily seen that the function of the word introducing this significant occasion is comparable to that of *'ēth* normally: reference to a definite occasion of unique significance. Its introductory function in this instance is both temporal and existential, so that it appears as a sort of apocopated formula: "The (new) situation is: you are broken by the seas into the depths of waters."

This interpretation opens the way for similar readings in the following three cases where it would be grammatically possible to omit the *'ēth* of the consonantal text or to point it *'atta*. The latter occurs twice in the MT itself, first in Ezek 23:43—*'attā yiznuh taznūthehā wāhīy'*. Considering the collective impersonal character of the verb, it may be pointed according to Kethibh thus: *'ēth yizneh taznūthāhh*, and rendered: "The situation is: they commit her whoredom, and she, too!" So also Ps 74:6, where the imperfect verb at the end of the

---

[1]) So BH and Fohrer, *Ezechiel*, pp. 155 f.

sentence indicates the condition of the on-going activity: "And the situation was (*weʿēth*): they were chopping down its panelling altogether with axe and hatchets." [1]) A justifiably confusing text is presented in Hag 1:2—*loʾ ʿeth-boʾ ʿeth-bēyth yhwh lehibbānōth*. It might somehow be possible to make some sense out of the MT, but the sentence is awkward and improbable, even if it be colloquial speech. The most generally accepted emendation is to change the first *ʿeth* to *ʿattāh*: "The time is not yet come . . .".[2]) But that would be the only case in the OT where this combination is used instead of *loʾ ʿōd*.[3]) The Kethibh may rather be pointed as a negative in correspondence to the above instances: *loʾ ʿeth bāʾ*, "The situation is not: the occasion of the House of Yahweh has arrived to build (it)." Thus two different, nonparallel uses of *ʿēth* occur in the same passage, the latter indicating the occasion of an intervening activity, the former referring to this occasion in the peculiar sense of an introductory directive (see pp. 132 f.).

In each case of this section, indication is made of the definite occasion of a significant activity that intervenes into the *status quo* of the course of affairs. Often, the intervening activity demands a decision. Yet, it is not the pregnant "decisive moment" of kairos-theology. The necessitated decision is always an obvious one, appropriate to the situation. The emphasis is not placed on the dilemma of deciding, but on the only good way to decide.

3. *An Intervening Event*

Again turning to the early chapters of Jeremiah, the familiar expression *bāʿēth hahīyʾ* is found in reference to an announced event that is not given an ordinary historical relationship in the course of events, but that interrupts with a force that is to change the normal course. Contrary to the present *status quo*, "on that occasion, they will call Jerusalem the throne of Yahweh" (3:17). The same use is employed in 4:11; 8:1; 31:1; Mic 3:4; Zeph 1:12; 3:19, 20a. In Mic 3:4, *bāʿēth hahīyʾ* is often omitted as a repetition of *ʾāz* in 4a (p. 88) and as a disturbance of the meter.[4]) But according to the accents, the

---

[1]) König reads with Q as a strengthened addition, *weʿattā* (*Psalmen*, p. 350).

[2]) A plausible conjecture by Hinckley G. Mitchell (*Haggai, ICC*, 30, 1912, pp. 32, 51) omits the first "time" as a dittography.

[3]) The related expression in Dt 12:9 has a different meaning: "not . . . until now".

[4]) Wilhelm Nowack, *Die Kleinen Propheten*, 3rd ed., *GHAT*, III:4, 1922, p. 214, and Procksch, *Kleine Propheten*, p. 108, also read with MT.

meter of the verse is 2+3, 3+3, as it stands, and the redundancy of temporal expressions is only apparent to the Western ear, whereas it is very common in Hebrew prophecy (*cf.* 5:1; 7:4, 11 f., 14 f.). Schmidt and Sellin wish to omit all instances in Zephaniah as glosses.[1]) But *wehāyāh bāʿēth hahīyʾ* in 1:12 is a good stylistic echo of *wehāyāh beyōm zebach yhwh* in v. 8 and of *wehāyāh bayyōm hahūʾ* in v. 10; it carries no implication of the absolute eschatological end (see pp. 95, 105). Even if the two final verses should be exilic or post-exilic,[2]) the use of *ʿēth* would not be foreign to the style of the author, for it helps to emphasize the intervention of the occasion of salvation. Sometimes the expression is augmented, as in the Messianic promise in Jer 33:15—"In those days and on that occasion (*bayyāmīym hahēm ūbāʿēth hahīyʾ*), 1 will make sprout for David a sprout of righteousness." The same combination appears in 50:4, 20; Joel 4:1 (see pp. 109, 116). If all three instances in Jer. are additions,[3]) the combined expression may be of late origin; at least it is used in Joel in connection with apocalyptic pictures.

The relevant occasion may be emphasized as a situation of peculiar quality and indistinct duration, rather than a specific moment, as in Am 5:13b (= Mic 2:3): *kīy ʿēth rāʿāh hīyʾ*—"for it is an evil situation" (see also Dan 12:1b; *cf.* pp. 95, 111 f., and Am 5:13a, p. 46), and in Dan 9:25—*ūbetsūq hāʿittīym*, "but in the distress of the times". The last instance represents a reversal of the usual position of *ʿēth* in such a genitive construction. This has become possible because of the occasional objectivization of *ʿēth* in later literature from a reference to the occasion to a designation of the occasion itself (see pp. 76 f.). Here it is the "distressful situation" that hinders the rebuilding of Jerusalem. In Job 38:22f. God is portrayed as storing snow and hail *leʿēth-tsār*—"for the situation of distress": distress for those who oppose him.

It may be the aspect of relevance to another occasion that characterizes an intervening event. In Isa 48:16, it is explained that Yahweh has brought a certain event to pass by showing how he announced it from the start, *mēʿēth heyōthāhh shām ʾānīy*—"from the occasion of

---

[1]) Schmidt, *op. cit.*, pp. 159, 165; Sellin, *op. cit.*, pp. 368, 372.

[2]) So Nowack, *op. cit.*, p. 319, and Horst, *op. cit.*, p. 183.

[3]) 33:14-26 is lacking in the LXX, and it is ordinarily considered a later gloss that drew from 23:1-8. The prophecy against Babylon, 50:1-51:58, is usually denied authorship by Jeremiah, but Rudolph (*Jeremia*, p. 274) notes that the fall of Babylon and return from the Exile were also concerns of Jeremiah, and attributes nearly all the material to him.

its coming into being, I was there". It is obvious that the reference is to the event of Israel's redemption from Babylon, which is the subject of the entire context, and not to secondary remarks about the Creation (v. 13) or the origin of the people (v. 1).[1]) This *ʿeth heyōthāhh* is acclaimed by Paul Volz as the highpoint, the decisive moment for the time of fulfilment.[2]) But the context speaks of the entire situation —the whole series of events—as "the highpoint". The "decisive moment" would perhaps have been the very beginning (*mēroʾsh*, *mēʿēth*), but this is mentioned here in this way simply to emphasize the fact that God's active presence has accompanied the events the whole time of their occurrence. There is no thought of "decisive moment" as the term is properly understood.

The end of a period of time is indicated in Ps 105:19—*ʿad-ʿēth boʾ-debārō*—"until the occasion of the coming of his word"; *i.e.*, until Joseph's prophecy was fulfilled. The eschatological passage on the Day of Yahweh in Zech 14 contains the promise of a new condition that is to interrupt the natural order that has existed since creation: "And there shall be 'one day' . . . and at evening-time (*leʿēth-ʿereb*) there will be light" (v. 7; see p. 22).

In a somewhat different way than in Dan 9:25 (p. 85), the plural may be used in later literature in a manner of objectivization (see pp. 76 f.). Adverbially, it may refer to the plurality of occurrence, as in Neh 9:28—"and you delivered them according to your mercy many times (*rabbōth ʿittīym*)". This thought of an indefinite number of "times" apparently made a late appearance in Hebrew, as it occurs otherwise only twice, likewise in later literature, in the form *peʿāmīym rabbōth*, Ps 106:43; Ecc 7:22. Probably the earliest example of objectivization occurs in Ezek 12:27 in respect to future situations—"and for distant occasions (*ūleʿittīym rechōqōth*) he is prophesying". A non-modified instance in Job 24:1 is presumably to be construed from the context as meaning critical situations, *i.e.*, occasions of unpunished injustice: "Why are not occasions (*ʿittīym*) hidden from the Almighty?" The verse is usually considered incomprehensible in its present form, and most commentators resort to textual correction.[3]) The difficulty

---

[1]) König (*Jesaja*, p. 400) and Duhm (*Jesaia*, p. 336) see reference here to the contemporary events.

[2]) *Op. cit.*, pp. 92 f.

[3]) *E.g.*, Franz Wutz (*Das Buch Job*, Eichstätter Studien III, Stuttgart: 1939, p. 88) omits *yāmāyw* and reads *ʿothīym weyēreʿū*, ". . . the sinners, who act wickedly without blushing".

seems to lie in understanding the *waw* joining the second half of the verse. It may well indicate a following answer to the question and not a continuation of it: "And (= then) those knowing him do not see his days." The intention is that the occasions of injustice might just as well be hidden from God, for the oppressed do not see the days of divine justice (v. 12). Thus the "occasions" are the situations of injustice and not, as often supposed, occasions of judgment.[1]) This connotation *ʿēth* never has of itself, but only from the context, as in Jer 27:7; 49:8; Ezek 7:7; 22:3 (pp. 82, 88, 106 f.). Contrary to apparent general opinion, *ʿēth* may indicate an occasion of judgment only on the basis of the immediate context because of its appropriate inherent meaning of a definite occasion, and not because it may have that meaning *per se*.

Further objectivization follows in the case of application to historical events, generally speaking. In Est 1:13, wise men were summoned by the king, *yodeʿēy hāʿittīym*—"who understand the events". Essentially the same expression appears in 1 Chr 12:33. This has been understood as the astronomical events in the heavens studied by the astrologers of Persia.[2]) That could hardly be the case, for the sons of Issachar are singled out for special citation by the Chronicler. It has been proposed to read *haddāthīym* in Est 1:13 to render "lawyers".[3]) Although this is not necessary, it does point to the clue in the second half of the verse: *kol-yodeʿēy dāth wādīyn*—the experts in law and custom. L. B. Paton should therefore be right when he says that it has to do with those familiar with historical precedents which rank next to laws,[4]) for it was an unusual situation for which there was no law. Thus the reference is to definite occasions of former judgment which are used as the guide-line for decisions in the present. A similar application is made in 1 Chr 29:30—"And the affairs of David (*wedibrēy dāwid*) ... behold, they are written ... and the events (*wehāʿittīym*) which came upon him." This is a very clear instance of indicating the historical occurrences themselves. It demonstrates how *ʿēth* as definite occasion was appropriate to be used in a general way for the significant historical events.

---

[1]) So Duhm (*Hiob*, p. 121), Fohrer (*Hiob*, p. 371), Weiser (*Hiob*, p. 183).

[2]) So Hans Bardtke (*Das Buch Esther*, KAT, XVII, 5, 1963, p. 287), and Rudolph (*Chronikbücher*, p. 109) to 1 Chr 12:33.

[3]) So Helmer Ringgren (*Das Buch Esther*, ATD, 16:2, 1958, p. 117) and Max Haller (with Kurt Galling: *Die fünf Megilloth*, HAT, 1:18, 1940, p. 118).

[4]) *The Book of Esther*, ICC, 13, 1908, p. 151.

The intervening event may also be one that has been determined for its interruptive purpose, as the double expression in 2 Sam 24:15 referring to the end of the pestilence: *mēhabbōqer weʿad-ʿēth mōʿēd*— "from the morning and until the occasion of appointment". As Keil observed, *mōʿēd* may here mean the appointed time for the daily religious assembly.[1]) The divinely-appointed "end" is also indicated in Jer 27:7 for Nebuchadnezzar's land: *ʿad bōʾ-ʿēth ʿartsō gam-hūʾ*— "until the coming of the occasion of even his own land", and in Dan 11:24 for the "despicable one" (v. 21): *weʿad-ʿēth*—"but until an occasion". The aspect of appointment has to do with the fact of the occasion and not with the definite temporality of its occurrence; the moment is left vague.[2]) The impending imminence of the appointed, intervening event of disaster upon Israel is dramatically emphasized in Ezek 7:7, 12: *bāʾ hāʿēth*—"The occasion has come!" (see pp. 87, 95, 106 f.) *The* definite occasion has arrived![3])

As in the foregoing sections, it has been demonstrated here, too, that the use of *ʿēth* with intervening occasions is concerned with the definite occasion for the significant occurrence without specific reference to precise temporality.

4. *Other Expressions with Intervening Occasions*

ʾāz is used particularly by the prophets and in poetry in connection with intervening events, but, as has been seen in other contexts, with an indefinite indication of temporal relationship. The earlier prophets use it sparingly: Amos not at all, and Hosea, Isaiah and Micah only once each. In Hos 2:9, it relates to a former state and in Isa 14:8 to a former experience (also Job 38:21; *cf*. Ps 89:20, where it refers to a former activity). But in Mic 3:4 it appears in parallel to *bāʿēth hahīʾ* (see p. 84). After condemning the present injustices of the Israelite rulers in the second person (vv. 1-3), Micah marks the change in both person and time with *ʾāz*: "Then they will cry to Yahweh, but he will not answer them . . ." This change of scene is strengthened by further emphasis on the surprising fact of Yahweh's action: ". . . and he will hide his face from them on that occasion . . ." The former indicates the temporal change, but indefinitely; the latter emphasizes the hard fact of the situation, and thus complements

---

[1]) *Die Bücher Samuelis, BCAT*, II:2, 2nd ed., 1875, pp. 394 f.

[2]) So Volz, *Jeremia*, p. 258.

[3]) Torczyner (*op. cit.*, pp. 106 f.) explains the masc. verb form with the fem. noun through a haplography.

the former by augmentation in degree without redundancy in kind. A similar abrupt change is also denoted in Ps 2:5; 40:8; 56:10; Job 33:16; Ecc 2:15. Usually, *'āz* indicates nothing more than the continuation or result of a situation, as in Jer 22:22—". . . and your lovers will go into captivity: surely, then you will be ashamed . . ." The same usage appears in Isa 33:23; 35:5; 58:8, 14; 60:5; Mal 3:16; Ps 19:14; 51:21a, b; 76:8; 119:6; 124:3, 4, 5; Job 9:31; 28:27; Prov 1:28. It may also be used in introducing a further aspect of the same situation, as in Jer 31:12 f.—"And they will come and shout . . . Then virgins will rejoice in dance . . .". The same sense is employed in 11:18; Hab 1:11; Ezek 32:14; Zeph 3:9, 11b; Isa 35:6; 58:9; Ps 96:12; Job 3:13. Thus, *'āz* is used to indicate an abrupt or expected temporal change in the situation or continuation of it, but true to its usual form, only as a rather vague reference to the situation itself.

mō'ēd may sometimes be understood as an intervening occasion, even though always an appointed one. In 2 Sam 24:15, it is used as the genitive in a construct connection with *'ēth* (see p. 88). If *mō'ēd* does not mean "assembly" here, it offers a good example of how the two expressions may complement each other: the one referring to the occasion as such and the other to its appointed aspect. They also appear in direct parallel in the intervening sense in Ps 102:14b (see p. 81), where the occasion for mercy is also an appointed situation: *kīy bā' mō'ēd*. So assured is the psalmist of Yahweh's merciful intervention on behalf of Zion that he heightens his reference to it from a "definite occasion" to an "appointed time". A similar, earlier case with respect to the appointed time for an intervening occurrence is presented in Hab 2:3—"For the vision is still (waiting) for the appointed time." The same sense is employed with preference in connection with a divine promise for the birth of a son (see p. 25) in Gen 17:21; 18:14; 21:2; 2 Kgs 4:16, 17. It also appears in a more general sense in Ex 9:5 and Dan 11:29. In every case, *mō'ēd* refers not simply to the occasion as such, but expressly emphasizes it as being definitely appointed.

Since *yōm* in the historical writings ordinarily refers to a situation of historical consequence (see pp. 55-59, 62-64, 67-71), it only appears a few times in this literature with respect to an intervening event. But worthy of special mention is 1 Sam 24:5, where David's men saw the opportunity for him to seize Saul in a cave—"This is the day (*hinnēh hayyōm*) of which Yahweh spoke to you . . ." The present day was the day for the long-awaited opportunity. The same sense is used in Jdg 4:14. Indication of the appropriate time for an action may be made with an infinitive in Mic 7:11a—*yōm libnōth gedērāyik*——"A day to build your walls!" The reference here is in particular to the temporal occasion of a certain day (see *yōm hūʾ*, vv. 11b, 12), and not, as with *ʿēth* (*cf*. 2 Kgs 5:26; Hag 1:4, *etc*., pp. 80 f.), to the situation itself. The significant day may be compared to other days according to its content and to the event that occurred on it, as the day when the sun stood still, Jos 10:14—"And there has not been such as that day (*kayyōm hahūʾ*) before it or after it." In a construction of relationship, reference may be made to the temporal occasion of an activity, as the day of eating the forbidden fruit, Gen 2:17; 3:5 (*beyōm ʾakālkā*), or the day of Yahweh's sending rain, 1 Kgs 17:14 (*ʿad yōm tēth-yhwh geshem*).[1]) The temporal relationship of a certain experience is indicated in David's Song, 2 Sam 22:19 (= Ps 18:19)—"They met me on the day of my calamity (*beyōm ʾēydīy*)" (*cf*. also 2 Kgs 19:3).

Some similarity may be seen in these instances to uses of *ʿēth*, for they do have reference to certain occasions. However, the distinctive meaning of *yōm* as "day" is always to be recognized: it emphasizes the present situation; it is the temporal situation for an occurrence; it stresses the close temporal relationship of certain occurrences. It could just as well be rendered "time" according to the use of this word in modern European languages: "this is the time . . .", "there has not been such a time . . .", "at the same time . . .", *etc*. This only indicates the semantical differences between languages, especially between Semitic and European languages, for *ʿēth* could only be employed in a few of the above cases, such as Gen 2:17; 1 Kgs 17:14; 2 Sam 22:19, but never with quite the same connotation as *yōm*. Thus the temporal expressions *ʾāz*, *mōʿēd* and *yōm* are also used according to their normal meanings with respect to intervening events.

5. The Prophetic "Day"

a. Relative and Qualitative Aspects

Most of the cases of *yōm* in the intervening sense appear in prophetic literature. Here it may be best to begin with the expressions of simple temporal relationship, as in Am 1:14, where Yahweh's fire is to consume the towers of Rabbah: *bithrūʿāh beyōm milchāmāh besaʿar*

---

[1]) See also 6:19, suggesting that the singular form is an old form of the infinitive.

beyōm sūphāh—"with a shout on the day of battle, with a tempest on the day of whirlwind". The connotation here is practically "on the same day", with emphasis on the close relationship of the occasions. The same holds true, for example, for Hos 5:9 and Isa 49:8aᵝ. The latter case occurs with *'ēth* (see p. 81), although *ūbeyōm yeshū'āh* is not an exact parallel, for it indicates not so much the propriety of the action as its temporal coincidence.

Reference may also be made to an experience as the content of a day, as in Jer 16:19, where Yahweh is the prophet's refuge: *beyōm tsārāh*—"in the day of distress". This usage, which also appears in 17:17; 18:17; 51:2; Isa 17:11b, *etc.* (*cf.* Prov. 24:10), corresponds to the use of *'ēth* in Jer 2:27; 15:11, *etc.* (p. 78). The general impression may be comparable, but the nuances are different: the former indicates the close temporal relationship and the latter the juncture of circumstances on a particular occasion. *yōm* retains its basic temporal connotation of "(the same) day" even when referring to the occasion of a particular event, as in Isa 10:3—"And what will you do on the day of punishment (*leyōm pekuddāh*)?" (so also Jer 12:3; 17:16, 18).

Similar reference is made to the relationship of an action in an infinitive construction: At the same time that Yahweh punishes Israel's sins, he will "punish" the altars of Bethel (Am 3:14): *beyōm pāqedī* (so also Isa 17:11a; Jer 27:22). These cases may be compared to such uses of *'ēth* as in Jer 6:15; 11:14, *etc.* (p. 82), but the same basic difference between emphasis on the temporal and occasional aspects may likewise be noticed here.

A certain qualitative aspect of the situation may also be connected with *yōm*, as in Am 6:3—"Would you be removers of the day of evil (*leyōm rā'*)?" (so also 8:10). This may be compared to the use of *'ēth* in 5:13b (p. 85), but the distinction between a qualitative experience and a qualitative situation is quite clear. The two expressions occur as parallel predicates in Jer 46:21 (p. 79; *cf.* also 30:7): *kīy yōm 'ēydām bā' 'aleyhem 'ēth pekuddāthām*—"For the day of their calamity has come upon them, the occasion of their punishment." Although it is significant that both words may be used so closely in parallel, it is seldom that words in parallel have exactly the same meaning or intention. They ordinarily serve to complement, supplement or augment each other. Here, too, a certain intensification is clearly visible as attention is directed first to the temporal aspect of the event, and then to the definite fact of its occasion. Each implies the fact of the reality of the occurrence; together they emphasize this fact. Similar usage also appears in 46:10; Isa 22:5, and, with the plural, in Hos 9:7 (*bis*).

The qualitative aspect may also be carried over to persons, as in Jer 50:27 in parallel with *'ēth* (also v. 31; pp. 79, 83)—"for their day has come, the occasion of their punishment". Although *yōm* is here immediately modified to indicate what is meant by simply "their day", it is obvious that the temporal occasion of a special personal experience is meant. This usage will be dealt with more thoroughly below (pp. 115-117). Of greater interest here is an expression such as that in Mic 7:4—"the day of your watchmen, of your punishment, has come!" This indicates that not the temporal occasion for a passive experience is meant, as before, but that for an active participation: the time has come for the watchmen to go into action. Similar in sense, though different in construction is Jer 31:6: *kiy yēsh-yōm kāre'ū nōtsrīym*—"For there is a day (when) watchmen call . . ."

b. "The Day of Yahweh"

The formula *yōm yhwh* has experienced various interpretations. R. H. Charles was of the opinion that the "Day of Yahweh" meant, in popular belief, a day of victorious battle for Yahweh's people over their enemies. Beginning with Amos, the prophets transformed this into an ethical conception as a day of judgment against Israel itself. In the Exile this was modified: Israel would be judged man by man but the Gentiles collectively. After the Exile, the concept was connected with the universalistic and nationalistic ideas of the Messianic Kingdom.[1]) This theory is supported by von Rad in so far as he sees the event of war as the origin of the concept. Thus the idea as such would have had no eschatological character, although it was later enlarged to cosmic significance.[2]) Following Hermann Gunkel's theory that eschatology originates in mythology and that the end of the world is described in the same terms as its creation,[3]) Hugo Gressmann also takes special note of the natural phenomena that often accompany the Day of Yahweh and he therefore objects to the premise that this concept was originally connected with a battle of

---

[1]) Charles' article, "Eschatology", in the *Encyclopedia Biblica*, II, is presented according to the review by Černý, pp. 27 f.

[2]) *Theologie des Alten Testaments*, II, pp. 133-137.

[3]) *Schöpfung und Chaos in Urzeit und Endzeit*, Göttingen: 1895, pp. 87, 318, 367-371.

Yahweh. He thus combined it with the Babylonian mythological idea of an eschatological world catastrophe.[1]) Sigmund Mowinckel found another use for the Day of Yahweh, and appropriated it in support of his theory of Yahweh's accession to the throne. Proceeding with the theory derived from the so-called "Accession Psalms" that "the content of eschatology originates from the cultic Feast of the Accession", he identified the Day of Yahweh with the day of Yahweh's accession and proclaimed this to be "the key to the whole of eschatology". According to Gunkel's above-mentioned theory, Mowinckel formulated the "formal principle of eschatology" that "the history of the End = the history of the beginning". Thus the cultic Day of Yahweh is a repetition and new creation of that which had been at the beginning: "Nach der Schöpfung wurde Jahwä zum ersten Male König; jeden Neujahrstag schafft er wieder die Welt und wird wieder König." [2])

The most thorough treatment of the Day of Yahweh as such is that by Ladislav Černý, who attempted to disparage the opinion of Charles and von Rad, that it originally meant a day of battle for Yahweh (*cherem*), on the grounds that this is only one aspect of the picture among many, for it is also the day of wrath, darkness, plague, theophany, *etc.*, and has furthermore a larger meaning and content for the future of the whole nation. Finding the "ideological sources" of the concept "deeply imbued in the native Hebrew tradition and connected with the memories of the nomadic past of the nation", and allowing only for the extra-mythological origin of the individual features, he repudiated Gressmann's theory of mythological origin. He also proved on grounds of evidence to the contrary, that Mowinckel's entire theory of Yahweh's enthronement does not in fact correspond to the Babylonian model, and that, if such a feast existed, it could not have furnished the origin for Israelite eschatology or for the Day of Yahweh. He concludes that "the original form of the Day of Yahweh must have been one of a fateful day decreed by Yahweh" when he secures the survival of his people in a glorious victory over their enemies. This battle was directed by Amos against Israel itself as an ethical judgment, but later received universal scope as a judgment on all nations. This idea was then extended to cosmic and eternal proportions and united with the concept of the Messianic

---

[1]) *Der Ursprung der jüdisch-israelitischen Eschatologie*, Göttingen: 1905, pp. 142-144.

[2]) *Psalmenstudien*, II, Oslo: 1922, pp. 226-229.

Kingdom. Yet, in every form, "*the Day of Yahweh is the decreed, dark, dreadful, destructive, and dangerous day*".[1]) Thus Černý produces his own theory for the popular origin and constant character of the idea, but follows the traditional lines outlined by Charles in tracing its appropriation and transformation by the prophets.

This study is not the place to examine and test the various theories, for the concern here is properly with the nature of the use of *yōm* in the respective formula and in its immediate contexts. Černý's unique definition actually enumerates the various aspects which the concept gradually acquired. The fact of primary importance in this context is the feature that remained constant throughout, that the Day of Yahweh was an occasion of victory for Yahweh over his enemies. In other words, it was an event of Yahweh's active initiative intervening in the normal course of human affairs. This basic fact of Yahweh's intervening action is substantiated in a review of the various occurrences of the term. Immediately preceding the descriptive passage, 5:18-20, Amos mentions the cause in v. 17: " 'For I will pass through your midst', says Yahweh." In the context of 1:7, 14, Zephaniah repeatedly refers to Yahweh's destructive judgment (vv. 2-4, 8 f., 12, 17 f.). The same holds true in the contexts of Ezek 13:5 (vv. 8 f., 13-15), Obd 15 (vv. 2, 4, 8), Isa 13:6a, 9 (vv. 3-5, 6b, 11-13, 17), Joel 1:15a; 2:1, 11b; 3:4; 4:14 (1:15b; 2:11a, 20; 3:3; 4:1 f., 4, 7 f., 12, 16, 21), Mal 3:23 (vv. 1 f., 5, 11, 17); *e.g.*, Isa 13:6 (= Joel 1:15): "Wail! for near is the day of Yahweh; as devastation from the Almighty it will come!" and Mal 3:17: "'And they will be mine', says Yahweh of Hosts, 'on the day when I act, a possession.'"

Other forms of the formula are listed by Černý [2]) which are undoubtedly closely related in expression and content. They likewise occur in contexts of Yahweh's intervening action: *yōm leyhwh tsebā'ōth* (Isa 2:12; *cf.* vv. 19, 21), *wehayyōm hahū' la'donāy yhwh tseba'ōth yōm neqāmāh* (Jer 46:10a; *cf.* v. 10b), *beyōm zebach yhwh* (Zeph 1:8; p. 31), *beyōm 'ebrath yhwh* (1:18; Ezek 7:19; *cf.* Zeph 1:3 f., 8 f., 21, 24, 27), *yōm 'aph-yhwh* (2:2, 3; Lam 2:22; *cf.* Zeph 2:5, 11-13; Lam 2:1-9, 17, 20), *yōm leyhwh* (Ezek 30:3; *cf.* vv. 8, 10, 12-16, 18 f.), *yōm nāqām leyhwh* (Isa 34:8; *cf.* vv. 2, 5 f., 11), and *yōm-bā' leyhwh* (Zech 14:1; *cf.* vv. 2-5, 12 f., 18). In every passage, the Day of Yahweh is characterized by Yahweh's warlike, devastating intervention.

---

[1]) *The Day of Yahweh and Some relevant Problems*, Prague: 1948, pp. 53-84.
[2]) *Ibid.*, pp. 17 f.

The question may well be put now, whether ʿēth could not have been used in these contexts just as well as yōm. As a matter of fact, ʿēth does occur in eight of the fourteen contexts. It refers to the evil of the situation in Am 5:13, to Yahweh's searching out the wicked in Zeph 1:12, to the occasion of punishment in Jer 46:21, to the approach of the fateful occasion in Ezek 7:7, 12; 30:3; Isa 13:22, and Zech 14:7, and to Yahweh's judgment of the nations in Joel 4:1 (see pp. 79, 84-88, 94, 105-107). As elsewhere, ʿēth also indicates in these instances a definite occasion. Why, then, didn't the prophets say, ʿēth yhwh?

The answer surely lies in the character of the Day of Yahweh as an occasion of battle, devastation and victory. When such an event took place, it always occurred on a certain *day*, and never on more than one day, for with sunset came the end of the fighting. Thus it was so important for Joshua that the day of the battle with the Amorites be prolonged, to enable the Israelites to complete their rout (10:12-14, 20). Each battle had its own day; it was this temporal characteristic that made it both unique and a historical reality. In fact, instead of saying "the Battle of Jezreel", it was said "the day of Jezreel" (Hos 2:2; *cf.* 1:4 f.). So other battles are named, *yōm midyān* (Isa 9:3; *cf.* v. 4), *yōm mitsrayim* (Ezek 30:9), and *yōm yerūshālāyim* (Ps 137:7a; *cf.* vv. 7b, 8).

It is therefore obvious that the formula *yōm yhwh* is synonymous with "the Battle of Yahweh". Thus von Rad should not be mistaken when he points to the miraculous circumstances that accompanied Israel's battles,[1] *e.g.*: the panic of God (Ex 15:14-16; 23:27 f.; Jos 2:9, 11, 24; 5:1; 7:5; 10:10; 24:12), the pillars of fire and of cloud (Ex 14:24), great hailstones (Jos 10:11), the halting of the sun and moon in their course (10:12 f.), power over darkness and water (Ex 24:27; Jos 24:7), earthquake and rain (Jdg 5:4 f.), thunder (1 Sam 7:10), the sound of marching in the trees (2 Sam 5:24), a mirage of blood (2 Kgs 3:12), the sound of chariots and of a great army (7:6), and the slaying angel (19:35). Therefore it is quite appropriate that Yahweh's great event be called "the Day of Yahweh".

Incidentally, other comparable expressions refer only to the temporal situation of the day itself, *e.g.*: birthday (Gen 40:20; Jer 20:14; Hos 2:5; 7:5 (*yōm malkēnū!*), Job 3:1-10), holy days of the Baalim (Hos 2:15), fateful day (*e.g.*, 1 Sam 26:10, p. 116), harvest day (Prov 25:13), snow day (2 Sam 23:20), and day of good fortune (Ecc 7:14).

[1] *Loc. cit.*, p. 136.

c. "On that day"

The most frequent *yōm*-formula used by the prophets is *bayyōm hahū*. This has been the subject of a thorough-going investigation by Peter Andreas Munch. He takes issue with Gressmann's opinion that it was an old *terminus technicus* as an introductory formula for prophetic promises and that it was objectively identical with the Day of Yahweh as the Day of the World Catastrophe and Renewal.[1] Munch identifies the formula as nothing other than a temporal adverb that had its origin in narrative; it never lost this adverbial character, even when used in prophecy. However, he holds that it is used in prophecy only as an editorial connective formula and never as a part of the original text of the oracles; it would therefore be no *terminus technicus* for the eschatological promises themselves, but only for the Judaism of later generations, which was so eschato-logically-minded that it "conceived all prophecy of the OT as escha-tology".[2]

Munch is undoubtedly right in establishing narrative as the original home of this formula in Hebrew literature, and maintaining that its original meaning had been "on the same day",[3] as has already been noted above (pp. 56 f.). His defense of its adverbial character is, however, unnecessary, for that is doubted by no one; in fact, it must always be a temporal adverb simply because of its form. Therefore, his point that the eschatological interpretation ceases quite naturally if it can always be understood as a temporal adverb [4] is of no conse-quence. His mistake may be clearly seen in his beginning with a contrast with the NT *terminus technicus*, ἡ ἡμέρα ἡ ἐκείνη, [5] which is both eschatologically intended and also a nominal expression, thus no adverb. Munch makes a strange oversight here, for he fails to note that this NT term occurs as an exact replica of its OT prototype in the very passages he cited: ἐν ἐκείνη τῇ ἡμέρᾳ (Mt 7:22; Lk 10:12; 2 Tim 1:18; 4:8; *cf.* the plural, *e.g.*, Mt 24:19). The nominative form also appears, of course (*e.g.*, Lk 21:34, and also in the plural, *e.g.*, Mt 24:22). This is actually analogous to the OT form *hayyōm habū*, which will be discussed below (p. 101). As for the objection to the

---

[1] *Der Messias*, pp. 83 f.
[2] *Op. cit.*, pp. 5, 8 f., 16 f., 25 ff., 56 f.
[3] *Ibid.*, p. 5.
[4] *Ibid.*, p. 6.
[5] *Ibid.*, p. 5.

eschatological sense, this transition was definitely accomplished no later than Daniel (*e.g.*, 10:2, 14; 12:13), and was but a step away from the earlier prophets.

With this misguided start, Munch proceeds to prove the non-eschatological character of the formula in every instance, including the frequent occurrences in the prophets. His method is very doubtful, for he presumes, on the one hand, the fragmentary character of the prophecies and their being later jointed together by editors, and, on the other hand, that the meter can always prove the secondary nature of the formula.[1]) The faultiness of the presumption of regular meter as a criterion is readily seen in the frequent cases where he is often forced to alter the text drastically in order to make his meter fit, *e.g.*, in Am 2:13-16; Isa 2:10-17; 7:18-25; Mic 2:1-5; Zeph 1:7-13; Zech 12:1-13:6.[2])

In Am 2:16, the reason why *bayyōm hahū'* is metrically superfluous is because *lo' yimtsā'* is added according to the LXX.[3]) But this is unnecessary, for the MT makes good sense in 3+3 meter as it is: "And the strong of heart among the mighty will flee naked on that day." In Isa 2:11 and 17, the refrain is intoned, "and Yahweh will be exalted alone on that day". It could naturally be expected to have a different meter than the rest of the context, but cannot be shortened without disturbing the rhythmical flow; neither is there any good reason to omit a temporal reference in a refrain or the refrain alto-gether. The four oracles in 7:18-25—each introduced by *bayyōm hahū'* —would be meaninglessly individualized if they were not related to each other, for each one describes only one aspect of a certain event. Thus they all supplement the announcement of the event in v. 17, with each instance of "on that day" adding emphasis to the pronouncement. In Mic 2:4, it is obvious that "on that day" does not fit into the general meter, but in the same way as "therefore, thus says Yahweh" in v. 3 and "one says" in 4b (*cf.* 3:1; 4:6; 5:9; 6:1). It does serve here as a connective formula, but to connect thoughts that closely belong together anyway.

Although both "and it shall be on that day, says Yahweh" in Zeph 1:10 and "and it shall be on that occasion" in v. 12 interrupt the meter as introductory phrases, "on that day" at the end of a line in v. 9 belongs to the 2 + 2, 2 + 2 meter of the verse. It is striking

---

[1]) *Ibid.*, pp. 17-20, *et passim*.
[2]) *Ibid.*, pp. 14-17, 21 f., 34-37.
[3]) So Sellin, *op. cit.*, p. 200; Weiser, *Zwölf Kleine Propheten*, p. 134.

that "on that day" occurs ten times in Zech 12:1-13:6 (12:3, 4, 6, 8 *bis*, 9, 11; 13:1, 2, 4). It always appears at the beginning of a verse, except for the second instance in 12:8; there it stands in the middle of a sentence, and there is no plausible reason to remove it. Some of the other cases are clearly introductory (12:3, 4, 9; 13:2, 4), but, if the attempt is made to find a meter, the others may be fit in without difficulty: 12:6 (3 + 2 + 2, 3 + 2, 2 + 2), 8 (3 + 3, 3 + 3, 3 + 3), 11 (4 + 4), 13:1 (4 + 4 + 2). Thus it appears that *bayyōm hahū*, whether belonging to the meter or not, could be used as an introductory formula for short sections within a prophecy, evidently as an expression of emphasis. That it belongs to the basic style of many prophecies and is no gloss whatsoever, should be seen from these examples. Further proof lies in the fact that it occurs in the midst of sentences and even at the end of a section (*e.g.*, Am 2:16; Isa 2:11, 17), and that many sections are begun without it or any other introductory formula.

Even though it may serve a purpose of emphasis, *bayyōm hahū* is always used by the prophets as a formula of temporal relationship, relating its modified statement to the preceding as a part of the same occasion.[1] It is as if it meant "in that battle" in a scene-by-scene description of a panoramic contest; yet it is not the battle itself—not the occasion as such—that is actually referred to, but the temporal circumstance, namely the day of the battle. Thus, returning once more to the passages just discussed, the strong of heart will flee when Yahweh attacks Israel (Am 2:16); Yahweh will be exalted when he rises up against the proud (Isa 2:11, 17); Yahweh will bring destruction from abroad, the survivor will only have curds and honey to eat, and vineyards will be turned into brier patches when Yahweh turns upon Judah (7:18, 20, 21, 23); the wicked will be taunted when Yahweh brings his evil upon them (Mic 2:4); Yahweh will punish the violent and unsuspecting and wailings will be heard from the city when the divine destruction comes upon Judah and Jerusalem (Zeph 1:9, 10, 12); and when Yahweh pits Judah and Jerusalem against the surrounding peoples, he will empower them to gain the victory, yet they will mourn because of their sins and be cleansed from them (Zech 12:1-13:6).

It is not necessary to list all the occurrences, but attention may also be called to some other examples: The songs of the palace will become

---

[1] *Cf.* Černý, *op. cit.*, p. 21.

wailings when Yahweh brings the end upon Israel (Am 8:3); Yahweh will break Israel's bow in Jezreel when he puts an end to its kingdom (Hos 1:5); he will remove the finery of the haughty women when he judges Jerusalem (Isa 3:18); the coastal inhabitants will be amazed when Assyria leads the Egyptians captive (20:6); courage will fail the royalty when Yahweh brings destruction upon Judah (Jer 4:9); he will break the yoke from his people's neck and save them when the occasion of distress comes upon them (30:8); the Ethiopians will be terrified when Yahweh sends the sword upon them and Egypt (Ezek 30:9); the mountains will drip with wine when he restores the fortunes of Judah (Joel 4:18). In one passage, the expression occurs adverbially without a preposition (*acc. temp.*): *yōm hū'* (Mic 7:11b, 12).[1]

Thus the phrase "on that day" connects the succeeding section of a prophecy to its preceding parts and serves as a means of emphasis by indicating the temporal relationship; yet, it does not refer to the occasion itself in the same way as *'ēth*.

d. Other Intervening Uses of *yōm*

Comparable to "on that day" is the plural form, *bayyāmīym hahēm*, which first appears in Jeremiah, as in 3:16— " 'And it shall be, when you multiply and are fruitful in the land in those days' says Yahweh, 'they will no longer say . . .' " Here it relates v. 16 to 15 temporally, and occurs again in v. 18 in a connective way: "In those days the house of Judah will come unto the house of Israel . . ." In much the same way in respect to future situations, it reappears in Jer 5:18; 31:29; 33:16; Joel 3:2; Zech 8:6, 23.

It may also be used in combination with *'ēth*: *bayyāmīym hahēm ūbe'ēth hahīy'* (Jer 33:15; 50:4, 20; Joel 4:1; see p. 85). The plural may be a parallel form to the singular "on that day". Yet, there is strong indication that the two joined expressions are not meant to be a repetition of the same idea. As does "on that day", "in those days" likewise indicates the temporal relationship of a future occurrence, but in a more general sense; instead of referring to the particular day it means a period, that is, the general situation. Thus, it is significant that it is combined with "on that occasion". As related but differing expressions, they denote an intensified emphasis.

---

[1] In v. 11b, it is obvious that the article for the demonstrative pronoun is due to a dittography.

"In those days" may also refer to a past situation, as in Ezek 38:17 and Zech 8:10 (*liphnē' hayyāmīym hahēm*), and, in the form *bayyāmīym hā'ēlleh* (vv. 9, 15), to the present situation. The plural may also indicate that the future situation involves an intermediate period before the culminating event: "For this is the covenant which I shall cut with the house of Israel after those days . . ." (*'acharēy hayyāmīym hahēm*, Jer 31:33). Similar reference to a future event is made by *layyāmīym 'asher*, Ezek 22:14—". . . at the days when I deal with you?"

The plural of "day" is also used by the prophets in other ways as a means to emphasize their announcement. The expression *yāmīym bā'īym* is first used by Amos to warn the Samaritans of the impending disaster: "The Lord Yahweh has sworn by his holiness that, behold, days are coming upon you, and they will take you away with hooks . . ." (4:2). It is always used for the same general purpose of emphasizing the fact of the prophesied event, although ordinarily in introduction to a section of particular importance: 8:11; 9:13; Isa 39:6; Jer 7:32; 9:24; 16:14; 19:6; 23:5, 7; 30:3; 31:27, 31, 38; 33:14; 48:12; 49:2; 51:47, 52. Similar is the emphatic declaration that the fulfilment of the prophetic visions is actually about to take place: *qāberū hayyāmīym* (Ezek 12:23).

A further variation is employed in Jer 25:34, *māle'ū yemēykem*—"For your days are full for slaughtering"; that is, the allotted period of time has lapsed. This manner of speaking occurs relatively frequently in the OT, some 27 times. It is usually used in a non-emphasized sense, *e.g.*, for the completion of an agreed (1 Sam 18:16), customary (Gen 50:3), normal (25:24), decreed (Lev 8:33) or simply of a certain (Ex 7:25) period of time, or for the completion of the period of a life-time (2 Sam 7:12), but also for the completion of the foretold period of seventy years' exile (Jer 29:10; 2 Chr 36:21). Indication of an indefinite period of time is made by *ya'arekū hayyāmīym* (Ezek 12:22)—"The days grow long." One more expression of importance is *be'acharīyth hayyāmīym*, which has already been discussed above (pp. 69 f.).

Mention may yet be made in this connection of the prophetic use of *hayyōm* and *hayyōm hazzeh*. The prophets use the terms in much the same way as Deuteronomy—or rather, *vice versa*, for it is Deut. that speaks of the past in a prophetic manner to actualize it for the present. Correspondingly, the prophets speak of the present situation as the occasion for Yahweh's intervention in the course of history, using the terms "today" and "this day" repeatedly to underline the reality of this fact. However, they are employed rather sparingly by the prophets, appearing first and most frequently (5 times) with the Deuteronomistic-minded Jeremiah, and six times with the post-exilic prophets (Hag., Zech., additions to Isa.). Thus, Yahweh made Jeremiah "today a 'fortified city' . . . against the whole land . . ." (1:18), and appointed him "this day over nations . . ." (1:10)[1])

One more form is *hayyōm hahū'* as predicate for Yahweh's day of devastation, as in Jer 30:7—"Alas! for greater is that day than any other like it!", 46:10 (see p. 94), and Zeph 1:15—"A day of wrath is that day!" It also occurs once without the demonstrative pronoun (*'al -hayyōm habbā'*), Jer 47:4—"Because of the day coming to destroy all the Philistines . . ."

It has now been shown in this section that the use of *yōm* in the writings of the prophets, whether in a construction of relationship or as a definite formula, always retains its original temporal connotation of "day". This "day" is to be understood in the singular as the temporal situation of a certain occurrence, such as a past or future event or the present situation, and in the plural as the indefinite temporal period of a particular situation.

Three essential points may be underlined: *First, yōm* always refers to the temporal relationship of an occasion and not ordinarily to the particular occasion itself. The only real exceptions are "the Day of Yahweh" and "the Day of Jezreel" (*etc.*, see p. 95), which signify the event of that day as well. *Secondly*, the use of *yōm* indicates decisively that the Hebrews had a very clear understanding of three-dimensional time according to the well-known categories of past, present and future. The different ways in which "day" is employed pointedly express which of the three temporal situations is meant, even when the verbal tenses do not strictly correspond, which is often the case in the prophets. It seems, therefore, that the temporal state is expressly stated in Hebrew by means of a temporal expression when it should be particularly emphasized, and not particularly by the verbal form. *Thirdly*, that precisely "day" became the most commonly used temporal expression is very significant, because the concept of time is thereby immediately coupled with the concept of event, for *every event takes place upon a certain day*. Each significant event has its own particular "day"; each significant period has its own particular "days".

---

[1]) The other instances of *hayyōm*: Jer 34:15; 40:4; 42:19, 21; Isa 38:19; 58:4; Zech 9:12; of *hayyōm hazzeh*: Jer 1:10; 44:2; Hag 2:15, 18, 19.

With this conceptual combination, it was but a short step for the Hebrews to take to an historical concept that conceived of events in a reasonable temporal relationship to each other. Thus, *yōm* establishes itself without serious competition as *the "work-horse" of the Hebrew concepts of time and history*. Yet, it received essential support from its more seldom but distinctive companion, *ʿēth*, in effecting *the solidified combination of time and event into one concept*. The latter, better rendered by "occasion", directs attention particularly to the occasion itself in placing it in a temporal relationship; thus it could be used as a handy aid when this aspect demanded special emphasis or clear expression. *Especially, then, in the usage of these two words, the Hebrew concept of time and history may be recognized and appreciated.*

Summary

1. *ʿēth* preserves in every case its basic use as a *reference to a specific occasion of peculiar quality and content*. It ordinarily indicates the relationship of events or states to each other; that is, it serves the purpose of denoting the conjunction of events or states existentially as well as temporally. In later literature, it may be objectivized to a designation of the specific occasion itself, generalized to an indefinite reference, or reduced to a superfluous augmentation or a temporal conjunction. The ordinary use may be contrasted with the employment of other temporal expressions: *ʾāz* is consistently used throughout for temporal relationship without implying any definiteness, although it may indicate a significant change or continuation of the situation. *mōʿēd* is consistently used in temporal situations to indicate or emphasize the appointed aspect of the situation. *yōm* in the singular ordinarily retains the basic implication of "day" *per se* as a temporal situation of reference, especially in earlier texts, but may in later texts indicate an indefinite temporal relationship. The plural *yāmīym* is very general in character, indicating an indefinite duration, period or situation in such a way that it may often be rendered "time" in the general sense.

2. Some aspects have often been previously interpreted temporally instead of subjectively. The present actualization of historical events in Deuteronomy and of future events by the prophets is not to be understood as a disregard for the temporal differences, but as a recognition of the subjective consequences of the past events upon the present or the present situation upon the future. Seemingly absolute temporal references in eschatological contexts are in fact relative; the state-

ments always refer to a transformation of the physical situation—perhaps even a suspension of the *measurement* of time—but never to a suspension of the two basic *categories* of time and space themselves. Some uses of *ʿēth*—and even of *yōm*—may refer to "crisis situations"; but such a reference is always dependent upon the context and is not made because of an inherent meaning in the temporal expression, except that *ʿēth* lends itself well because of its basic indication of a definite occasion, and that *yōm* is often preferred for no other reason than to provide a temporal reference as a means of emphasis upon the fact of the occasion.

3. *ʿēth* may be used in a temporal reference with an ulterior motive, so to speak, for the purpose of substantiating or emphasizing the reality of a certain occasion, whether a sworn oath, a past historical event, or a foretold future occurrence. With respect to historical situations, it often indicates the causal historical relationship between occasions or the semblance of an historical setting. In comparison with other temporal expressions, it proves itself the most appropriate because of its definite reference to the occasion as a conjunction of events; but since it lacks a clear-cut indication of the temporal aspect of the particular situation, it has not been used with special frequency, except where its distinctive character could be used to good advantage. As could be expected, *ʾāz* indicates no more than a general temporal reference for historical situations, and *mōʿēd* is used in this connection only secondarily and incidentally. *yōm*, however, is also employed, in both singular and plural, to indicate historical causal relationship or the semblance of an historical setting, although it often refers only to an indefinite temporal relationship in historical situations. Both it and *ʿēth* may be used in their capacity as temporal references to emphasize the intended *tempus* of past, present or future, which is otherwise simply left to the context. They therefore prove unquestionably the existence of these *tempora* in the Hebrew concepts of time and history. In exceptional use as a designation for a significant occasion itself, *yōm* may in this way combine the concepts of time and event, which is done by *ʿeth* as a matter of course. Although it may seem to us modern Westerners that Hebrew had an inadequate vocabulary for the expression of its historical consciousness, this may be attributed to the lack of a desire to express temporality with absolute preciseness.

4. The determined, decisive acts of God are referred to in many contexts; decisive in an historical or intervening event is God, not

the decision of man (*cf.* Jer 8:12; Ezek 7:7, pp. 79, 88). In so doing, God does not act without reasonable cause nor impinge upon man's freedom of will when making use of him to accomplish his purposes. This is in fundamental contrast to other ancient Near Eastern religions that attributed the cause of events to the unchangeable forces of nature or to a council of gods who acted purely arbitrarily. God's intervention does not produce a suspension of time, either (see p. 7). Infinite, transcendent God condescends instead to man's finite limitations, restricting his activity to dimensions appropriate for human experience, such as time and space. The peculiarity of the OT proclamation does not demand a peculiar concept of time, but rather a peculiar relationship to God within temporal existence.

These considerations form much of the foundation for a basic understanding of the Hebrew concept of time and of the close relationship between the concepts of *time, event and history*.

CHAPTER FOUR

THE USE OF *'ETH* WITH AN OCCASION OF FINAL DESTINY OR GIVEN POSSIBILITY

One more major category of the usage of *'ēth* remains to be considered. A later and secondary derivation, it received notable employment in only a few writings, although it apparently came to be well known in the language as a whole. This category is concerned with destiny and possibility, and may be divided according to the uses that deal with a destined end for a people or history, with death as fate, and with a given possibility for every occasion.

A. The Concept of a Final Destiny

The concept that there is a beginning and an end for something in a temporal context may possibly have originated with the first comprehended experiences of birth and death. But the concern here is not with the ultimate origin, the development and the various forms of expression for the concept, but rather with the application and meaning of the word *'ēth* in this context, and with the relationship of this usage to the concept of time. The earliest extant application of *'ēth* within this general category was made not to a man's death but to the end of a people in the sense of a fate or destiny. The distinction between the end of a people within the course of history and the end of the course of historical events itself should become clear in the course of the examination.

1. *The Destiny of a People*

If the judgment of the majority of scholars is to be accepted that the Song of Moses (Dt 32:1-43) and Isa 13 are of exilic or postexilic origin,[1] the earliest instances of connecting *'ēth* to the idea of a final destiny for a people may have been prompted by the shock of the Exile, or even already by its threat. In one instance (1:12), Zephaniah applies the expression to his description of the "Day of Yahweh", which in vv. 2-6 and 18 (*cf.* 3:6, 8) seems to signify the absolute end of all life upon the earth. But the rest of the oracle shows that only a limited destruction is intended. It is not to be the end of the life of

---

[1] So Rost (*op. cit.*, pp. 38 f.), Dillmann (*Jesaia*, p. xxv), Marti (*Jesaia*, p. xvi).

man upon earth and therefore of history, but only the end of the wicked within Jerusalem (1:8-13) and Judah (*cf.* 2:7) and of certain neighboring nations (2:4-15). Similar extremes are expressed in Isa 13, but only the destruction of the wicked and of Babylon are meant here, despite the use of such expressions as *kol-hāʾārets* (v. 5).

The life of man in the dimensions of time and space—in the course of historical existence—is to continue as before "the great Day of Yahweh" (Zeph 2:7b, 9b; 3:9-20). It may be noted that, even if all or part of the closing promise of salvation, 3:9-20, is consigned to the work of well-meaning optimists,[1]) it should be recognized that the proclamations of total annihilation are outbursts of radical zeal that wish to emphasize expressly the definite fact of the impending destruction. The underlying tone pictures only a limited destruction and a following continuation of existence in a purified manner. This is repeatedly seen, for example, when that which is meant in 1:3 by *ʾādām* is more closely defined as "the wicked", "the remnant of Baal" and "the name of the idol-priests" (v. 4), and those who have turned away from Yahweh to worship other Gods (5 f.).

The other instances of *ʿēth* in contexts with the Day of Yahweh are likewise concerned with a "limited", not absolute end: Am 5— the end of the unjust in Israel; Jer 46:13-28 and Ezek 30:1-19—the end of Egypt (see Jer 46:28—"For I will make a finish of all the nations where I have scattered you (Jacob), but of you I will not make a finish"); Ezek 7—the end of Israel; Isa 13—the destruction of Babylon; Joel 4 and Zech 14—the judgment of Israel's oppressors (see pp. 94 f.).

Other instances of *ʿēth* in references to a "limited end" occur with striking frequency in Jeremiah with respect to Yahweh's impending judgment of Judah (6:15; 8:12), idols (10:15=51:18), Egypt (46:21), Edom (49:8), and Babylon (27:7; 50:27, 31; 51:6, 33b). The same may be said of Israel's perverse generation in Dt 32:35 (see p. 79) and of the despicable usurper of Dan 11:21-24. Although classified as singular occasions because of their intervening character, the cases in Jer 27:7; Ezek 7:7, 12, and Dan 11:24 (see p. 88) could just as well be assigned to this section according to their explicit indication of the end of a certain people. The other instances are less explicit in this aspect, including the comparison in Jer 51:33b to the reaping of harvest (see p. 27).

---

[1]) *Cf.* Procksch (*Kleine Propheten*, p. 147) and Horst (*Kleine Propheten*, p. 186).

Even more explicit instances of this usage appear especially in Ezekiel (see 7:7, 12; p. 88), where there is to come upon the king of Israel "his day, at the occasion of the End-punishment" (*be'ēth 'awon qēts*; 21:30). The same expression is also applied in announcing the end of the wicked of the Ammonites (v. 34) and in retrospection over the past punishment of Israel at the hands of Mount Seir (35:5b). In the passage of the "Day of the Lord" against Egypt (30:1-19, pp. 94 f., 106), the expression *'ēth gōyim yihyeh* appears in parallel to *weqārōb yōm leyhwh* as the definite occasion of doom upon Egypt and her allies (v. 3). The city Jerusalem is personified in 22:3 (see p. 108), as well as Babylon in Isa 13:22; the end of both is expressed with the phrase *lābō' 'ittāhh*, which can best be rendered, "that her occasion may come".[1])

Considering the frequent appearance among the prophets of the concept of a final destiny for a nation or community, it must have been an idea that had always been a part of their milieu, beginning with Amos' very explicit *bā' haqqēts*—"The end has come upon my people Israel" (8:2), which Franz Hesse has identified as the basic tenor of his entire proclamation.[2]) Using the verb *swph*, Amos also prophesies the end of many houses in Israel, 3:15. The "end-idea" finds expression in nominal and verbal forms throughout many of the literary prophets. The same phrase *bā' haqqēts* is appropriated by Ezekiel in 7:2b, 6aβ, and without the article in v. 6aα; *qēts* occurs alone in vv. 2a, 3, and otherwise in Hab 2:3aβ (*cf.* also Lam 4:18b *bis*). *hatstsephīyrāh* in Ezek 7:7a, 10, parallel to *qēts*, remains a riddle without a satisfactory solution.[3])

The phrase *be'acharīyth hayyāmīym* has already been discussed (pp. 69 f.) and defined as a term for the end of a certain period of time by the prophets. *'acharīyth* appears alone in the same sense in Jer 5:31 ("but what will you do at the end of the matter?"), Isa 46:10 and 47:7, evidently referring to the outcome of certain events. The end of a people may also be denoted by *kālāh*, nominally in a negative sense in Jer 4:27; 30:11b; 46:28b (*bis*), and positively in 30:11a; 46:28a; Zeph 1:18; it is employed in verbal form in Isa 21:16; Ezek 30:13. *shbth* is also employed for this concept in Hos 1:4; 2:13; Ezek 30:18; Isa 13:11. There yet remain the instances

---

[1]) So Torczyner (*op. cit.*, p. 107) to Isa 13:22, and Karl Heinrich Cornill (*Das Buch des Propheten Ezechiel*, Leipzig: 1886, p. 311) to Ezek 22:3.

[2]) "Amos 5, 4-6, 14 f.", *ZAW* 68 (1956), p. 13.

[3]) So Zimmerli, *op. cit.*, pp. 161 f.

with *yōm*, which are really adaptations to the "corporate personality" from the idea of the end of an individual. In Jer 25:34, the days of the princes of the nations are filled (*mlʾ*) for slaughtering (*cf.* Lam 4:18); the day of the Babylonians for their punishment has come, 50:27(-31); in Isa 13:22bβ, Babylon's days will not be prolonged (*nmshn*); and Jerusalem itself has brought its days near (*hqryb*), Ezk 22:4.

These expressions sometimes occur in rather close proximity or even parallel to ʿ*ēth* in the same general sense (Ezek 7:7b, 12; 22:3; 30:3; Isa 13:22bα; see pp. 87 f., 106), but with different shades of meaning. Because of the extreme brevity of the relevant statements in Ezek 7:2-12, the basic differences cannot be clarified on the basis of this passage alone. However, it is obvious that the very employment of several synonyms for the same subject demonstrates that the subject is being approached from different angles of observation in order to give a full description. In 22:4, "your day" and "your years" indicate particularly the temporal aspect of the coming event, evidently in the sense of Jer 25:34. The verbal forms in Ezek 30:13, 18; Isa 13:11, indicate the cessation of a condition, which ʿ*ēth* could only express with the aid of other words. The distinction is most clearly seen in Isa 13:22, where ʿ*ēth* is placed in parallel to the indefinite temporal reference *yāmīym*. It is therefore clearly not meant to be a close parallel at all; the former indicates the definiteness of the occasion and the latter the cessation of the preceding period of time.

From these considerations it is seen that, among other expressions indicating varying aspects, the word ʿ*ēth* was also an appropriate term for *the prophetic idea of the final destiny of a people*. It could express the aspect of "definite occasion", but without denoting an absolute end. As R. H. Charles long ago pointed out, a distinction must be made between the eschatology of the prophets and that of the apocalyptists, the latter alone having the idea of a catastrophic End.[1] Prophetic eschatology is almost always characterized as the expectancy of a divine intervention into the present situation or in the immediate, impending future; it does not belong to the distant future.[2] However, this immediate expectancy of the critical event of judgment or renewal is sometimes overplayed in the temporal cate-

---

[1]) *Religious Development*, pp. 17, 21.

[2]) See Kurt Galling: "Die Geschichte als Wort Gottes bei den Propheten", *ThB* 8 (1929), p. 171; Weiser: *Glaube und Geschichte im Alten Testament*, pp. 85, 87; Delling, *Das Zeitverständnis des Neuen Testaments*, pp. 41 f.; Ratschow, "Anmerkungen zur theologischen Auffassung des Zeitproblems", p. 374; Hesse, *loc. cit.*, pp. 2 f., 14; Marsh, *The Fulness of Time*, p. 64.

gory, so that the heavily emphasized stress upon the present in the sense of a pregnant "Kairos"[1]) cannot do full justice to the uniqueness of the concept. The prophets are attributed with a view of time that has concentrated all *tempora* into the "here and now" of the present; [2]) the future is nothing more than the lengthened now.[3]) This concentration on the present even leads Werner Vollborn and John Marsh to the opinion that the past and future are actualized in the present, which means a suspension of time itself (see pp. 7-9).

A concept that concentrates the past and future *tempora* in the present hardly corresponds to the prophetic view of time. The foregoing examination shows that the impending event, however imminent, nevertheless remained in the future. The present situation is always distinguished from the future as the situation of preparation and announcement.[4]) It is in this sense that the so-called actualization of the future in the present is unveiled as actually involving the preliminary consequences of, particularly, a change of attitude: "Seek good and not evil, so that you may live" (Am 5:14). This is the now of "today". "To-morrow" is imminent, and may in fact be so imminent that it is about to burst into present moment. But the key words here are the oft-repeated expressions *bayyōm hahū'*, *bayyā-miym hahēm*, *be'achariyth hayyāmiym*, *yōm yhwh*, and even *bā'ēth hahiy'*, which all indicate a specific temporal situation; "that day or occasion" is not "now" or "today", but "tomorrow" or, simply, "in the future" (see pp. 69 f., 84 f., 92-99).

Further mention may be made of *qārōb*, which appears 18 times in relevant prophetic pronouncements,[5]) and of *'ōd me'at*, which occurs five times.[6]) The impending event is "near"—perhaps immediately near; but "near" is still "there" and not "here". Or, the event will come in "yet a little while", which is very soon, but not yet "now".

The "prophetic perfect" is often taken advantage of in arguing for the actualization of the future in the present.[7]) However, the seeming

---

[1]) See Marsh, *loc. cit.*; Eichrodt, "Heilserfahrung und Zeitverständnis im Alten Testament", p. 113.

[2]) See Scott, *The Relevance of the Prophets*, p. 150; von Rad, *Theologie des Alten Testaments*, II, pp. 115 f.

[3]) *Cf.* Muilenburg, "The Biblical View of Time", pp. 246 f.

[4]) *E.g.*, Am 4:12; 5:4-7; Hos 10:12; Isa 1:16-20; Jer 3:12-14; 22:2-4; Zeph 2:3; Ezek 3:16-21.

[5]) Zeph 1:7, 14 *bis*; Jer 48:16; Ezek 7:7, 8; 12:23; 22:4; 30:3 *bis*; 36:8; Isa 13:22; 51:5; 56:1; Joel 1:15; 2:1; 4:14; Obd 15.

[6]) Hos 1:4; Isa 10:25; 29:17; Jer 51:33; Hag 2:6.

[7]) Robinson (*op. cit.*, p. 137) calls the prophetic perfect a sort of "timelessness".

absoluteness of *bāʾ*, "it has come", is consistently modified by such temporal references as *qārōb* and *ʿōd meʿat*. This modification of the prophetic perfect adapts the certainty of the event already determined to the reality of the category of time. The event is subjectively assured and in this respect it already produces effective consequences in the present. But these are only the advance consequences. The event itself is coming "on that day": it is not yet "here", it is only "near". It still belongs in reality to the future. Thus, the prophets do not give evidence in their proclamation of the impending "kairos" that they possess a special sense of time. Their appreciation of the usual three *tempora* has been emphasized by Charles, Hans Wildberger, and especially Walther Eichrodt,[1]) who points particularly to the contrast by the prophets between past generations and the present one and to the completely new character of the coming salvation event: "Es bleibt demnach bei der Realität eines in die Zukunft sich erstreckenden objektiven Zeitverlaufs als der Daseinsform des Geschöpfs, die keine Flucht in einem vor oder über aller Zeit vorhandenen Heilszustand ermöglicht, sondern von dem kommenden Heil ihre Bedeutung empfängt." Whether the impending event is salvation or judgment, as proclaimed future occurrence it may effect significant consequences in the present situation of the listeners.

The further observation may be made that all the temporal references indicate in effect that the proclaimed event is to occur on a particular day or definite occasion, but do not reveal the temporal moment. This demonstrates that primary emphasis is laid upon the *fact* of the occasion and that God does not determine the *moment* in advance, but takes advantage of the opportunities presented by human action to effect his will. Neither the activity of man nor the temporal occasion is determined, but only the eventual outcome.

The so-called "eschatology" of the prophets did not therefore introduce a new concept of time that felt the actualization of the past or future *tempora* in the present. In fact, it was not even eschatology at all, in the proper sense of the word, for a "limited end" is not yet an end. This prophetic view has been well formulated by C. H. Ratschow:[2]) "Am Ende aller Dinge steht nicht Unendlichkeit, sondern 'kommende Tage' und endlich der 'Tag Yahwes' oder der

---

[1]) Charles, *loc. cit.*, pp. 22 f.; Wildberger, *op. cit.*, p. 84; Eichrodt, *loc. cit.*, pp. 114-116.

[2]) *Loc. cit.*, p. 374.

'Tag des Heils'. Der Begriff der Tage also umfaßt den Gesamtzusammenhang des Handelns Gottes wie des Geschehens der Welt, und das Gespräch verläuft nicht auf der Linie einer Zeit-Ewigkeit-Dialektik, sondern bei der Frage, ob dieser Tag, wie füglich postuliert werden darf, Licht sei, oder ob man nicht der prophetischen Rede zu folgen habe, die von diesem Tage Finsternis aussagte (Am 5, 18 f.)." The prophets did not foresee an end to time, history or the world, but only an end to a certain people. As ordinarily the case with the People of God, they foretold only a "provisional end", that is, merely an end to the misfortune of the present situation or immediate future (wickedness and judgment = darkness), that would be followed in the more distant future by restoration (justice and peace = light). There is truly a basic difference between apocalyptic and prophetic eschatology: that between true eschatology and historical intervention. Instead of being termed "eschatology", the prophetic concept would better be named *"destiny"*—the corporate destiny of a certain people within the future course of history as it has been planned by God.

2. *The Final Destiny of History (Daniel)*

There is only one book in the OT where the "definite occasion" of *ʿēth* is employed together with the concept of an absolute end of the world's course of historical events, and that is Daniel's apocalypse. This term occurs 15 times in Chs. 8-12 in various connections, including five instances in contexts where only the absolute eschatological "End" may be understood. These cases are linguistically nearly identical, consisting of the genitive construction *ʿēth qēts* introduced by one of three prepositions, *ʿād, le,* or *be.*

A clear witness to the final character of the expression is offered by 11:40, where the history of the conflicts between the world powers reaches its last stage. Here, as the final "act" begins prior to the decisive intervention by the "great prince", Michael (12:1), "at the time of the End" is used for the only time in respect to an event in the course of the "history". It is thus evident that the absolute End is meant here, not as a short moment, but in the sense of a final "act": [1] the "situation of the End". Since the genitive in this construction appears without the article, it is probably best to treat it as an appositional relationship: "the End-situation", or "the final

---

[1] See von Rad: "ἡμέρα", *TWNT* II, p. 949.

Situation". The only other immediate temporal references to the End in this passage are the four occurrences of ʿēth in 12:1, which refer to it as "that situation" and as "a situation of distress" (see pp. 51, 60, 85).

This End-situation is twice announced in advance with ʿēth. In the next-to-last "act" of the apocalyptical drama, it is said that the wise are to be purified "until the End-situation" (11:35a). This is immediately followed by a parallel, kīy-ʿōd lammōʿēd; the sufferers must wait until the End comes, "for it is yet (kept) for the appointed Time". This last expression is found in various forms, including one with ʿēth the first time it appears. In 8:17, Gabriel announces to Daniel that the vision which he had just seen "is for (= concerns) the final Situation". Two verses later, an appositional combination is employed, where reference is again made to the same vision, that lemōʿēd qēts—"is for the final Appointment". These two words are separated in 11:27, where it is indicated that the machinations of the kings of the North and South will be of no avail, "for the End is yet for the appointed Time". One other similar usage is met in 8:26, which, however, indicates that the vision is not to be fulfilled soon, kīy leyāmīym rabbīym—"because it is for many days (hence)". The same sense is intended in 10:14b with the single word layyāmīym.

The other two relevant cases with ʿēth come toward the close of the book after the account of the final course of events, where Daniel is told that he should "keep the words secret and seal the book until the final Situation" (12:4). Essentially the same announcement appears in v. 9, except that the verbs are passive participles instead of infinitives. There also appears basically the same expression, although without ʿēth, in 9:26bβ, where it is foretold that "until the End there will be war". Similar reference to the End is made in the final verse, 12:13, where Daniel is instructed: "But you go (your way) till the end (laqqēts); and you will rest and will stand according to your lot at the End of the days (leqēts hayyāmīyn)."

qēts is also employed in regard to the End in 12:6, where Daniel asks: ʿad-māthay qēts happelāʾōth—"Until how long is (=How much longer is it until) the end of the wonders?" One further parallel appears twice, first in a construct relationship in 8:19a, where the eschatological events are named a "curse", namely, when Gabriel was to make known to Daniel "what will be at the end of the curse" (beʾacharīyth hazzāʿam). The other case, 10:14a, again concerns the revealing to Daniel of "what will happen to your people at the end of the days" (*be'acharīyth hayyāmīym*). Discussed more thoroughly above (p. 69), this last expression had been found to be merely a general reference to a future situation elsewhere in the OT. However, it is evident that it refers to the absolute End in this case, considering the following expression pertaining to the fulfilment of the vision, which is stereotyped in content and intention, if not strictly in form.

Precisely this last observation warns against presuming that the various terms in this apocalypse have been employed as *termini technici*. Not only are *'ēth*, *mō'ēd*, and *'acharīyth* used as interchangeable parallels with *qēts*, but they all also appear elsewhere in expressions that do not pertain to the End itself. *'ēth* occurs in the relative sense in 9:21, 25; 11:6, 14, 24; 12:11 (see pp. 30, 51, 76 f., 85, 88), besides the instances already mentioned in 12:1 (see pp. 111 f.). *mō'ēd* is used for the determined occasion for the king of the North to invade the South again (11:29), and for appointed "time, two times, and half a one", which denote the interposing periods before the End (12:7; *cf.* the corresponding expression in Aramaic with *'iddān* in 7:25). *'acharīyth* indicates the end of the rule of the four kingdoms in 8:23. Even *qēts* is made use of in the relative sense, denoting in 9:26bα the end of the "annointed one", in 11:45 the end of the King of the North, and in 11:13 the end of an indefinite period of time (*shānīym*). Mention may also be made of the two cases of the Aramaic *sōphā* in ch. 7, which refers to the complete destruction of the dominion of the eleventh king (v. 26), and to "the end of the matter" (*dīy-millethā'*, v. 28).

The opinion is sometimes held that *'ēth* corresponds to the apocalyptical concept. For instance, Gerhard von Rad implies that Daniel used it for this reason in contrast to "the Day of Yahweh", "die nur eine akute Krisis bedeutet".[1]) However, since *'ēth* also appears in the Day-of-Yahweh texts because it corresponds well to the concept (see p. 110), it follows that it is employed in both contexts as a secondary synonym, not as a primary term.

It may now be concluded that *qēts* alone is used expressly in Daniel as a *terminus technicus* in relation to the absolute eschatological End because of its frequent use denoting the End itself, often without the article, as if it were a proper noun. The other expressions are only appropriated as synonyms in similar fashion as had also been done in narrative and prophetic literature, being employed because

---

[1]) *Loc. cit.*

of their individual basic meanings of "definite occasion", "appointed time" and "latter end". Although the characteristic meanings of these expressions refer specifically to an event of definite finality, they do not suggest that the exact temporal moment has been determined; Daniel's "weeks of years" would refer at most to the certain year in which the End is to come.

In this section, a major difference becomes obvious between the views of prophecy and apocalyptic toward the historical situation. It was seen above (pp. 105-111) that the prophets see before them a transformation that is to affect a certain people or peoples, or perhaps even all peoples, but that pertains only to the relative destiny of the historical situation. With respect to the temporal references, the characteristic expressions may be generally represented by *bayyōm hahūʾ*, which looks to the future as an abrupt, radical intervention, yet as the continuation of historical time which is to be continued further.

In contrast, Daniel presents a carefully worked out description of the chronological sequence of the coming events that proceed from the present situation. He very consciously and deliberately writes a plan for history corresponding to his religious conviction.[1] The course of the events is indeed directed to a transformation brought about by a divinely determined intervention. But it is fully conceived as the final and absolute End for all events; its characteristic *terminus* is *qēts*. Human history comes to a close and is replaced subjectively and existentially by the Messianic kingdom and temporally by everlasting life for the "saints" (7:13-18, 27; 12:1-3).[2] As Charles has said: "The apocalyptist sought to get behind the surface and penetrate to the essence of events, the spiritual purpose and forces that underlie and give them their real significance. With this end in view apocalyptic sketched in outline the history of the world and of mankind, . . . the ultimate triumph of righteousness, and the final consummation of all things. . . . Apocalyptic and not prophecy was first to grasp the great idea that all history, alike human, cosmological and spiritual, is a unity—a unity following naturally as a corollary of the unity of God preached by the prophets." [3]

The fact that an apocalyptist like Daniel had a truly historical viewpoint is seriously questioned by von Rad because he depicted

---

[1] *Cf.* Weiser, *loc. cit.*, p. 98.

[2] See H. W. Robinson, *op. cit.*, p. 147.

[3] *Loc. cit.*, p. 24.

the salvation event as eschatological and not within the course of history, as did the prophets; furthermore: "Bei einem derart determinierten Geschichtsablauf kann der Entscheidung der Menschen nur eine untergeordnete Bedeutung zukommen; sie sind ja nur bedingt die Träger des Geschehens, und deshalb entbehrt die Darstellung auch der wirklichen geschichtlichen Spannung." [1]) However, even when the salvation event puts an end to history, it is a part of the historical course of events; it is the last event and therefore does not itself take place beyond history.

That the apocalyptists leave no room to man for decisions to affect the course of events, is actually a misunderstanding, for the view of events is characterized throughout as effected by human undertakings which, as in the prophets, cut each other short. Thus, here, too, God makes use of the machinations of man to work out his temporary judgments upon the wicked and over-ambitious. The only essential difference is that the apocalyptists believe that God's decisive intervention will not be by human agent alone but also through his "heavenly hosts", and not in the midst of the historical course but as the final occurrence of all events in the spatially and temporally limited world. Thus the belief in the universal God led to an historical universalism that postulated an end to all history as the goal of God's control of it and plan for it.[2])

B. Death as Man's Natural Destiny

In the usual OT view of death, it is considered as "the natural end of life, when it comes in the fulness of time to one already 'satisfied with days'" [3]) (*zāqēn ūseba' yāmiym*, Gen 35:29; Job 42:17). This is the *destiny* of man: natural and final. It is both an expected occurrence and the proper and fitting culmination of the normal earthly life. In a temporal sense, the event of the natural death may be expressed as above, or as the occasion "when your days are full (*kiy yimle'ū yāmeykā*) and you lie down with your fathers" (2 Sam 7:12; *cf.* Jer 25:34; Lam 4:18; 1 Chr 17:11). This "satisfaction" or "fulness" of days is the proper, expected time for death. In this sense, natural death after a long life is pictured in Job 5:26 as going "with vigor to the grave, as sheaves go up in their season" (*be'ittō*). So it was, too, when

---

[1]) *Theologie des Alten Testaments*, II, pp. 314, 317 f., 328.

[2]) See H. H. Rowley: *The Relevance of the Apocalyptic*, 2nd ed., London: 1947, pp. 152, 154.

[3]) H. W. Robinson, *op. cit.*, p. 93.

"the days of David to die approached" (*wayyiqrebū yemēy dāwid lāmūth*, 1 Kgs 2:1; see Gen 47:29). Thus death may also be termed the end of a person, as that of the unjust rich man in Jer 17:11 (*be'achariythō*), as that of every man in Ecc 7:2 (*sōph kol-hā'ādām*); or as that of the "annointed one" in Dan 9:26 (*weqitstsō*; *cf.* Lam 4:18).

Although this is an occasion to be expected, its temporal arrival is not determined at a fixed moment, as is demonstrated when David refuses to put an end to Saul, for "his day may come, that he die" (*yōmō yābō' wāmēth*, 1 Sam 26:10; *cf.* Ps 37:13). This uncertainty [1] is explicitly expressed in Ecc 9:12—"For man does not even know his occasion (*'eth-'ittō*); like fish that are seized in an evil net and like birds seized by the snare, like them the sons of man are trapped on an evil occasion (*le'ēth rā'āh*), when it falls upon them suddenly" (see p. 78). The reference to death in vv. 2 f. with *miqreh* is surely more than "chance" or "happening"; [2] it ought rather to be rendered: "for everyone there is one destiny". It is meant that good and bad alike die; therefore, the wise will lead their life with this end in view (7:2-4; 9:4f.).

That the temporal occasion is not seen as a divinely determined event is particularly clear in 9:11—*kīy-'ēth wāphega' yiqreh 'eth-kullām*, "for occasion and happening meet them all". According to the context, both of the parallels are used negatively here [3] with respect to death. Therefore, despite the "reflective syntactic context" of this usage, James Barr is hardly right in claiming an application of *'ēth* to "time in general". [4] The context is obviously referring to the particular occasion of the destiny of death. "Time" itself does not meet anything, but rather the occurrences for which it is the temporal sphere. Furthermore, the whole context of Ecc. is reflective. Although the divine judgment is meant in these cases, [5] it is presented as the natural destiny of every man and beast; only, the occurrence may come unexpectedly. In this sense, *'ēth* may indicate an occasion that, as H. W. Robinson has said, "meets you on your path through life", according to the basic meaning he derived for it etymologically. Unfortunately, Robinson brands Koheleth's time-consciousness as

---

[1]) *Cf.* Barr, *Biblical Words for Time*, p. 99.

[2]) So H. W. Robinson, *op. cit.*, pp. 68 f.

[3]) See 1 Kgs 5:18; *cf.* Robert Gordis: *Koheleth—the Man and His World*, 2nd ed., New York: 1955, pp. 297 f.

[4]) *Loc. cit.*, pp. 99 f.

[5]) So Leupold, *op. cit.*, pp. 219-221, to 9:11 f., and Loretz, *op. cit.*, p. 201; see above, pp. 152-158.

being "as un-Hebraic as we should expect to find in a book from which the sense of history is absent".[1])

As an ordinarily natural occasion, death may also occur unnaturally under extraordinary circumstances. In other words, it may come prematurely, before the proper, expected temporal occasion for it: *lāmmāh thānūth belo' 'ittekā*—"Why should you die not (yet) at your occasion?" (Ecc 7:17; also Job 22:16). This premature death is considered in these cases as a just punishment for the wicked, as also in Ezek 22:3 f., where wicked Jerusalem has caused its occasion to approach (*cf.* also Isa 13:22; see p. 107). It is with this idea that the death of the "despicable" King of the North is mentioned (*ūbā' 'ad qitstsō*, Dan 11:45; see p. 113).

Other occurrences of temporal expressions with respect to death merely indicate the temporal relationship of the occurrences as: "And it was about the occasion of her dying . . ." (1 Sam 4:20; see p. 38); and: "For the lad will be a Nazirite of God from birth until the day of his death" (*'ad yōm mōthō*; Jdg 13:7; *cf.* 2 Sam 6:23; 20:3; Ecc 7:1).

Occasionally, *'ēth* appears to denote the destined occasion of death without further modification, as if it could contain this meaning inherently (see esp. Isa 13:22; Ezek 22:3; Job 22:16; Ecc 9:11 f., pp. 106 f., 116 f.). However, this is no more true of *'ēth* than of the other temporal expressions; *yōm* in Ps 37:13, *'achariyth* in Jer 17:11, *qēts* in Dan 11:45 and *sōph* in Ecc 7:2 all denote the death-occasion without closer modification. It is evidently unnecessary to name the occurrence by its *terminus technicus* in order for it to be understood; what is meant is clear in all of the above cases from the contexts. Not a specialized term for the occasion of death, *'ēth* takes a place among other expressions which differ from each other in their shades of meaning, whether specifically implying the temporal situation (*yōm*), the culmination of life (*'achariyth, qēts, sōph*), or the definiteness of the occasion (*'ēth*).

C. Occasion as Given Opportunity (Koheleth)

The view of time of the "Preacher" is often singled out in the OT as unique. Apparently expecting to find evidence of the salvation history everywhere, H. W. Robinson and Gerhard von Rad accuse him of having no sense of history and "no concern with a redemptive

---

[1]) *Op. cit.*, pp. 109, 112, 121; so also Muilenburg, *op. cit.*, p. 234.

past, and no vision of a Messianic future".[1]) To the contrary, Kurt
Galling commends Koheleth as the first from the area of OT wisdom
"der die Geschichtlichkeit der Existenz—in tormentis—entdeckt
und thematisch behandelt hat".[2]) Whereas Robinson and Masao
Sekine do not find Koheleth's view of time typical for the OT,[3])
James Barr finds nothing extraordinary, even if the concept of "time
in general" should be included.[4]) H. L. Ginsberg identifies the view
as predestination,[5]) but Oswald Loretz defines it as a regulation by
God of the right moment for an event,[6]) and C.H. Ratschow understands
this "right time for something" as the basic meaning of ʿēth in the
OT.[7])

Since some cases of ʿēth in Koheleth have been discussed above
without any appreciable evidence of uniqueness within the OT as a
whole (see pp. 28 f., 44, 78, 82, 116 f.), the apparently problematic
cases should be the remaining ones in chs. 3 and 8. Here, the instance
in 3:1 obviously finds its interpretation in the verses 2-8, which
likewise form the basis for the instances in verses 11 and 17, finding
yet an echo in 8:5 f. Therefore, it would be logical to begin with the
central passage, 3:2-8, in order to arrive at an appreciation of this
particular usage of ʿēth in Koheleth.

This remarkable passage, a "Catalogue of Seasons",[8]) an anaphora
in the form of a "complexio duorum oppositorum",[9]) employs ʿēth 28
times in succession, each time in a construct relationship to an infinitive, except for the last pair, where nouns are used. The first obvious
observation is that this is a list of predicate constructions where the
predicate itself is unexpressed, "there is a . . ." In fact, the real subject
is lacking, for all of the infinitives (and even the two nouns) express
something that is done by, or that happens to, someone. This subjective someone is not mentioned, yet it is apparent that his implicit
role is essentially passive, for it is dependent upon the "occasions".
It may be said, then, that this someone is properly the object of the

---

[1]) Op. cit., p. 121. Cf. von Rad, Theologie des Alten Testaments I, p. 454.
[2]) "Das Rätsel der Zeit im Urteil Koheleths", ZThK 58 (1961), p. 1.
[3]) H. W. Robinson, op. cit., p. 121; see Muilenburg, op. cit., p. 235.
[4]) Loc. cit.; see below, p. 116.
[5]) "The Structure and Contents of the Book of Koheleth", SVT III, 1955,
p. 140.
[6]) Op. cit., pp. 200, 252-254, 314.
[7]) "Anmerkungen zur theologischen Auffassung des Zeitproblems", p. 380;
see above, p. 10.
[8]) Gordis, op. cit., p. 51.
[9]) Galling, Prediger, p. 61.

occurrences. It is this certain someone who passively experiences birth and death (v. 2), war and peace (v. 8).

The construction of the opposed pairs is obviously no accident. Galling understands this as a choice between two possibilities: man is always confronted with a decision.[1]) But that would imply an "either-or", which is not represented in the syntactical construction with a simple *waw*. Galling bases his view on H. J. Stoebe's interpretation of *'ēts hadda'ath tōb wārā'* in the Paradise account. Stoebe resolves the difficulty of the article with *da'ath* instead of with *tōb wārā'* by proposing that the last two words were an addition by the Yahwist, although he renders it in the usual manner, "the Tree of the Knowledge of Good and Evil". He proceeds further to read too much into the figure of speech on the basis of other instances, concluding that it signifies the capacity to judge between that which helps a person in his life and that which hinders one.[2])

However, he evades the clear witness of the negative cases that mean simply "nothing", as in Gen 31:24—"Watch yourself, lest you speak with Jacob from good to evil (*mittōb 'ad-rā'*)." Those cases that involve a decision are expressly indicated with *hbyn* (1 Kgs 3:9), *m's*, *bchr* (Isa 7:15 f.), or *drsh* (Am 5:14; *cf.* v. 15, Mic 3:2), while *yd'* means simply recognition or sensual perception (2 Sam 19:36). Thus Stoebe misses the whole point of 2 Sam 13:22, where Absalom's refusal to speak to Amnon "either good or evil" was a sign of deep personal enmity; it meant *complete* avoidance, that he spoke nothing to Amnon at all. Thus, positively, *tōb wārā'* must mean "everything", that is, all that stands between these two extreme poles.[3])

As for the grammatical construction for the name of the tree in Paradise, the possibility that the last two words be an addition solves nothing, for the Yahwist must have known Hebrew well enough not to leave a glaring grammatical error. This expression may best be handled as an apposition: "the Tree of Knowledge—(both) Good and Evil" (*cf. kā'ēth chayyāh*, p. 25). The pair of opposites modifies *hadda'ath* in a descriptive sense, indicating not the object or content of the knowledge, but its extent, as if to say, "the Tree of all-encom-

---

[1]) *Ibid.*

[2]) H. J. Stoebe: "Gut und Böse in der Jahwistischen Quelle des Pentateuch", *ZAW* 65 (1953), pp. 196-201.

[3]) So Gerhard von Rad: *Das erste Buch Mose. Genesis*, 6th ed., *ATD*, 2-4, 1961, p. 65.

passing Knowledge". Similarly, the announcement in Jdg 13:7 that Samson should be a Nazirite "from birth until the day of his death" intends to signify his entire lifetime. Thus the opposite pairs are a Hebrew idiom for expressing the whole of something.[1]

In this sense, the pairs of 3:2-8 present radically opposed events that mean to include every shade and degree of related occurrence that may be placed between their poles. It is therefore of major significance that the list begins with birth and death—the beginning and final events of human life—and finishes with war and peace—the most extreme states of existence. These already imply that every human experience and existential condition is symbolically meant to be included. The intervening pairs comprise no attempt whatsoever to literally mention all possible events in a person's life. It is their number that is of greater importance: they form seven double pairs, which in itself symbolizes wholeness. Therefore, the pairs represent all the possibilities that may take place within the range of human activity and experience.[2]

Special mention may be made of the first infinitive, *lāledeth*, which is usually rendered passively, "to be born", in order to correspond to *lāmūth* as the extreme experiences in the life of the same person.[3] But the argument nevertheless seems weak, as laid out, *e.g.*, by Walther Zimmerli: "Der Infinitiv kal *ldth* steht hier als nackter Verbal-begriff da. In der Parallele zu *mwth* gerät er trotz seiner aktiven Form in passive Bedeutung". [4] H. C. Leupold judiciously points out that the support based on a comparison with infinitives in Jer 25:34 and Hos 9:11 is of doubtful value and that the LXX found no difficulty in translating τοῦ τεκεῖν.[5] It all depends upon what one wishes to have understood. If all the events are to pertain to the same person, a passive interpretation is demanded. However, the active meaning, "to bear", proves to be of even greater significance. For nowhere does Koheleth apply his reflections to a single person, except when speaking of himself, 1:12-2:20. Thereafter, he always speaks of *hāʾādām* in the general sense, "a man". It should then be expected that he does not mean all the events in the life of any particular man in 3:2-8, but rather *all the events* that occur within the range of *all*

---

[1]) *Cf.* Galling, *loc. cit.*; Loretz, *op. cit.*, p. 188.
[2]) *Cf.* Loretz, *op. cit.*, p. 253, and Leupold, *op. cit.*, p. 83.
[3]) *E.g.*: Galling, *loc. cit.*, p. 58; RSV; *Zürcher Bibel*.
[4]) *Op. cit.*, p. 167, n. 1.
[5]) *Op. cit.*, p. 84.

human life. In this sense, the giving and losing of life form perfect opposites.

Having established the fact that Koheleth is concerned here with all events in human life, it will be worthwhile to examine their character more closely. The repetitive *'ēth* is often identified with the καιρός of classical Greek and modern philosophical theology: "the decisive moment".[1]) Barr's investigation has, on the one hand, proven that καιρός began to lose this specific meaning in post-classical Greek and certainly does not retain it with any degree of consistency in either the LXX or NT. On the other hand, he has indicated that Paul Tillich's use of the word in his philosophical presentations has likely "led some readers to expect this as the natural meaning of the ancient word". [2]) It was no later than 1922 that Tillich first used καιρός in the philosophically weighted sense of a moment of crisis that demands a decision. Although he connected it directly and particularly to the "fulfilled time" of the appearance of Jesus as the Christ as the most significant turning-point in history, he did not presume to have identified his philosophical "Kairos" with the use of any Biblical word.[3])

It is then significant that no mention was made of *'ēth* as "point of time", let alone "decisive time" or "critical time", until after Tillich had made an impression upon his contemporaries. The first to apply the weighted sense of καιρός to the OT was apparently Galling in 1929, who cites Tillich as his source. In this first stage, however, he only applied the concept to the prophetic view of the present and future as "fulfilled time".[4]) This opinion was quickly echoed by Johannes Hempel,[5]) but the first semantical application was apparently effected by Gerhard Delling in 1938, who affixed it at once to καιρός in the NT and LXX and to *'ēth* in the OT.[6]) Thereafter, it became "every man's thing" in both the conceptual and semantical applications.

In taking a cue from Barr, a glance at 3:2-8 quickly shows that there is no consistency in indicating either a moment of time or a

---

[1]) So Walther Zimmerli (with Helmer Ringgren): *Sprüche/Prediger*, *ATD*, 16:1, 1962, p. 169; Hans Wilhelm Hertzberg: *Der Prediger*, *KAT*, XVII:4, Gütersloh: 1963, p. 103; Vollborn, *op. cit.*, p. 25.

[2]) *Biblical Words for Time*, pp. 31-53.

[3]) *Op. cit.*, pp. 9-28.

[4]) "Die Geschichte als Wort Gottes bei den Propheten", p. 171.

[5]) *Op. cit.*, p. 32.

[6]) "καιρός", pp. 456-465.

critical or decisive time. In the first place, scarcely any of the experiences or activities may be conceived of as occurring within the space of
a moment—surely not "to keep" (v. 6), "to keep silent" (7), "of war"
and "of peace" (8). Further, hardly any may be termed a critical
or decisive time, *e.g.*, "to weep", "to laugh" (4), "to embrace", "to
refrain from embracing" (5), "to seek", "to lose" (6), "to rend" and
"to sew" (7). Finally, many cases are not such as present a possibility
for decision, or are at least ordinarily reactions or the expression of
emotions: "to bear", "to die" (2), "to heal" (3), "to weep", "to
laugh", "to mourn" (4), "to lose" (6), "to love", "to hate", "of war"
and "of peace" (8).

It must therefore be concluded, first, that Koheleth does not have
moments of time in mind, but rather *occasions* or *situations*. Secondly,
he does not mean critical or decisive occasions, but rather *all* occasions
whatsoever. Thirdly, he does not mean situations for decision, but
rather *all* situations that are presented in the daily course of life,
situations that may involve all possibilities: emotional reaction or
passive experience, as well as decision for a particular activity. The
simple and plain fact is that Koheleth showed no evidence here or
elsewhere of any influence from the philosophy of Greece [1]) or of
Tillich.

Accepting this fact that Koheleth did not have decision-situations
in mind for 3:2-8, it is not only the "kairos"-concept that must be
divorced from the passage, but also the interpretation of Ratschow.
For, as Barr has already pointed out,[2]) Ratschow's discussion "shows
the contradictoriness of combining" Biblical material with non-
Biblical philosophical material. Ratschow indeed does an invaluable
service by analyzing the modern figure of speech, "I don't have any
time". He demonstrates how the mental attitude that produces this
figure of speech in modern society is really a sign that man is closed
to his outside world. The remedy to this essentially non-Christian
relationship is a change of attitude from "having time for something".
Such a change in attitude frees a man from being a slave to time:
"dann heißt die Freiheit: Warten, bis es Zeit sei". [3])

---

[1]) It has been the invaluable service of Loretz in his thorough examination of
outside influences upon Koheleth to prove this fact (*op. cit.*, p. 56), as Gordis
(*op. cit.*, pp. 51-58) did before him in lesser detail.

[2]) *Loc. cit.*, p. 150.

[3]) *Loc. cit.*, pp. 377-379.

Although Ratschow's insights into the contemporary understanding of time and his answer to it are worthy of serious consideration, he tries to find linguistic correspondence to his concept in the Bible. This he believes to have found in 'ēth, whose basic meaning he identifies as the "rechte Zeit für . . ." He then proceeds with the semantically impossible method of assigning different shades of meaning to the various grammatical forms: genitive constructions denote an activity or occurrence at the appropriate time-moment; the addition of a personal suffix indicates that something occurs when God has ordered it or simply at the proper time or opportunity; and the junction to an infinitive with le indicates the time for a particular activity, "was der Prediger zu einem Zentrum seines Denkens macht". Not overlooking the many instances where 'ēth denotes the temporal relationship of a narrative or implies repetition "at every time", he characterizes these uses as "Eindringen der anderen Zeitbegriffe in dies verhältnismässig geschlossene Bedeutungsgefüge, die diesem Zeitverständnis von Hause aus fernliegen". His next step is to identify his time concept with the use of καιρός in the NT, and then to come to the conclusion: "Zeitbegriff und Zeitdenken sind für das Alte wie für das Neue Testament anscheinend im wesentlichen an die Zeit-für, sowohl als Zeit-sein-für wie als Zeit-haben-für, geknüpft." [1] Criticism of such a method that correlates vocabulary with mental sense perception has been provided effectively enough by Barr, which he names "illegitimate totality transfer"—reading one meaning of a word into all of its cases.[2]

Yet, Ratschow comes very close with his concept of the Kairos-moment to Koheleth's idea of the occasion. Most other Kairos-adherents think of it as a critical or decisive moment that, pertaining to man's own activity, amounts to a "moment of decision". But Ratschow explains: "Diese Zeit-für kennzeichnet das Gelingen gründende Offensein, Gelegensein, Günstigsein für dies oder das, also den oben näher gezeichneten Tatbestand des Offenseins-für als Augenblick oder Kairos." [3] This openness for every situation that comes upon a man is approximately what Koheleth is advocating in

---

[1] *Ibid.*, pp. 380-384. It is too bad that a closer examination of the linguistic evidence cannot substantiate this conclusion, which Ratschow uses to support his declaration for the contemporary Christian: "Glaube, in der Zeit-für ausgesagt, ist dann die Erschlossenheit für den Kommenden."

[2] *Op. cit.*, p. 218.

[3] *Loc. cit.*, p. 382.

distinction to the usual Kairos-idea that every situation demands a responsible decision. Both Koheleth and Ratschow foster a general attitude of openness to each situation. Ratschow points out that everything has "seine ganz bestimmte Zeit-für",[1]) but Koheleth sees this aspect from another angle. Man's openness to the situation is basically an acceptance of that which comes, whatever and whenever that may be. This is essentially not a "time-for" that emphasizes the appropriate moment for a particular activity, but rather an "occasion-when" that primarily stresses the passive acceptance of the occasion as such whenever it may come. It seems, therefore, that the basic idea concerns *not the temporal aspect* but *the concrete structure of the situation*. Further, its intention is to check man's willful action in disregard to the facts of the particular situation, and to show that the occasion is given to him that he may take advantage of it.

This seems to be Koheleth's concern throughout. His principal theme in a negative sense, that "all is a breath" (*hakkol hābel*), clearly announced in 1:2,[2]) is directed against all of man's striving to produce something new, better or lasting; the experience of life through the generations proves that this is useless (1:3 f., 9-11, 14). Mankind may thus be compared to the processes of nature that likewise produce no changes (1:4-7). These natural processes are magnified by von Rad into the "trostlosen Kreislauf aller Dinge" that supposedly exemplifies the non-historical and "gemeinorientalische zyklische Denken" of Koheleth.[3])

However, Loretz has proven in his thorough investigation that such cyclical thought did not exist in Israel or even in Mesopotamia, so that one cannot speak of it as generally Oriental. Koheleth's point here is rather that man fails to comprehend the reason behind the natural processes,[4]) because he always tries to structure his life according to his own imagination instead of according to the possible situations that are given to him. After arguing against such senseless striving in various areas of life (1:16-2:23), Koheleth concludes that the only enjoyable life is the one that accepts what is given from God's hand, for it is obvious that those who always strive for more

---

[1]) *Ibid.*, p. 381.
[2]) *Cf.* Loretz, *op. cit.*, p. 216.
[3]) *Theologie des Alten Testaments*, I, pp. 453 f.; *cf.* H. W. Robinson, that for Koheleth "time consists of endless cycles of repetitions with nothing new" (*op. cit.*, p. 121).
[4]) *Op. cit.*, pp. 251, 254 f.

than that only labor under the divine curse (2:24-26). Having established his principal argument, the remaining ten chapters elaborate
the theme in detail, demonstrating its truth in the various situations
of life, negatively and positively. It is therefore appropriate that the
elaborated application of the thesis begins in ch. 3 with an artistically
symbolical reference to all possible events that may happen in the
course of human life. As far as human life is concerned, the thesis is
universal; it has applicability to every conceivable occasion.

In this context, then, the remaining instances of ʿēth in Koheleth
may be understood. The instance in 3:17 is itself clear, although the
final word, shām, has caused many a headache because of its apparently
awkward position. An alteration is often attempted, usually to sām
—"he (God) has appointed", but it is not the right position for the
verb.[1]) Some retain the word as it is, and the best interpretation is
that made by Zimmerli, who considers it a direct modification of the
accompanying verbal noun and relates it very logically to the foregoing "place of justice" in v. 16.[2]) It is in any case clear from the
context that God is the actual subject who, despite the injustice in
the courts, has ordained that there nevertheless be an eventual possibility for justice: "an occasion for every matter and over every
undertaking there". Although restricted to the court situation, this is
obviously an echo from vv. 2-8 and particularly from the introductory
verse which, in typical Hebrew fashion, concisely announces what
follows.[3])

The parallel expression zemān in 3:1 appears only here in Koheleth.
This fact should already indicate that a meaning basically different
from that implied by ʿēth is not to be expected. Although zemān as a
word borrowed from Aramaic ordinarily means in Hebrew a fixed or
established time, it also appears in Biblical Aramaic in ways that correspond exactly to uses of ʿēth. In the form bēhh zimnāʾ, "at that time",
it occurs as a relative temporal reference in Ezra 5:3; Dan 3:7 f.; 4:33,
and as zimnīyn telāthāh, "three times" (cf. rabbōth ʿittīym, Neh 9:28),
in Dan 6:11, 14. It may thus be considered as a parallel that has been
chosen because it can correspond closely in meaning. The statement
in 3:1, "for everything there is a time, and an occasion for every
matter under the heavens", is then to be regarded as a preliminary
summary that corresponds precisely to the following detailed state-

---

[1]) See Hertzberg, *Prediger*, p. 101.
[2]) *Prediger*, p. 175.
[3]) See Cassuto, *Genesis*, p. 20.

ments; every possible event that may transpire in the world of man is included—there is a given possibility for each one.

As in 3:17 above, the immediate context following the catalogue likewise names God as the actual subject who orders the occasions. In answer to the rhetorical question implying the hopelessness of seeking gain through striving (v. 9), Koheleth replies in effect that the striving for something else beyond the extent of the possible is senseless, for that with which man can best occupy himself is simply given (*nthn*) to him by God (10). Then follows (11) the assertion that could well be called Koheleth's basic positive thesis: *ʾeth-hakkol ʿāsāh yāpheh beʿittō*—"Everything he has made beautiful on its occasion." The meaning is essentially the same as in v. 1, only that God is expressly identified as the actual subject of the given occasion. This thought is somewhat elaborated in v. 14, where it is held that, in distinction to undertakings of men (see 1:9-11, *etc.*), it is only the work of God that has lasting quality, "and God has done (it) that they should fear him". Therefore, since man cannot comprehend the underlying purposes of God (11b), there is nothing better for him to do than to enjoy what God has given him, including his work (12f.).

What is therefore urged is not a materialistic hedonism as seen by Aarre Lauha,[1]) but a submission of the free will to the divine. Thus Martin Luther's comment is understandable: "Dies Buch sollte billig den Titel haben, dass es wider den freien Willen geschrieben wäre." [2]) Actually, as seen above, Koheleth does not polemicize against man's free will, but against his disregard for God's gift of advantageous situations that he foolishly ruins. Many have found evidence here of skepticism, determinism or even fatalism,[3]) but Loretz has surely recognized the real intention: "Der Sinn dieses unberechenbaren göttlichen Handelns ist nach Qohelet, dass die Menschen das Werk Gottes nicht begreifen. Von fatalistischer oder deterministischer Bestimmung des Lebens durch Gott ist keine Rede." [4])

Had Koheleth meant that God determines every occasion for man without allowing man the possibility for freedom of action, he would

---

[1]) "Die Krise des religiösen Glaubens bei Kohelet", *SVT* III, 1955, p. 188.
[2]) Cited by Hertzberg, *loc. cit.*, p. 227.
[3]) See Johannes Pedersen: "Scepticisme israélite", *RTP* 10 (1930), p. 349.
[4]) *Op. cit.*, pp. 253 f.; *cf.* Leupold, *op. cit.*, pp. 28-30, and Zimmerli, *loc. cit.*, pp. 137-139.

scarcely have used *ʿēth* when a much more fitting word was at his disposal: *mōʿēd*. Elsewhere in the OT, whenever stress is to be placed upon an occasion as specifically appointed or determined, *mōʿēd* is used. This applies to appointments by man (1 Sam 9:24; 13:8, 11; 20:35; 2 Sam 20:5) as well as by God, such as the promised birth of a son (Gen 17:21; 18:14; 21:2; 2 Kgs 4:16 f.), the end of the pestilence (2 Sam 24:15), the regular migration of the birds (Jer 8:7), the harvest of wine (Hos 2:11), and the occasion for Yahweh to have mercy on Zion (Ps 102:14), where it serves to complement *ʿēth* with a more precise meaning (see pp. 25-28, 89). Further, divinely determined appointments are mentioned in reference to the plague of cattle (Ex 9:5), the time of the vision (Hab 2:3), the time of judgment (Ps 75:3), the appointed End (Dan 8:9; 11: 27, 35), the futile invasion of the South by the King of the North (11:29), and the appointed periods preceding the End (12:7. see p. 113), not to mention the divinely appointed times for the observance of feasts (*e.g.*, Ex 13:10; 23:15; Dt 16:6; 31:10). Although an *argumentum e silentio* furnishes no conclusive proof, the fact that Koheleth never uses *mōʿēd* may at least be an indication that he is not thinking deterministically.

As God has given ordered existence to nature, so he also gives man the occasion to lead an ordered life. But most men are rebellious and disorderly over against God and the situations that he offers them. Their life therefore seems futile. But the man who submits to God's will and accepts each occasion as a gift from God may lead a happy life in what the NT would call "faith". Such a man is for Koheleth the truly wise man who waits for and recognizes the occasion and judgment given by God, and does not question the situation as, *e.g.*, when receiving an order from the king—"then occasion and judgment (*weʿēth ūmishpāt*) knows the heart of the wise man" (8:5). Galling would omit this verse as a contradiction to the following: [1] "Because for every matter there is an occasion and a judgment, for the evil of man is great upon him, that no one knows what will be . . ." (vv. 6-7a). However, the wise man recognizes only the possibility of the given situation (5), not even he can foresee the future, which becomes a tempting snare for those who try to plan for it (6-8).[2] It is not for man to alter the occasion that God has given him, neither is it in his

---

[1] "Stand und Aufgabe der Kohelet-Forschung", *ThR* 6 (1934), p. 358.
[2] *Cf.* Zimmerli, *loc. cit.*, pp. 217 f.

place to be his own judge or effect his own justice, for this, too, is governed by God (*cf.* 3:17, p. 125) The double expression is not a hendiadys, for it refers on the one hand to the occasion given to man, and on the other hand to God's eventual judgment of the situation.

The principal distinction to be noted is that the whole emphasis of Koheleth is not laid upon the temporal aspect of the given possibility, namely, that each one comes at a certain determined moment. His main argument is not directed against the man who does not recognize the right time for a certain matter, but rather against the man who is not content to accept the opportunity within its given limits and tries to overplay the situation and strive for something beyond his reach. The right time may be discerned by anyone, but only the God-fearing is wise enough to limit himself to the extent of the possibility given by God. Therefore, the primary factor is *not the moment*, but *the given occasion*.

Similar belief in the divine initiative for creating an opportune situation within the course of the individual's life appears with ʿēth in Est 4:14b. Mordecai makes it plain to Esther that help will come for the Jews, if not from her, then "from another place, . . . and who knows if you have not for an occasion as this (*leʿēth kāzoʾth*) come to the kingdom?" (see v. 14a, p. 46). Of course, the agent of the help can be understood as none other than God. Passing mention may also be made of Jdg 13:23 (see p. 37).

It may be concluded that the emphasis on the *concrete structure* rather than on the temporal aspect of the situation gives further demonstration of the fact that the Hebrew concepts of *time and event* were inseparably fused together. In addition, Koheleth in particular represents a unique view in early Judaism that every occasion which comes upon a man in the course of his life is *an opportunity given to him by God*. It is neither an opportunity to strive for something that is not within his reach, nor an occasion in the sense of a divine demand for a particular decision. Rather, it is an opportunity given to man for the purpose of making the most of life that lies within his human capacity, in short, to enjoy its pleasures and tasks and not to be disheartened by its difficulties, sorrows and injustices. This *"living according to the occasion"* was not based on constant decisions but on an attitude, and the basis of this attitude was not human reason or will but the submission of the same in fear and faith before God.

Summary

The various subjects of this chapter present the following conclusions:

1. It may be observed that *ʿēth* appears in no connection as a *terminus technicus*. Except for the lone example among temporal expressions in the considered context, namely, *qēts* as the *"End"* (p. 113), all relevant expressions retain their usual meanings and are employed not as synonyms, but in complementary fashion to indicate the particular aspects of the occasions. *ʿēth* is consistently and appropriately used as *"definite occasion"*. The first occurrence of *ʿēth* in relationship to an occasion of destiny appears in an early narrative context (1 Sam 4:20, p. 117) as a temporal reference with respect to an individual's death. It appears more frequently in the prophets as temporal reference for the impending event, which already receives the characterization of a *"final"* event in Amos (8:2, p. 107). However, *ʿēth* is not used in this way of referring to the event itself until Ezekiel (7:7, 12; 30:3, p. 88; *cf.* Isa 13:22, p. 107), due to the fact that its objectivization was a comparatively late phenomenon. In late post-exilic literature, it then came to be used in this way for an individual's death, the eschatological End and the given occasion.

2. It is not essentially the temporal aspect of the particular occasion that is consistently indicated by *ʿēth*, but rather the *fact* of the occasion itself. It is applied by the prophets to the definite fact of the impending divine intervention, by the apocalyptist Daniel to the definite fact of the eventual End, by various witnesses to the definite fact of the destiny of death, and by Koheleth to the definite fact of man's given possibilities. Stress may be laid upon the fact of the occasion as being determined by God, but not upon the temporal moment. Obviously, it is the *subjective factor ad personam* that plays the decisive role, and not the temporal factor.

The concept of destiny probably originated with the natural destiny of death common to all men. Death comes as a consequence, either naturally as the culmination of a long life, or prematurely, as the result of a wicked life. A corporate people may also have a final destiny, assured in fact by the divine will. But this is seen in prophetic literature as an end only to a certain people or peoples within history, and not in the eschatologically absolute sense. What really deserves the term "eschatology" is the apocalyptic view of the universal destiny of all peoples in the spatial and temporal sense: the absolute End of history.

3. References to specific occasions in man's private life concern the *given opportunities* for activity and experience; his action or reaction in the particular situation are left up to him. Further, these given possibilities are not actually temporal moments but *occasions* or *situations*; they are not necessarily critical or decisive times, for *all* situations are included; they are not necessarily times for decision, for many of them are occasions that rather involve *passive experience* or *emotional reaction*.

4. Further evidence has been presented on the basis of the witness of the prophets against the supposition that the impending destiny for a people involves actualization of the announced event in the present situation or a suspension of time *per se*. The recognition of the *tempora* is not only recognized but expressly substantiated by prophets as well as apocalyptists, who compare the future event, which nevertheless possesses uniquely new character, to the closed events of the past and the peculiar aspects of the present. Yet, the present is essentially effected from both past and future, for the consequences of the past form the presuppositions of the present and the announcement of the future may produce a consequential change in the present attitude.

5. The ultimate agency of *God* is the actual factor behind the concept of destiny for a people, history, and individual man with respect to death and even with respect to the given possibilities of his activity and experience. In prophecy and apocalyptic, this is particularly expressed as an intervention by God in time and history, which implies both his freedom in the temporal sphere as well as his accomodation to its limitations. Whereas the fact of man's death is set by God and may even be determined in individual cases of judgment upon the wicked, the divine agency is not so deterministic that it excludes human freedom of action. Instead, God either takes advantage of man's actions to effect his own will, or he offers opportunities to man's advantage.

CHAPTER FIVE

'ETH AND TEXTS OTHER THAN BIBLICAL HEBREW

The discoveries of Hebrew texts in the ruins of Lachish, in the Cairo Genizah, in the caves of Qumran and at Murrabba'at in the Judean Desert provide some passages with significant cases of *'ēth*. The texts from Old Testament times supplement the understanding of some uses in Biblical Hebrew, and the later texts give evidence of new usages that indicate differences in the concept of time. Of further interest are the uses of related forms in early Aramaic texts. First to be considered are the texts from Murrabba'at and Lachish, which date from the era of the first literary prophets. Then, the Hebrew text of Jesus ben Sira, the Damascus Codex and the texts from Qumran belong to the Early Jewish or Intertestamental Period. Of further importance in this later period, particularly for the younger influences on the NT, is the translation of *'ēth* in the LXX.

A. EARLY HEBREW LETTERS

1. *The Murrabba'at Letter*

The Murrabba'at Letter (Mur 17), written on papyrus in old Hebrew characters, offers only a few lines from the beginning of a letter. The opening greeting is followed in the second line by this interesting introduction to the body of the letter: *w'th 'l tshm' lkl dbr 'shr ydbr 'lyk*. Excepting for the moment the first word, this may be rendered as a request not to be influenced by secondary rumors in distinction to the actual report contained in the letter: "do not listen to every word which one says to you . . ." J. T. Milik, who published the extant text of the letter, characterizes *'th* as the introduction to the body of the letter: "and now".[1] This phonetical form *'att* would be compared to that found in the Lachish Letters (pp. 132 f.) and in Ezek 23:43 and Ps 74:6. However, with respect to the cited Biblical passages, it has been found that they well represent a peculiar use of *'ēth* and not a variant writing for *'attāh* (see pp. 83 f.).

---

[1] (With P. Benoit and R. de Vaux) *DJD* II, p. 96.

Milik supports his argument with reference to 2 Kgs 5:6, where *weʿattāh* introduces the body of a letter,[1]) as also in 10:2—"And now, when the letter comes to you . . ." However, the witness of the early Aramaic texts (pp. 134-138) points to a difference in the use of the forms *kʿth* and *kʿnth* on the one hand and *kʿn* on the other. The first two words are only used for introducing the main body of a letter or the solution to a problem, as *ʿth* in Mur 17:2 and in the Lachish Letters, while *kʿn* is employed as *ʿattāh* in its normal usage in Biblical Hebrew. But an exceptional use of *kʿn* in place of the otherwise exclusive use of *kʿth* and *kʿnth* shows that the body of a letter may also be introduced by "now" instead of the usual *termini technici* (pp. 134 f.). The cases in 2 Kgs 5:6; 10:2, therefore correspond to this non-technical variation.

Thus, *ʿth* in Mur 17 would correspond to the peculiar usage of *ʿēth* identified in Ezek 23:43; 27:34; Hag 1:2 and Ps 74:6 (pp. 83 f.), indicating, in contrast to the formalistic greeting, the specific situation: "Now, the situation is: do not . . ."

2. *The Lachish Letters*

In the six letters found in the excavations of Lachish, *ʿth* appears some ten times, including the conjectures for damaged texts. Three instances correspond to Mur 17, above, introducing the body after the greeting, as in 4:2: *wʿth kkl ʾshr shlch ʾdny kn ʿsh ʿbdk*—"Now, the situation: As everything that my lord has sent, so has your slave done . . ." The same may well be conjectured for 3:4, for three letters are lacking precisely where the introductory formula would come: "(Now, the situation:) Your slave has sent a letter to the 'open one' . . ." The same circumstance in 5:6 provokes the conjecture *ʿth*: "(The situation:) Your slave has returned the letters to my lord."

The other seven instances of *ʿth* in the Lachish Letters appear in the unique formula *ʿth kym*, always within the greeting. That these two words constitute a particular formula is obvious from the regularity of their occurrence and from the two cases where they are repeated (2:3; 5:2 f.). The publisher of the letters, Harry Torczyner, presumed a correspondence between this formula and the singular expression *ʿthh zh* in 6:2, which seems to serve the same purpose. Thus he identifies *ʿth* in all cases in the letters as a short form for

---

[1]) *Ibid.*

'attāh and corresponds *zh* with *kym*.[1]) This *zh* would be understood according to the context in the sense of the Biblical adverb or supporting particle "then, just", as in Gen 18:13—"Why then (*lāmmāh zeh*) did Sarah laugh?" The same combination as in Lachish 6:2 occurs three times in the OT: 2 Kgs 5:22 ("Behold, just now two young men have come to me"), 1 Kgs 17:24; Ruth 2:7.

With this, Torczyner derives the *kym* from the Accadian adverb *kiām*, "so, thus", relating it to the Hebrew words *koh*, *kēn*, *kak*. It would have the same ending as *pith'om*, and would be pointed analogically *keyom*. He also finds this "new" Hebrew word in the OT where the Massoretes have written it *kîy hayyōm* (1 Sam 9:12), *kehayyōm* (9:13; Neh 5:11), or *kayyōm* (Gen 25:31, 33; 1 Sam 2:16; 1 Kgs 1:51; 22:5; Isa 58:4; 2 Chr 18:4).[2]) However, this solution appears improbable for at least the three instances where the article is written in the consonantal text. Furthermore, it is not impossible that *yōm* be employed in an adverbial construction in the sense of "today" in the cited passages. It must be remembered that time was reckoned by the day rather than by the hour; what happened "today" was of temporal urgency. Thus 1 Sam 9:12, for example, may be rendered: "Hurry now, for today (= just now) he has come to the city."

The Lachish formula may then be pointed *'ēth kayyōm*. A literal translation may seem strange to Western ears, but not without sense: *yshm' yhwh 'th 'dny shm'th shlm 'ēth kayyōm 'ēth kayyōm*—"May Yahweh let my Lord hear tidings of peace on an occasion as today, an occasion as today" (2:1-3). The formula recurs in four other greetings: 4:1; 5:2 f.; 7:2; 8:2. It need cause no difficulty when a greeting does not contain the formula, as in Letter 3, or when it is replaced in 6:2 by *'thh zh* ("just now").[3]) This usage of *'ēth* may be compared to *kā'ēth māchār*, "as on this occasion—tomorrow" (pp. 34-39). The latter is a strengthened reference in an oath or promise to the fact of the specific situation in respect to the morrow, and the former is a strengthened reference in a wish to the fact of the specific situation with respect to the present day.

The instances of *'ēth* in the early Hebrew letters supplement, therefore, the normal usage in the OT, indicating a definite occasion

---

[1]) *Op. cit.*, pp. 80, 108 f.

[2]) *Ibid.*, p. 111.

[3]) *Cf.* H. Donner and W. Rölling: *Kanaanäische und aramäische Inschriften*, I, pp. 36, 196.

that may also be characterized as a *specific situation with a temporal aspect*. Where it introduces the body of a letter it further indicates the *juncture of circumstances*, that is, the turning-point between the formalistic greeting and the facts of the matter in the body.

B. Early Aramaic Texts

1. *Empire Aramaic*

The oldest extant recorded Aramaic is generally referred to as "Empire Aramaic", being used as the *lingua franca* of the Persian Empire in the Sixth to Fourth Centuries B.C. For instance, the phrase *wk'th shlchth lk* occurs on an ostracon as the introduction to the body of a letter following the greeting.[1]) It may be rendered in the same way as Mur 17 and Lachish 3:4; 4:2; 5:6 (see above), only including the prefixed particle of comparison: "Now, according to the situation, I send to you . . ." The same use is employed in all of the thirteen letters published by G. R. Driver, nearly all of which were sent from the chancery of one Arsham, Persian satrap of Egypt, during an absence from his seat of office.[2]) In one letter, the term appears twice, the first time in the midst of the greeting: "Peace and prosperity for you! Now, according to the occasion, there is peace here with me—may there also be peace with you! Now, according to the situation: there are certain Cilicians . . ." (5:1-2).

This same term is also used eight times in the body of letters, but always as the introduction to a command of the superior to his subordinates as the solution to the problem situation which had just been reviewed in the preceding sentence, for example: "Also he has sent a complaint about you, saying: 'The wine that was in Papremis and all the harvest of the land Nechtichur he has taken and appropriated.' According to the situation: restore all the wine, the harvest and anything else that you have taken" (12:5-7; so also 11:2; 12:9). In five cases, a certain formula is employed: "According to the situation, Arsham says thus: . . ." (3:6; 4:2; 8:3; 10:4; 12:3).

2. *Egyptian Aramaic*

The same epistolary use of *wk'th* found in Empire Aramaic appears in the Aramaic papyrus documents of the Jewish community of

---

[1]) Mark Lidzbarski: *Ephemeris für semitische Epigraphik*, III, Giessen: 1915, pp. 23 f., No. C:3:3 f.

[2]) *Aramaic Documents of the Fifth Cent. B.C.*, Oxford: 1957, pp. 4, 9, 19, 21-37, 103.

Elephantine, Egypt, toward the end of the Fifth Century B.C., for example: *shlch ʾchy bkl ʿdn wkʿth shlchth lk*—"Peace, my brother, at every time. Now, according to the occasion: I am sending to you . . ." [1]) The more usual spelling of this introductory formula is *wkʿnth*.[2]) A significant exception to these cases is the employment of *kʿn* in three instances for the same purpose, although it ordinarily means simply "now" in Aramaic.[3]) This usual reference to the present situation as such appears repeatedly in the body of documents, for example: "These goods I gave in affection to Yehoyishma; now I want to recover them." [4]) As *kʿn* normally corresponds to *ʿattāh* in Biblical Hebrew, so the exceptional use in place of *wkʿth* in introducing the body of a letter corresponds to this exceptional use of *weʿattāh* in 2 Kgs 5:6; 10:2 (p. 132). It therefore becomes possible to distinguish between the technical use of *ʿth* in Hebrew and *kʿth* (or *kʿnth*) in Aramaic, and the non-technical substitution of *ʿattāh* in Hebrew and *kʿn* in Aramaic.

3. *Old Testament Aramaic*

In the Aramaic portions of the OT, the three instances of *ūkeʿeneth* and the lone case of *ūkeʿeth* (Ezra 4:17) are usually interpreted according to *keʿan*, which appears some twelve times as "now". This conclusion is not without foundation, for besides the single occurrence of *keʿan* in simple reference to the present situation, Dan 2:23, all other instances may seem to involve the technical usage that has been attributed above to *kʿth*. However, it must first of all be remembered that *kʿth* and *kʿnth* belong exclusively to the epistolary style of introducing the body of a letter following the greeting. They also appear in this same way in OT Aramaic: Ezra 4:17 ("To Rehum the commander . . ., peace. Now, according to the occasion: The letter which you sent to us . . ."), 4:11; 7:12. The instance in 4:10 is merely anticipatory, having been inserted at the end of the list of the subscribers to the letter, which constitutes an interpolation after the letter had already been announced in v. 8.

---

[1]) Lidzbarski, *op. cit.*; see also *Inscriptiones Aramaicas Continens* (*CIS* II), No. 151:3.
[2]) Lidzbarski, *op. cit.*, II, Giessen: 1908, pp. 229 f., 233 f., 237-241, Nos. H: a:1, K:a:1, b:1, L:1, M:b:2.
[3]) *Ibid.*, No. C:b:1, pp. 219 f.; Eduard Sachau: *Drei aramäische Papyrusurkunden aus Elephantine*, Nos. I:4, II:2, 7, 10, 12, 14.
[4]) Emil G. Kraeling: *The Brooklyn Museum Aramaic Papyri*, No. 7:41 f., pp. 206 f.

ke'an is used five times in letters, but never in place of *ūke'eneth* as the introduction to the body. It does indeed appear as a sort of formula in the sense of "therefore", but always within the body for the purpose of introducing a further circumstance of the matter being presented, whether a warning (Ezra 4:13), proposition (4:14; 5:17), or command (4:21; 6:6). In this respect, it is employed in much the same way as some of the cases of *k'th* in letters of Empire Aramaic (p. 134). This indicates the possibility of variation between the two expressions within the body of a letter. This variation can scarcely have been historically conditioned, for both groups of letters belong to the Fifth Century. However, it appears that the use of *ke'an* represents a freer style in distinction to the more formalistic *ke'eth*, which was probably a *terminus technicus* for introducing an order as well as the body of a letter. The six instances of *ke'an* in Daniel are of less relevance here, for they all occur in oral addresses instead of letters, although their function is similar. Following preliminary remarks, it may precede reference to further circumstances of the situation (5:15) or to the concluding statements to the matter (3:15; 4:34; 5:16; 6:9).

The usage of the relevant expressions in OT Aramaic substantiates the technical epistolary usage of *ke'eth* (*ke'eneth*) in distinction to *ke'an*.

4. *Palestinian Aramaic*

Considering the literary form of the extant fragmentary Palestinian targums to the Pentateuch, it is not surprising that the expressions *ke'eth* and *ke'eneth* are not to be found here. However, *ke'an* appears frequently, sometimes in the usual sense of *'attāh* in Biblical Hebrew as "now", *e.g.*: Gen 48:21; Dt 27:1, 10.[1]) Yet, even here it is not a translation of *'attāh*, but an insertion, in the last two instances replacing *hayyōm*: *diy'anā' ke'an mephaqqēd*—"what I am now commanding". Interestingly enough, the other instances of *ke'an* in these targums are employed as a translation of the Hebrew *nā'* (*e.g.*, Gen 30:14, 27; 37:32; 44:18), or in the same sense in emphasizing a command, petition or question (*e.g.*, 31:27; 37:27; 38:17; Ex 5:22 *bis*).[2])

Among the Dead Sea literature, an Aramaic apocryphon to Genesis was discovered, which was still in the process of being examined

---

[1]) See Paul Kahle: *Masoreten des Westens*, II, pp. 23, 27 f.
[2]) *Ibid.*, pp. 17 f., 21, 23.

when the columns 19-22 were published.[1]) The only expression in this section relevant to this investigation is *k⁽n*, which occurs five times. A sixth instance is discernible on a fragment of col. 5, but too little of the text remains to warrant a passable interpretation. Three cases (20:23; 22:29 f.) correspond to Hebrew *nā⁾* and *ke⁽an* of the Palestinian targums. The other two instances present a unique usage in the sense of a temporal conjunction to indicate the succession of activities in the report of a journey, as: "(I arrived) at the river 'Karmon', . . . 'Then' we (left?) our land (and) I crossed the seven heads of this river . . ." (19:12; so also l. 13). It may be that the report was intended to be understood in the present tense, in which case a literal rendering of *k⁽n* would be very appropriate: ". . . Now we (are leaving) . . .".

Apart from these two exceptional instances, the use of *ke⁽an* in Palestinian Aramaic presents a contrast to that of earlier Aramaic, serving the function of an emphatic particle.

5. *Babylonian Aramaic*

The Aramaic used by the Jews in Babylonia in the first centuries of the Christian era, as it has been preserved in the Babylonian targums Onkelos and Jonathan,[2]) is also of interest in this context as one of the earliest translations of Biblical Hebrew. The rendering of *⁽ēth* in the targums does not require much treatment, since it is always given by *⁽dn*, except for one instance. In 2 Kgs 5:26, TJ renders *hsh⁽ h hy⁾*—"Is this the hour . . .?"—for the Hebrew *ha⁽ēth* (p. 80). This reflects the use of *shā⁽āh* in Aramaic (6 times in Daniel) and of ὥρα in the LXX and NT, often where *⁽ēth* could be used (p. 152).

It would go well beyond what is necessary for this section to consider each one of the many occurrences of *k⁽n* in the targums. But comparing some fifty instances of *⁽attāh* with its equivalent in the targums, it is seen that it is rendered mechanically with *k⁽n*. One exception is formed by Gen 29:34, where TO with *zmn⁾ hd⁾* ("this time") renders only the Hebrew *happa⁽am*, omitting the preceding *⁽attāh* ("now this time").

Otherwise, *k⁽n* is often used in these targums to render the Hebrew *nā⁾*, as also in the Palestinian targum (above). In one case, it replaces *⁽ōd*; where the Hebrew reads "you are still exalting yourself" in

---

[1]) Nahman Avigad and Yigael Yadin: *A Genesis Apocryphon*, Jerusalem: 1956.
[2]) See A. Sperber: *The Bible in Aramaic*, I, II, Leiden: 1959.

Ex 9:17, TO renders *'d k'kn*—"until now . . ." (also Jos 14:11,
TJ). Thus, in distinction to the earliest witnesses from the Fifth
Century (pp. 134-136), the usage in the later Aramaic of the Pales-
tinian and Babylonian targums is rather unified.

Attention may yet be called to Lev 16:21, which reads in Hebrew:
weshillach beyad-'îsh 'ittiy—". . . and he will send (it) by a man ready".
The adjective is suspect, not only because it appears only here in
Hebrew, but also because it, as a supposed derivative from *'ēth*, is
attributed with a function from the context that does not correspond
to its derivation. An adjective from *'ēth* should properly be one that
particularly modifies the occasion and not a person, as, for example,
"a timely arrival". Therefore, the most likely step would be to read
'āthiyd, which carries precisely the meaning demanded by the context
in reference to a person (Job 3:8; 15:24; Est 3:14; 8:13; [1]) Aramaic:
Dan 3:15). The translation in TO supports the sense of the context,
although with a different nuance in meaning: *byd gbr dzmyn*—". . . by
a man who is appointed". The passive participle of *zmn* does not
indicate a certain relationship to the peculiar meaning of *zemān*,
"time", in correspondence to the supposed relationship between
'ittiy and *'ēth*, for the meaning relates only to the objective aspect
of the situation, and not at all to the temporal.

C. INTERTESTAMENTAL HEBREW

1. *Jesus ben Sira*

The wisdom literature of the OT and its apocrypha gives evidence
of a great deal of interrelationship. The Wisdom of Jesus ben Sira
(Ecclesiasticus) is more closely related to Proverbs and the Wisdom
of Solomon, and Koheleth more closely to Job. Yet, Sira gives
evidence of having been familiar with Koheleth and his ideas, even if
he differed in his approach and answer to life's problems. These he
handled as a traditional Chakham, identifying wisdom with the
Torah and holding to the principle of reward and retaliation.[2] But
one secondary concept from Koheleth that made an influence on
Sira was the idea of the "given occasion" (pp. 125 f.). The frequent
and essentially significant instances of *'ēth* by Koheleth have provided
insights into this unique segment of Hebrew thought. Similarly,
Sira furnishes numerous cases that represent a further application
of this particular concept of time.

---

[1] Read with Q: *'athiydiym*.
[2] See esp. Gordis, *op. cit.*, pp. 26, 32-38, and Loretz, *op. cit.*, pp. 197-208.

Considering that ʿēth occurs twelve times in the twelve chapters of Koheleth apart from the 28 instances in the catalogue of 3:2-8, it appears in the Hebrew of Sira in almost exactly corresponding frequency. About two-thirds of the Hebrew text being extant,[1]) ʿēth appears some 37 times in the 50 chapters. Many of the cases correspond exactly, or nearly so, to uses in Koheleth and other books of the OT, which will become clear in the course of the discussion. It seems advisable to follow the outline of procedure established in the previous chapters.

One disputed reading offers evidence that Sira makes use of ʿēth with respect to the natural chronological order of time. The Hebrew text of 43:6 reads: wgm yrch yrch ʿthwth shbwth. The LXX offers little help with its rendering, εἰς καιρὸν αὐτῆς, and two marginal readings likewise represent rather substantial differences: ʿth ʿth and ʿd ʿth.[2]) However, the HT is not at all improbable when considering the context, which describes the moon as the regulator for setting the times, especially in vv. 6b-7a: "... ruling the limit and an everlasting sign, by which is the appointed time and the times of the statute". [3]) The second yrch will certainly be a verbal form meaning "to set the date" (part. yōrēach or impf. yērach), as in Arabic.[4]) The last word in the line could make good sense as the infinitive of shbth (cf. Lev. 23:32; 25:2), or as shebūth in the astrological sense. Thus the line may be rendered: "And also the moon sets the times of observing the Sabbath", or, "of fortune". In either case, it would be a unique use of ʿēth, the only case of employing the plural for natural time. Yet, this is not too improbable, since both the plural and the objectivization of ʿēth had been practiced since Ezekiel.

Reference to the appropriate occasion for an action according to custom or social propriety appears in 4:23 in the same sense as Prov 15:23, 25:11 (p. 29): ʾl tmnʿ dbr bʿthw,[5]) "Do not withhold a word on its occasion." The virtue of speaking propitiously appears again in 20:6 f.—"... and there is one who is silent because he notices the

---

[1]) See Rudolf Smend: *Die Weisheit des Jesus Sirach*, Berlin: 1906.

[2]) The former is preferred by Smend (*op. cit.*, p. 45) and Norbert Peters (*Das Buch Jesus Sirach oder Ecclesiasticus*, *EHAT*, 25, 1913, p. 365), while the RSV and Andreas Eberharter (*Das Buch Jesus Sirach oder Ecclesiasticus*, *HSAT*, VI:5, 1925, p. 141) follow the LXX.

[3]) *Cf.* A. Schlatter: *Das neu gefundene Hebräische Stück des Sirach*, Gütersloh: 1897, p. 43.

[4]) See Hans Wehr: *Arabisches Wörterbuch*, Leipzig: 1956.

[5]) So Syriac, see Smend, *op. cit.*, p. 44.

occasion (*rʾh ʿth*); a wise man is silent until the occasion (ʿ*d ʿth*), but
a fool does not watch the occasion (*yshmr ʿth*)." In a similar case of
social propriety, MS C reads in 4:21, *wbʿth hshb qphwdh*: [1]) "Let not
your hand be extended to receive, and on the occasion of returning,
(not) closed." These cases, particularly the last one, border on the use
for the given occasion as employed by Koheleth. They demonstrate
further how the latter was the precursor of the logical development
in Sira. Reference is made to an occasion of social appointment in
32:11—"At the appointed occasion do not linger behind" (*bʿth
mphqd*).[2]) This may be compared to the appointed times in Ezra
10:14; Neh 10:35; 13:31 (p. 31).

Temporal relationship in the comparative sense is indicated by
the HT for 35:26bα—*kʿth chz yz ym*, "precious is his favor in the time
(*bzmn*) of distress, as on the occasion of storm clouds . . ." [3]) This
use may be compared with Ezek 16:57 (p. 38).

There is likewise one instance of simple relationship in the form of
a temporal conjunction (as 2 Chr 20:22; 24:11; 29:27; pp. 41, 43).
In 11:22, the foolishness of the rich man's satisfaction with his goods
is denoted: "Then when (*kāʿab*) he says, 'I have found rest, and
now (*wʿthh*) I shall eat (= enjoy) my goods,' he does not know what
kind of day is coming on which he must leave it to another and die."
This is essentially the same idea as in Ps 39:7; 49:11; Ecc 2:18, 21,
26; 3:22; 4:8; 6:2, 12; 8:7; 9:12 (p. 116); 10:14, but it carries the
thought further by combining the aspects of knowing neither what
follows nor when one dies.

Whereas only two cases of interrupting occasions occur in Koheleth
and none in Proverbs, *ʿeth* is used in this way 16 times in Sira, revealing
affinity especially to the prophets and Psalms. With respect to an
intervening experience, linguistic relationship to the Song of Moses
(Dt 32:35, p. 79) is shown in 3:31—". . . and on the occasion of his
stumbling (*wbʿth mwtn*) he will find support." The construction of
ʿ*d ʿth* with a verbal form, as in Mic 5:2; Ps 105:19 (pp. 82, 86), is
employed in 4:17 for the unique statement concerning personified
wisdom: ". . . and until the occasion (when) his heart is filled with
me" (*cf.* Prov 2:2, 10). The same construction also appears in 12:15

---

[1]) *Cf.* Smend, *ibid.*, p. 47.
[2]) *Cf.* Peters, *op. cit.*, p. 265.
[3]) In keeping with the LXX (ὡς νεφέλαι ὑετοῦ), the conjecture is usually
made to *kāʿab* (so Hermann Strack: *Die Sprüche Jesus' des Sohnes Sirachs*, p. 28),
which, however, produces a redundancy without exact parallel.

with respect to an insolent person: "Until the occasion (when) one can stand, he does not appear." [1]

The well-known expression *b'th tsrh* (Isa 33:2; Jer 14:8; 15:11; 30:7; Ps 37:39; Neh 9:27; pp. 78 f.) is used in 8:9 ("Because from them (= the aged) you receive understanding, on the occasion of distress to return advice") and 40:24 ("a brother and a companion are also at the occasion of distress").[2] A closely related expression is *b'th tswqh* in 37:4 concerning a "fair-weather" friend: "on the occasion of distress he stands aside". Of significance is the fact that some of the cases imply a "given situation" for the appropriate action, especially 8:9; 37:4 and 40:24 (see pp. 127 f.).

Reference is made to an intervening event with *wb'th nqm* (*cf.* Jer 51:6, p. 81) in 5:7, "and on the occasion of vengeance you will be swept away".[3] Similar is the "situation of drought" (*b'th btswrth*) in 35:26b (see p. 140). Noah is praised in 44:17 as becoming a "substitute" [4] for those who perished "on the occasion of annihilation" (*l'th klh*). Good fatherly advice is given in 4:20, "My son, watch the occasion of abundance (*'th chmwn*) and beware of evil." [5]

The construction *'th 'shr* as a temporal conjunction, as in Ecc 8:9; 2 Chr 25:27 (see pp. 76, 82), is employed in 38:13. But with the addition of *ysh*, *'th* is also a predicate: "Because there is an occasion when success is in his (= the physician's) hand." The expression *'th r'h* occurs frequently in the OT, and even as a predicate in Mic 2:3 (=Am 5:13b; *cf.* Jer 30:7; 51:6; Dan 12:1b, pp. 78, 81, 85), but in 11:27 it is used as an active subject: "The occasion of evil causes (one) to forget luxury." Reference here is clearly to the occasion, but the LXX interprets it temporally: κάκωσις ὥρας (so RSV: "The misery of an hour").

Untimely old age is referred to in 30:24 with *wbl' 'th* ("And not (yet) at the occasion, anxiety makes (one) old"), which is used in Job 22:16 and Ecc 7:17 for the occasion of death (p. 117). That such

---

[1] The line is usually read according to the LXX (ὥραν μετὰ σοῦ διαμενεῖ, "he will stay with you for a long time"), but it should be clear that it is meant to be complementary in thought and not temporally earlier than the following one: "and if one stumbles, he will not offer support".

[2] Rendering of the text according to Smend's reconstruction (*op. cit.*, p. 30).

[3] This is the reading of MS C, followed by the LXX.

[4] *Cf.* Strack, *op. cit.*, p. 73; Israel Lévi: *The Hebrew Text of the Book of Ecclesiasticus*, p. 85.

[5] *chmwn* is usually omitted with the LXX (so Eberharter, *op. cit.*, p. 28, and RSV), but it does not need a clear parallel to make sense, since the thoughts change rapidly in the context.

old age comes too soon is certainly implied, but the direct indication is to the abnormalcy of the situation, as the abnormal flow of blood in Lev 15:25 (p. 25). Primary emphasis is on the situational aspect, not on the temporal. The temporal aspect seems to be implied only because old age and death come just once in a person's life.

Sira betrays a dependence on Koheleth by making rather frequent use of his concept of the "given occasion", eleven times in all. Koheleth actually applied his idea only generally (3:1, 11, 17), for his catalogue of specific occasions (3:2-8) only serves the purposes of establishing the truth of the general principle, and his reference to obeying the king's commands without objection (8:5, 6) proceeds from the specific situation but makes a generality out of it for every occasion (see pp. 125-128). This general thought is echoed twice by Sira in the same words: *ky hkl b'thw ygbl*, "Because everything prevails on its occasion" (39:21, 34). As Ecc 3:11, 17, the context here likewise ascribes this "everything" to God: "The works of God—all of them are good, and every need on its occasion (*b'thw*) will have abundance" (39:16; *cf.* v. 33—"to every need on its occasion he gives abundantly").

There is ample evidence elsewhere that Sira carried the idea logically further in applying it to the specific, special occasion in human life. He speaks of drinking wine on its given occasion (*b'thw*, 31:28), of refraining from displaying cleverness when the occasion does not allow it (*wbl' 'th*, 32:4), and of receiving one's reward for righteous work (*b'thw*, 51:30b).[1]

One distinctly new usage appears in this connection, and that is the construction *l'th* without further modification, that is, apparently with the article. Thus, in 10:4, reference is made to God's rule of the earth, "and a man for the occasion (*w'ysh l'th*) he will raise up over it". Comparable to the storing up of snow and hail for the situation of distress in Job 38:23 (p. 85), the dangerous beasts and the sword of revenge "are (kept) in the storehouse, and for the occasion they are summoned" (39:30). Likewise, Elijah is described as being "prepared for the occasion" (48:10). A variation of this use appears in 12:16, where it is said of the enemy that "if he finds occasion (*mts' 'th*), he will not be satisfied with blood". The simplest interpretation is to

---

[1] The reading of HT in v. 30a, *btsdqh*, is altered by Lévi (*op. cit.*, p. 76) and Smend (*op. cit.*, p. 62) to *bl' 'th* with the LXX (πρὸ καιροῦ—"before the time") and Syriac, but for no other good reason, unless it should be applied to the judgment after death, as Peters does (*op. cit.*, p. 446).

think of the "right time", the "appointed time", or "opportunity"[1]).

The basic thought here, however, seems to be the advantageous juncture of two situations. Such a *"juncture of occasions"* is the underlying thought for *'ēth* which makes it so applicable as a so-called "temporal" reference. This aspect, however, indicates primarily the fact of the relationship or meeting of the factors that produce an occasion or event; the temporal aspect is secondary. The new feature contributed here by Sira is the application in a positive sense and in such a way that it is only implied by the grammatical construction and the context. This "right situation" is the closest that Hebrew comes before the turn of the millennium to expressing what we mean with "at the right time". The "definite" or "given" occasion has become the *"right situation"*.

2. *The Damascus Codex and the Dead Sea Scrolls*

The generally accepted procedure is followed here of grouping the Damascus Codex of the Cairo Genizah with the scrolls and fragments discovered near Qumran. Temporal expressions seem to occur in this body of writings with an unsurpassed frequency in Hebrew literature, and the word *'ēth* is not one of seldom appearance. Thus it has retained a position of particularly familiar usage in Hebrew from the time of Deuteronomy and Jeremiah up to the dawn of the Christian Era. As in the case of Sira, many of the 42 occurrences of *'ēth* in the published Dead Sea Corpus are essentially comparable to uses in the OT. But there are also some unique and altogether new cases that even give evidence of a peculiar view of time. Most of these peculiar cases are to be found in the Manual of Discipline, which also includes many more instances than in any other writing, namely 18. But they will also be handled here according to the systematical division employed in the foregoing chapters.

Reference is made in DC 10:14 f. to the occasion of sunset as the beginning of the Sabbath: "No one shall do work on the sixth day from the occasion when the disk of the sun is (*mn h'th 'shr yhyh glgl hshmsh*) distant by its width from the gate." [2]) Shemaryahu Talmon

---

[1]) So Othmar Schilling: *Das Buch Jesus Sirach* (Herders Bibelkommentar), Freiburg: 1956, pp. 57, 167; RSV (48:10) and Peters, *op. cit.*, p. 107; RSV (12:16) and Eberharter, *op. cit.*, p. 53.

[2]) Text of DC from Solomon Zeitlin: *The Zadokite Fragments* (*Jewish Quarterly Review*, Monograph series, No. 1), Philadelphia: 1952.

believes this sentence to be a gloss by a later Karaite or Rabbanite copyist who objected to the prevailing view in the DSC for a solar calendar year and for beginning the day with morning, thus adding this statement to set the beginning of the Sabbath at the exact moment of sunset.[1]) However, it should be noticed that the Sabbath is being spoken of. As U. Cassuto has pointed out, the common procedure in the OT is to begin week-days in the morning according to the Canaanite practice, but to begin the Sabbath and festivals in the evening according to the old nomadic practice.[2])

The cited statement at first appears to be in the style of the Rabbis. But as A. Dupont-Sommer has observed, the passage on the Sabbath (10:14-11:18) is to be distinguished from Rabbinical laws through its greater strictness.[3]) Thus the observance of the Sabbath is not only of great importance for the viewpoint represented in the DSC, but it also gives evidence to similar precise chronological reckoning. Talmon apparently made an unfortunate textual error that seemed to add weight to his argument: "The verb *yts'* in biblical and mishnaic language always denotes the setting of the sun, whereas the verb *bw'* denotes its rising. In the language of the Scrolls the opposite is the case."[4]) However, the only other instance in the DSC that may be applied here is 1 QM 18:5, which combines *shmsh* and *bw'* in reference to sunset in the same way as above and elsewhere in Hebrew literature. Since DC 10:15 offers no direct contradiction within the DSC, there is no reason to suppose that it is a gloss.

The use of *'th* here is, however, noteworthy, for it apparently is used emphatically in the sense of "exact moment".[5]) It is to be compared to the cases discussed above (pp. 21-23), especially to *le'ēth bo' hashshemesh* in 2 Chr 18:34. It has been demonstrated there that it was not the moment of occurrence that was actually indicated, but rather the *fact* of it that is characterized as the coincidence of occasions. Although still more closely defined in DC 10:15, it is likewise the peculiar occasion that is meant. *'ēth* proves itself appropriate in referring to an occasion that is constituted by the juncture of specific factors.

---

[1]) "The Calendar Reckoning of the Sect from the Judaean Desert", *Scripta Hierosolymitana* IV, 1958, pp. 192 f.

[2]) *Genesis*, pp. 29 f.

[3]) *Les écrits esséniens découverts près de la Mer Morte*, Paris: 1959, p. 166, n. 3.

[4]) *Op. cit.*, p. 190.

[5]) See Dupont-Sommer, *op. cit.*, p. 167, "du moment où".

Another application in the chronological sense appears in 1 QH 12:7 f., where the psalmist praises God and kneels for prayer continually, that is, at all chronological turning points: at evening and at morning, as well as continually "at every birth of occasion, at the foundations of time, and in the course of the festivals in their order..." (*bkwl mwldy ʿth yswdy qts wthqwphth mwʿdym bthkwnm*).[1] *mwldym* is used elsewhere in the plural form but for a single birth (3:11 *bis*), and so indicates the beginning of the particular chronological occasion.[2] *qts* appears frequently in the sense of temporal relationship (*e.g.*, 12:4, 6, 22, 26) or in the plural form for time periods (*e.g.*, 1:16, 24; 8:31; 13:20; 18:30), as well as in the singular for temporal situations (*e.g.*, 3:28; 1QS 3:23; 4:16; 1 QM 1:4), so that the concrete beginnings of temporal situations or periods are meant here. Although *thqwphh* can mean "turning-point", as in 3:5 f., it indicates, in singular form with a plurality of festivals, the round of festivals made in a year (see 1:24; 1 QS 10:3, 6; Ex 34:22; *cf.* the circuit of the sun in Ps 19:7). Thus the occasion (*ʿēth*) and temporal situation (*qēts*) meant here are the chronological times according to the calendar regulations for prayer and festivals established by divine ordinance (*cf.* 1 QM 12:9).

A temporal reference to a natural occasion is made in 1 QH 8:23 —"and in the time of heat (*wbʿth chwm*) he will retain a refuge". Dupont-Sommer, with "saison de la chaleur",[3] indicates a season of year which would correspond to the use of *ʿēth* for the seasons of harvest (Jer 50:16) and rain (Lev 26:4; Dt 11:14; 28:12; Jer 5:24; Ezek 34:26; Zech 10:1; Ezra 10:13; see pp. 25-27).

One case in particular seems to indicate appropriate activity according to the social order (see pp. 28 f.): "and to learn all prudence found in accordance with the occasions" (*lphy hʿthym*; 1 QS 9:13).[4] According to the context, the "occasions" are not simply objectivized but are even modified by the established order (9:12).

As already implied in the last case, the most characteristic use of *ʿth* is that applied to an appointed situation (see pp. 29-32). It is also

---

[1] Text of 1 QH from Eliezer Sukenik: *Otsar ha-Megilloth ha-Genuzoth*, Jerushalaim: 1955.

[2] Millar Burrows (*The Dead Sea Scrolls*, New York: 1955, p. 414) renders it here "generations", although it refers properly to the occasion of generating and not to the period of a generation; so Dupont-Sommer, "genèses" (*op. cit.*, p. 253).

[3] *Op. cit.*, p. 243.

[4] Text of 1 QS from Burrows, ed.: *Plates and Transcription of the Manual of Discipline (The Dead Sea Scrolls of St. Mark's Monastery*, II), New Haven: 1951.

significant that six of the nine cases occur in 1 QS alone. Reference
is made in 1 : 14 to the appointed calendar dates for festivals according
to divine ordinance:[1]) "and not to digress in any one of all the words
of God in their times (*bqtsyhm*), and not to advance their occasions
(*'thyhm*), and not to delay with all their festivals (*mw'dyhm*)". The three
relevant expressions illustrate admirably their capacity for parallelism
without necessarily implying identity of meaning. They indicate the
various aspects, respectively, of temporal relationship, definite occasion and established appointment.

It appears, however, that not only the festivals were given a
definite date by divine ordinance, but also the whole year was strictly
divided into set periods. The members of the community are charged
to "learn all prudence found in accordance with the (various) occasions (see 9 : 13, p. 145) and the ordinance of the (specific) occasion"
(*w'th chwq h'th*, 9 : 14), as well as to walk "in the regulation of the
(specific) occasion" (*wbthkwn h'th*, 8:4). Furthermore, they were to
"administer true knowledge and righteous judgment for the choosers
of the Way, each according to his spirit according to the regulation
of the (specific) occasion" (*kthkwn h'th*, 9 : 18), and to "be zealous for
the ordinance and its (specific) occasion" (*lchwq w'thw*, 9 : 23). Similarly, those elected to office were to be chosen "according to the
occasion" (*lphy h'th*, DC 10 : 5), that is, for a certain, definite period.
Thus, in 1 QS 9 : 14, the members were enjoined to "hold firmly to
the elect of the (specific) occasion (*wbbchyry h'th*), according to his
will" (= God's will, see 9 : 13).

Dupont-Sommer pays too little attention to the tenor of these
passages and their pre-occupation with definite periods of responsibility when he defines this expression as "le 'Décret du Temps',
c'est la Loi divine qui préside à la succession régulière des périodes
des saisons, des heures". On this basis, he concludes that the Qumran
sect thought of the action of every hour foreseen and determined
by God, "le souverain maître du Temps".[2]) However this may
possibly be indicated by other evidence (he cites here 1 QpHab 7 : 13 f.)
it is not to be concluded from the above *'th*-passages, where "Time"
and "God" as the "Lord of Time" do not as abstract, philosophical
concepts fit into the context of the concrete situations of regulated
terms of service. One would at best refer to the classical "time"

---

[1]) *Cf.* Dupont-Sommer, *op. cit.*, p. 89, n. 4.
[2]) *Op. cit.*, p. 110, n. 2.

passage in 1 QH 12:4-8, where it might at first appear that *'th* means "Time" in the absolute sense. However, as pointed out above to 12:8 (p. 145), *'th* in the midst of chronological terminology refers to a chronological occasion or period. The passage 1 QpHab 7:13 (with *qytsy 'l*) refers to the historical periods that precede the time of the eschatological End (*hqts h'chlwn*, 7:12). Therefore, they cannot be treated in connection with the general context of either 1 QS 8:4-9:26 or 1 QH 12:4-8.

Further, reference is made in 1 QM 15:5 to the established time (*mw'd*) of the War for reading the appropriate prayer according to the "Book of the Order of Its Occasion" (*sphr srk 'thw*).[1] It may be noticed that it is *mw'd* and not *'th* that refers to the "decisive moment" of the War. A similar usage also appears in what may be a reference to the Book of Jubilees: *sphr mchlqwth h'thym lywblyhm wbshbw'wthyhm*, "the Book of the Divisions of the Times according to Their Jubilees and in Their Weeks" (DC 16:3 f.).[2]

Besides these nine cases of *'th* that refer primarily to an appointed occasion, the fact that a peculiar concept of temporal regulation is common to the DSC also comes to view in the calendar regulations in 1 QH 12:8 (p. 145) as well as in two passages that primarily indicate direct relationship to singular occasions. These instances involve 1 QM 14:13 and its equivalent in the corresponding passage 4 QM^a 11[3]—*nrwmmh thph ('rthkh bkwl) 'thym wmw'dy th'wdwth 'wlmym 'm m(bw)' ywmm wlylh wmwts'y 'rb wbwqr*—"we exalt (your honor on all) occasions and set dates of everlasting attestations with the advent of day and night and the exits of evening and morning". Although the conjectured reading is plausible here, it would represent a contrast to the Biblical use of the singular, *bekol 'ēth* (see pp. 43 f.). This indicates an objectivized reference to the established occasions themselves, as the parallel *mw'dym* implies.

An entirely unique use of *'th* in double form is presented by a group of four passages. In 1 QS 8:15 and 9:13 reference is made to the Law of Moses or Will of God that has been revealed "time after time" (*'th b'th*; in 9:13—*l'th b'th*). This may be compared to similar expressions in late Biblical Hebrew for "day by day": *yōm beyōm* (Neh 8:18; 2 Chr 30:21), *leyōm beyōm* (24:11) and *le'eth-yōm beyōm*

---

[1]) Text of 1 QM from Sukenik, *op. cit.*

[2]) *Cf.* Chaim Rabin: *The Zadokite Documents*, Oxford: 1964, p. 75, n. 1.

[3]) See C.-H. Hunzinger: "Fragmente einer älteren Fassung des Buches Milḥamā aus Höhle 4 in Qumran", *ZAW* 69 (NF 28, 1957), pp. 131-151.

(1 Chr 12:23, pp. 44 f.).[1]) As in the last passage that nullifies the specific connotation of 'ēth by combining it with an indefinite phrase, so this unique double usage amounts to a similar nullification of definiteness. The same is true for the comparable phrase in DC 12:21 and 1 QS 9:12, where reference is made to the ordinances that are to be obeyed "according to the regulation, time after time"—'th w'th. This construction corresponds to yōm wāyōm (Est 3:4) and yōm yōm (Gen 39:10, p. 45). These instances do not represent objectivization, as is usually indicated in respect to the last two cases where, for example, Johann Maier renders "gemäß der Ordnung der jeweiligen Zeit" for 1 QS 9:12.[2]) This translation is hardly possible grammatically, for it involves a genitive construction with an adverbial phrase.

Comparable to the unique case in Est 4:14a (p. 46), b'th hzw'th in 1 QS 9:20 refers back to the future occasion of preparation (9:19, see p. 149) with respect to "everything found to do at this time". In the next line (21), it is implied that this occasion of utmost significance is a period: "And these are the regulations of the Way for the prudent in these times (bymym h'lh)." Comparable to Isa 18:7 (p. 46), b'th hahy'h in 1 QS 9:5 identifies the occasion of the significant future event (9:3—bhywth 'lh, "when these things take place") as the occasion for separating a sacred house for Aaron (so also 1 QM 18:3).

One of the two cases of reference to a past occasion in the historical sense occurs in the historical resumé at the beginning of DC. In 1:13, the time of the Teacher of Righteousness is identified as the fulfilment of Hos 4:16—"that is the time about which it was written". For the grammatical construction hy' h'th 'shr see Ecc 8:9 (p. 82), and for the relationship to the historical setting of a certain period, the use in Jdg 11:26 (p. 60) may be compared. A similar construction is used in the other instance, 4 QT 21 (b'th 'shr—"on the occasion when"), which relates Joshua's ceasing "to praise and to confess with songs of praise" to his curse of Jericho (Jos 6:26).[3])

A large group of nine instances relates primarily to specifically singular, intervening occasions. In comparison to the frequent references in the OT to occasions of distress and punishment (Jer 8:12; 30:7, etc., pp. 78 f.), 4 QpIsa b 2:2 reads: whyh b'th pqdth h'rts

---

[1]) Cf. also Dt 14:22 (shā'āh shā'āh) and 15:20 (shā'āh beshā'āh).
[2]) Die Texte vom Toten Meer, I, München: 1960, p. 39.
[3]) Text of 4 QT from J. M. Allegro: "Further Light on the History of the Qumran Sect", JBL 75 (1956), pp. 89-95.

—"and it shall be on the occasion of the punishment of the land".[1])
Similarly, the eschatological End is identified in 4 QF 2:1 as: *hy'h*
'th hmtsrph hb('h)—"this is the time of the coming trial".[2]) This
midrash of selected passages clearly represents the eschatological
concept of late Jewish apocalyptic, with the weighted, repeated use of
b'chryth hymym ("at the End of the days", 1:2, 12, 15, 19) in the sense
of Dan 10:14 (pp. 70, 112 f.), and of *'wlm* in the sense of "eternity" as
a future state of being (1:4 f., pp. 17-19). Almost exactly the same
construction appears in 4 QpPs 37 2:19, where the reference is to the
time of the trial that came upon "the priest and the men of his council".[3]) Further reference to negative circumstances is offered by the
fragment 1 QHf 45:2—"(he will) hunger to death at the time of
transgressions" (*b'th 'wwnwth*).[4]) Expressions comparable to Jer 30:7
are also presented in 1 QM 1:11 f. and 15:1; the former reads:
why'h 'th tsrh '(l kw)l 'm pdwth 'l—"And this is the occasion of distress
(for all) the people of the redemption of God." A. M. Habermann
conjectures an occasion of individual stress on a certain fragment:
(*'th*) *ywrwny mbny ('hrwn)*—"(on the occasion of) throwing me out
from the sons of (Aaron)".[5])

The eschatological War is characterized by 1 QM 1:5 as follows:
"That is the occasion of salvation (*'th yshw'h*) for the people of God
and the time of rule (*wqts mmshl*) for all the men of his lot." It is
evident here that *'eth* and *qets*, although each may refer to a temporal
period, are parallel only in kind and not in purpose. The former relates
the situation to the singular, intervening event of salvation, while
the latter implies that this event constitutes the beginning of the
lasting dominion of the Sons of Light (1:1).[6]) Living according to
the principles of the community belongs to the "time of clearing the
way to the desert" (*'th pnwth hdrk lmdbr*, 1 QS 9:19 f., see p. 148).[7])
A fragmentary midrash of Isaiah offers little basis for interpretation,
but Habermann's plausible conjecture in 1:4 allows for an objec-

---

[1]) See J. M. Allegro: "More Isaiah Commentaries from Qumran's Fourth
Cave", *JBL* 77 (1958), pp. 215-221.

[2]) Text of 4 QF from Allegro, "Further Light on the History of the Qumran
Sect".

[3]) Text of 4 QpPs 37 from Allegro, *ibid.*

[4]) See Sukenik, *op. cit.*

[5]) *'Eda we-'Eduth, Three Scrolls from the Judaean Desert, The Legacy of a Community,*
Jerusalem: 1952, p. 124.

[6]) *Cf.* Burrows, *op. cit.*, p. 390.

[7]) *Cf.* 8:12-14 and Isa 40:3 against Maier, *op. cit.*, p. 39.

tivized usage: (*bbw' h*)*'th* [1])—"(at the arrival of the) occasion". This may be compared to the instance in Jer 27:7 (p. 88).

As in the Florilegium (see 4 QF 2:1, p. 149), '*wlm* appears repeatedly in the DSC in the sense of "eternity" [2] as the temporal factor in the future state of salvation. Uniquely enough for Hebrew, it is used twice in a genitive construction with '*th* in 1 QSb. In 4:26, the consecrated priest is to partake in the council together with the saints "for time everlasting and for all the periods of eternity"— *l'th 'wlm wlkwl qtsy ntsch* (so similarly in 5:18 with the preposition '*m*).[3] This eternal state is designated here by '*ēth* in parallel to the plural of *qēts*, which can only mean a reference to the entire everlasting *duration*. This represents a stark contrast to the employment of '*ēth* for the *occasion* of the End in Daniel, which, although it may be a situation of some temporal duration, is never more than a temporally limited one (pp. 111-114). For it is after the End that the saints are blessed with everlasting life (7:13-18, 27; 12:1-3). Thus the above construction with '*wlm* serves on the one hand to intensify the idea of eternity as a situation of definite significance, but, on the other hand, it changes the intention of this definiteness from that of a particular occasion to that of a constant condition. '*ēth* has here lost its character of referring to a juncture of events or conditions and is applied to a condition itself.

In conclusion, it is noteworthy that '*ēth* in the DSC often serves the same purpose as in the OT. It may indicate *temporal relationship* in the sense of denoting the *juncture of circumstances*, and it ordinarily refers to a *specific occasion*. However, it may also represent the trend in later Biblical Hebrew toward *objectivization* and *indefiniteness*, which is carried further in some points, such as the objectivized reference to "all occasions" in 1 QM 14:13, the indefinite reference to repeated situations "time after time" in 1 QS 8:15, *etc.*, and the reference to a state of everlasting duration in 1 QSb 4:26; 5:18.

The typically unique use of '*ēth* in the DSC is a further *objectivization of the appointed occasion*. The basis of this idea is not that of the "given occasion" as in Koheleth (pp. 124-130), but of a systematically ordered calendar. Everything has become ordered and regulated. When the individual is confronted with a particular situation, he does not need to make a decision, but turns instead to the set regulation for the occasion.

---

[1]) *Scrolls from the Judaean Desert*, Tel Aviv: 1959, for the text of 4 QpIsa b.

[2]) So also Jenni's conclusion (*op. cit.*, pp. 247 f.; *cf.* above, pp. 17-19).

[3]) Text from *DJD* I, plates xxv-xxix.

Because this whole system of regulations is seen as the revealed will of God, it is not merely legalism, but an attempt to combine legalism with divine predestination. For the sake of his faithful elect, God has overcome the "time problem" by using temporal dates and periods to build a structural form for their worship, as revealed in his Law. Thus the concept of time is expressed very concretely with respect to these set periods. This concept is expressed further through other temporal words, but particularly by using the otherwise common *yōm*. Instead of *'ēth*, *qēts* finds a unique application in reference to the temporal situation or period, and the frequent use of *mō'ēd* emphasize the appointed aspect. Thus the usual OT emphasis on the temporal situation as one of specific event or of historical significance recedes gradually into the background under the influence of the concept of legalistic predestination.

D. THE SEPTUAGINT TRANSLATION

In the Septuagint translation of the canonical Hebrew Old Testament, *'ēth* is usually rendered by καιρός. Yet, this is not the case in nearly 100 instances, so that the words cannot be easily identified. Statistics have been presented by Gerhard Delling,[1]) but it would be well to review them here with certain additions and corrections. The following words are employed to render *'ēth*, the occurrences in Sira being supplied in brackets: καιρός—198 (26), ὥρα—24 (5), ἡμέρα —9, ἡνίκα—4, χρόνος—3, εὐκαιρία—3, νῦν—3, ἄν—3, ὡς—2, πρός—1, εὔκαιρος—1, ἄωρος—1, καθώς—1, ὅταν—1, τότε—1, ἄκαιρος—(1). To these must be added 40 (5) instances where *'ēth* is not rendered, because of a variant text—5 (2), because of omission within the phrase —29 (3), or of the relevant passage—6.

It is significant that none of the translations for *'ēth* may be regarded as a *terminus technicus* for any particular use. καιρός is frequently regarded as the word for "moment of time".[2]) However, it is used in 132 cases for temporal relationship where the relationship or juncture of events is meant and not a temporal moment *per se*, e.g., ἐν καιρῷ θλίψεως ὑμῶν ("in the time of your distress", Jdg 10:14), ἐν παντὶ καιρῷ ("at every time", Ps 10:5; see pp. 43, 78). Furthermore, some cases refer to a condition or period, *e.g.*: οὐκ ἐν καιρῷ τῆς

---

[1]) *Das Zeitverständnis des Neuen Testaments*, pp. 50 f.
[2]) See Delling, *loc. cit.*, p. 49; Vollborn, *op. cit.*, p. 25; Marsh, "Time, Season", p. 258.

ἀφέδρου αὐτῆς ("not in the time of her issue", Lev 15:25), ἐν τῷ καιρῷ τοῦ γήρως αὐτοῦ ("in the time of his old age", 3 Kgs 15:23; pp. 25 f.). Although the frequent expression for reference, bā'ēth hahī', is usually given by ἐν τῷ καιρῷ ἐκείνῳ (Gen 21:22; Dt 1:9, etc.), it may also be rendered ἐν τῇ ἡμέρᾳ ἐκείνῃ (Jos 6:26; 3 Kgs 8:65; Zeph 1:12; Dan 12:1b; 2 Chr 13:18), ἐν ταῖς ἡμέραις ἐκείναις (Jer 3:17), ἐν τῷ χρόνῳ ἐκείνῳ (38:1, HT: 31:1), κατὰ τὴν ὥραν ἐκείνην (Dan 12:1a), or simply τότε (Isa 20:2; pp. 48-51, 60 f., 64, 84 f.).

Considering that the usual temporal unit in Biblical Hebrew is "day", it would be logical that, if 'ēth meant a definite situation in the temporal sense, this peculiarity would be emphasized in translation by "hour", which was common to both contemporary Aramaic and Greek. But ὥρα is not used frequently enough to be significant, and even then, it is employed 19 times for occasions of relationship, e.g., πᾶσαν ὥραν (Ex 18:22), εἰς ὥρας ("in those hours", Dan 11:6; pp. 44, 76 f.). Sometimes it is used for occasions that are particularly emphasized as definite or determined, so that it appears to be a special means of emphasis, although this occurs too seldom to be of general consequence, e.g.: the appointed time for the end of the pestilence in 2 Kgs 24:15 (ἕως ὥρας), the proper time for gathering in the flock in Gen 29:7 (οὔπω ὥρας), the evening sacrifice in Dan 9:21, and the End-situation in 11:40 (καθ' ὥραν συντελείας; pp. 28, 88, 111, 153). However, the End-situation is also rendered by καιρός (11:35; 12:4) and even once simply by ἄν (12:9; p. 112).

The fact that 'ēth may be rendered by indefinite temporal expressions indicates that the translators did not strictly consider it as a particular temporal moment. It is given by ἡμέρα (e.g., ἐν ἡμέρᾳ σωτηρίας—"on a day of salvation", Isa 49:8), χρόνος (e.g., "it is a difficult time for Jacob", Jer 37:7, HT: 30:7), and νῦν (e.g., "as now", Ezek 16:57). It may further be rendered by adverbs or conjunctions that simply indicate the temporal relationship: "he would not (οὐκ ἄν) have made us hear these things" (Jdg 13:23), "whenever" (ὅταν, Est 5:13), "and it happened as (καὶ ἐγένετο ὡς) they brought in" (2 Chr 24:11), "as (καθώς) being melted from heat" (Job 6:17) "when it happened" (ἡνίκα ἐγένετο, Isa 48:16), and "then" (τότε, 20:2; pp. 37, 43 f., 80, 85, 161).

This lack of considering 'ēth as a "decisive moment" becomes especially obvious through the comparatively large group of 29 instances where it is omitted in translation without a hint of a variant HT.

This may be the result of combining several words, as the rendering of *lachakamīym yode'ēy ha'ittīym* in Est 1:13 by τοῖς φίλοις (p. 87). But it is usually caused by regarding the temporal reference as an expendable unit that may just as well be implied in the obvious sense of the passage. Thus, *be'ittō* is omitted in Ezek 34:26 ("I shall give you rain") and *ba'ēth hahīy'* in Est 8:9, which is modified by a distinct chronological reference (*bachodesh hashshelīyshīy*; pp. 26 f., 60).

It is noteworthy that the omission takes place regularly in reference to the time of day, indicating that *'ēth* was no longer recognized as referring to a juncture of occasions, but was only seen to be superfluous, *i.g.*: πρὸς ἑσπέραν—"at evening" (Gen 8:11), ἕως ἑσπέρας ταύτης—"until this evening" (Jos 8:29), μεσημβρίας—"at noon" (Jer 30:16), and δύνοντος τοῦ ἡλίου—"when the sun had set" (2 Chr 18:34), as well as the time of year: ἐν τῷ ἐπιόντι ἔτει ἐν τῇ ἐξόδῳ τῶν βασιλέων—"when the year arrived at the going forth of the kings" (1 Chr 20:1; pp. 21 f.). The lone exception is the reference in Dan 9:21 (p. 30) that is significantly rendered: ἐν ὥρᾳ θυσίας ἑσπερινῆς—"at the hour of the evening offering". *'ēth* is likewise regarded as unnecessary in passages where it had been reduced already in Hebrew to an indefinite temporal conjunction, as ἐν τῷ ἄρξασθαι—"when they began" (2 Chr 20:22; 29:27, p. 41).

This fact that the translators of the LXX frequently interpreted *'ēth* indefinitely or regarded it as an expendable element of temporal references, indicates that its particular significance was no longer understood. This is also seen in many of the cases where καιρός was employed despite the fact that an unusual reading in Greek results, *e.g.*: ὡς ὁ καιρὸς αὔριον ("as the time tomorrow", 1 Kgs 9:16), ἐν ταῖς χερσίν σου οἱ καιροί μου ("in your hands are my times", Ps 31:16), ἐν καιρῷ ("at (the) time", Dt 32:35), ἕως καιροῦ ("until a time", Isa 8:23), κατὰ καιρόν ("according to a time", 60:22; pp. 37, 40, 79-82). The impression is thereby made that καιρός does not always do justice to *'ēth* because it is limited to the temporal aspect. Thus it is sometimes simply omitted due to a redundancy that is felt in Greek if καιρός were used, which does not hold true in Hebrew when *'ēth* is used. The rendering of καιρός in these cases creates the impression of a mechanical, literal translation. The "definite occasion" of *'ēth* cannot always be identified by the "temporal occasion" of καιρός.

Therefore, the representations by Delling, who implies that the primary use of χαιρός in the LXX signifies "decisive moment",[1]) and John Marsh, who relates *ēth* directly to this meaning of χαιρός,[2] are misleading. These opinions have already been repudiated by James Barr, who further exposed the futility of making a crass distinction between χρόνος and χαιρός in both the LXX and NT.[3]) He also revealed the weakness in Oscar Cullmann's distinction between χαιρός as a "point of time defined by its content" and αἰών as a "duration of time".[4]) Cullmann had actually identified these words with his own view of time as made up of a line of decisive moments as the components of salvation history on the one hand, and time as an entirety on the other. He thus did not take into account the polysemy of the words that alone make it impossible to conceptualize or hypostatize them.[5]) If the salvation history is constituted by a line of decisive times, they are not to be identified with the use of χαιρός but with the very occasions themselves according to their evaluation in the Scriptures. It may not be surprising, then, that Cullmann does not regard his position as being affected by Barr's criticism, for it is actually derived from his general conception of the NT, independent of the lexicography.[6]) It thus follows that Cullmann's entire argument over the distinctive uses of αἰών and χαιρός is both irrelevant to his subject as well as misrepresentative for an understanding of the words. As Barr pointed out,[7]) it cannot be expected that the vocabulary stock should correspond exactly to the pattern of thinking about time. Neither can it be assumed that the peculiar meaning of a certain word may be adequately rendered by an equivalent in translation. χαιρός was apparently the best possibility for translating *ēth*, but proved inappropriate in many cases because of a difference in meaning. Distinctions must thus be made between the two words in their languages, but especially between the various uses employed for each word.

Summary

1. The normal usage of *ēth* in the Hebrew OT is substantiated by the instances in early Hebrew letters, where a *juncture of circumstances*

---

[1]) "χαιρός", pp. 459 f.; *Das Zeitverständnis des Neuen Testaments*, pp. 49, 52.

[2]) *Loc. cit.*

[3]) *Biblical Words for Time*, pp. 34-46.

[4]) *Christus und die Zeit*, pp. 50-60.

[5]) Barr, *loc. cit.*, pp. 47-53, 58-81. *Cf.* also the criticism by Rudolf Bultmann: "Heilsgeschichte und Geschichte", *ThLZ* 73 (1948), col. 663.

[6]) *Loc. cit.*, p. 27; see pp. 45 f.

[7]) *Loc. cit.*, p. 80.

is indicated, as well as by many of the cases in the extant Hebrew texts of Sira and the DSC, particularly in regard to the indication of temporal relationship and singular, definite occasions.

2. The late Hebrew texts of Sira and DSC represent the trend already begun in the OT toward the *objectivization* of ʿēth to denote an occasion *per se* and its generalization as an indefinite reference. One aspect is presented by Sira, where the "given occasion" of Koheleth is further objectivized as the "right occasion". The DSC carries out objectivization in a chronological sense, applying ʿēth to the regulated times of a systematized calendar.

3. The use of relevant expressions in early Aramaic letters corresponds closely to that of the Hebrew letters, so that a technical epistolary style may be identified for ʿēth as well as for keʿeth and keʿeneth, in distinction to ʿattāh and keʿan. The use in later Aramaic for kʿn undergoes a change, being reduced in most instances to an emphatic participle in the sense of the Hebrew nāʾ, except where it is used to translate ʿattāh.

4. The translation of ʿēth in the LXX indicates that it was not regarded as a particular temporal moment. In fact, it is clear that the translators no longer understood the real significance of ʿēth. It is obvious that it does not coincide with its usual equivalent, καιρός, which primarily denotes only the "temporal occasion" instead of the "definite occasion".

These various texts offer both similarity and differences to the usage of ʿēth in the OT, especially representing the trend in thought in the first centuries after the last canonical writing of the OT.

Excurse 2

Etymology of ʿēth

a. The Various Proposals for Derivation

Many different proposals have been made in the past for the etymological derivation of ʿēth. As a biconsonontal word, it has presented something of a riddle, for it has been widely thought that Hebrew words with only two radicals are to be derived from triliteral verbal roots.[1]) If this is the case, one of the original radicals must have been

---

[1]) See J. Barth ("Vergleichende Studien, I: über biliterale Nomina", *ZDMG* 41 (1887), pp. 603 ff.), Kautzsch (*op. cit.*, §§ 30a, f, g, m, 81a, 82, 83a), and Alexander Heidel (*The System of the Quadriliteral Verb in Akkadian*, Assyriological Studies 13, Chicago: 1940, p. 134).

dropped or assimilated. An assimilation in the *th* of *'ēth* had apparently taken place; when vocalization was introduced, the traditional pronunciation demanded a *daghesh forte* in the plural (*'ittīym*—Ezek 12:27, *'ittōthay*—Ps 31:16) and with suffixes (*e.g.*, *'ittēk*—Ezek 16:8), as well as in the probable derivatives *'attāh* (Gen 11:6) and *'ittay* (1 Chr 2:35).[1]) It is possible that the *th* itself may be an addition to the root, having assimilated the final radical.

1. The first possibility for a plausible derivation is that *'ēth* be derived by suffixing a *th* to a *l"h* root and assimilating the middle radical.

Mention may first be made of *'dh* ("pass over", Job 28:8). Wilhelm Gesenius first derives *'ad* ("eternity, future", Isa 30:8) from *'dh* in the sense of the progression of time. He then considers *'ēth* to be a contraction from a feminine form, *'edeth*, of the substantive *'ad*.[2]) However, it is unlikely that *'ad* can be derived from *'dh*, for the final *h*-syllable always requires retention of its vowel. This prevents the assimilation of a radical, even if the *h* has been converted to a *th*. Then, too, *l"h* verbs are originally either *l"w* or *l"y*. Thus the second vowel of the root is long, which is restored in many of the forms by a *y* before the ending. The connecting vowel is always used before suffixes when the *h* is dropped, thus preventing any assimilation. It is only in the shortened forms of the imperfect that the final syllable is omitted.[3]) Thus it is unlikely in the formation of derivatives that the final *h* would be changed to a *th* without the formation of a long vowel written *plene* with *y* or *w*.

A more popular proposal is *'nh*.[4]) This root presents possibilities for semantical relationship in the meaning "answer". Yet, the probability is slight, going over a detour with "response" to perhaps "turning-point". More important, as with *'dh* above, the following examples show that the final radical, even if changed to a *th*, cannot be assimilated with the middle radical: Qal perf. fem. *'ānethāh* (1 Sam 4:20), inf. *'anōth* (Ex 32:18), part. suf. *'onēhū* (1 Sam 14:39).

---

[1]) See Kautzsch, *op. cit.*, §§ 19b, f, 20a, b, 1. See also the argument presented above, p. 138, that the *hapax legomenon 'ittīy* (Lev 16:21) be a misspelling for *'āthīyd*.

[2]) *Thesaurus philologicus criticus linguae hebraeae et chaldaeae Veteris Testamenti*, Leipzig: 1840.

[3]) See Kautzsch, *op. cit.*, 75.

[4]) Proposed by: J. Levy: *Chaldäisches Wörterbuch über die Targumim*, Köln: 1959 (repr.), p. 572; Friedrich Delitzsch: *Prolegomena eines neuen hebräisch-aramäischen Wörterbuchs zum Alten Testament*, Leipzig: 1886, p. 115; Jakob Barth: *Etymologische Studien zum hebräischen Lexicon*, Leipzig: 1893, p. 17; A. Ungnad: *"Zur babylonisch-assyrischen Grammatik*, II, p. 177.

2. Another group of possible roots for a derivation of ʿ*ēth* is where one radical of the root is assimilated into a *th*-radical. Paul Kahle assumes a derivation from the ‴ʿ root ʿ*thth*.[1]) However, it is properly a radical that closes a syllable with a short vowel which is assimilated into the beginning consonant of the following syllable, as long as both consonants permit it. For instance, the Qal perf. 1. pers. sing. of *mwth* would ordinarily be *mathtiy*, but the *th*-radical closing the first syllable is assimilated into the following *th* of the suffix to build the shortened form *mattiy*, Gen 14:19. Because ʿ*ēth* contains a long *tsere*, the original form should have had a long vowel in the first syllable.

3. The root ʿ*dth* is proposed by Hans Bauer and Pontus Leander, that is, the Accadian word ʿ*idtu*, "agreement".[2]) Similarly, Friedrich Delitzsch expresses the opinion that the Aramaic root ʿ*nth* might be a possibility, as also Acad. *ēttu, ittu*, "when", "time", from *ēn-tu*.[3]) Although the roots ʿ*dth* and ʿ*nth* are not extant in Hebrew, they would at least present theoretical possibilities.

4. The final plausible root for consideration is *yʿd*, which has been proposed by Conrad von Orelli.[4]) Here, the *y* of the *p"y* root is dropped, the feminine *th* is added and assimilates the second radical from the segholate form ʿ*edeth*. There is no comparable extant form from this root; to the contrary, the known derivatives seem to witness against the step: ʿ*ēdāh*, "assembly" (1 Kgs 12:20), *mōʿēd*, "appointment" (Jdg 20:38), *muʿādāh*, "designation" (Jos 20:9). But the probability is at least theoretical, considering the example of the inf. const. of *yld*—*ledeth* (Gen 4:2). Of particular interest is the contracted form *lālath* in 1 Sam 4:19, which need not be a textual error.[5]) At least this derivation can furnish a tempting basic meaning for ʿ*ēth*: "determined, right time". It could then be further related to Ethiopic ʿ*edemē* ("appointed time"), Syriac *waʿdoʾ* ("term"), Arabic *waʿada* ("appointment"), and especially Aram. ʿ*iddān* ("time").[6]) Yet, where a *th* is suffixed to the root, there is no example of assimilation with

---

[1]) *Der masoretische Text des Alten Testaments nach der Überlieferung der babylonischen Juden*, Leipzig: 1902, p. 68; so also Bergsträsser, *op. cit.*, § 26i.

[2]) *Op. cit.*, 51z.

[3]) *Op. cit.*, pp. 34, 116.

[4]) *Op. cit.*, p. 47.

[5]) Against Buhl, *loc. cit.*, and Koehler, *loc. cit.*

[6]) See Augustus Dillmann: *Lexicon Linguae Aethiopicae*, Giessen: 1864; Carl Brockelmann: *Lexicon Syriacum*, 2nd ed., Halle: 1928; Wehr, *op. cit.*; Baumgartner, *op. cit.*

the *d*: Ugaritic *'dt* ("assembly"), Syr. *'idto'* ("congregation").[1]) Thus
the etymological evidence remains inconclusive. Incidentally, the
Aram. *'iddān* is actually to be derived from another but related root,
'dh, according to Accd. *adānu* ("set time"), Ugar. *'dn* ("season"),
Syr. *'eddān* ("moment"), Arab. *'addān* ("certain time").[2])

b. The Possibility of an "*'n*-Family"

Some of the proposals for deriving *'ēth* from *'nh* have connected
the root with temporal words in other languages, such as Accd. *inu*
("when"), *ēttu* ("time"), Phoen. *'ny* ("time"), Aram. *ke'an*, *ke'eneth*,
ke'eth ("now").[3]) Thus the attempt has been made to find a common
etymology for all of these expressions.[4]) However, Assyriologists
recognize two different roots here. Accd. *ēttu* is not related to a
temporal category, but is connected with *ittu* ("sign"; *cf.* Heb. *'ōth*).
The temporal expressions *inu* ("at the time of, when"), *inūma* ("now,
when"), and *inūmi* ("at that time"), are found only as adverb, preposition or conjunction, and not as a verb or noun.[5]). There is also
no plausible argument for establishing a relationship between *'nh* and
Accd. *inu*, and it would seem advisable to avoid such a connection,
particularly because of the structural improbability (see p. 156).

The previous proposals for a derivation of *'ēth* from a triliteral
verbal root all prove to be unsatisfactory. Indeed, ever since Caspar
Neumann in 1693, some Hebraists have advocated the theory that
all triliteral Hebrew roots stem from biliteral ones.[6]) Attention may

---

[1]) See Joseph Aistleitner: *Wörterbuch der ugaritischen Sprache*, Berlin: 1963;
Cyrus H. Gordon: *Ugaritic Manual*, III, Roma: 1955; Brockelmann, *loc. cit.*

[2]) See *The Assyrian Dictionary of the Oriental Institute of the University of Chicago*;
Wolfram von Soden: *Akkadisches Handwörterbuch*, Wiesbaden: 1962.

[3]) See W. Röllig: *Kanaanäisches Glossar (Kanaanäische und aramäische Inschriften*,
III, from: H. W. Haussig: *Wörterbuch der Mythologie*), Stuttgart.

[4]) So Barth, *op. cit.*, p. 17; Buhl, *op. cit.*, ad loc.; Baumgartner, *op. cit.*, ad loc.;
Delitzsch, *op. cit.*, pp. 34, 116.

[5]) *CAD* and von Soden, *op. cit.*, ad loc.

[6]) G. Johannes Botterweck (*Der Triliterismus im Semitischen erläutert an den
Wurzeln gl kl ḳl*, Bonner Biblische Beiträge 3, Bonn: 1952) came to this conclusion,
and presents a review of the following advocates of the theory: Neumann (p. 11),
Wilhelm Gesenius (p. 11), F. W. M. Philippi (p. 16), S. T. H. Hurwitz (pp. 24 f.)
and G. R. Driver (p. 28). H. Ewald differentiated between biliterals for "Gefühls-
und Deutewurzeln" and triliterals for "Begriffswurzeln" (p. 12), and H. Bauer
differentiated between aorist roots for biliterals and perfect roots for triliterals
(p. 20). See esp. Hurwitz: *Root-Determinatives in Semitic Speech* (Contributions to
Oriental History and Philology, VI), New York: 1913, pp. 35 f., 107; and Driver:
Problems of the Hebrew Verbal System (Old Testament Studies, 2), Edinburgh:
1936, p. 5.

then be called to the possibility of a biliteral nominal root, ʿn. Such a root would have an originally temporal meaning, perhaps even as the noun "time" or "occasion". However, it is also quite possible that it was originally only a word of temporal reference as the above-mentioned witness in Accadian indicates: adverb, preposition and conjunction. This root would have belonged to the early stock of the Semitic family of languages, thus finding access to the various dialects. The various appearances of the root in the several Semitic languages constitute therefore a family of related temporal words.

As is already indicated by the parallel forms keʿeneth and keʿeth to keʿan in Aramaic, the addition of the nominal feminine ending th to the root is a real and typically Semitic possibility. This is also evidently the explanation for the formation of Ugaritic ʿnt, "now".[1] With the example of keʿeth, a parallel is already given for the assimilation of the n of the root into the th of the feminine ending. It is possible that the feminine ending was added in order to give the word a substantival connotation. This early use as a substantive may be reflected in the epistolary forms in Heb. (ʿēth) and Aram. (keʿeth), which have been identified as distinctive terms in comparison with Heb. ʿattāh and Aram. keʿan (see pp. 131-138). A further step would have been the formation of the derivative ʿattāh, "now", with the locative ending that serves a temporal function in emphasizing the present situation.[2]

This "ʿn-family" is best characterized semantically by the fact that its members are ordinarily used only for purposes of *temporal relationship* without evidencing a definite meaning in the sense of, e.g., mōʿēd, ʿiddān or zemān. It would be very tempting to carry these considerations further in searching for an explanation why it was that the common word in Hebrew for "time" came from this otherwise relatively insignificant family of words. It could even be imagined that ʿēth was consistently used only in the form of a temporal reference in early passages because of its etymological origin. However, that would lead the investigation too far astray into mere speculation. Interesting though the etymological considerations may be in comparison with the use of a word, a study that is directed toward a clarification of the *usage* and its implications for the broader temporal

---

[1] So Gordon, *op. cit.*, to Aqhat I:154, 161 (ʿnt.brh.pʿlmh, "now he has fled for eternity"), and 154, 162, 168 (ʿnt.pdr.dr, "now and for evermore"). Compare the parallel expression in I:167 f.: lht.wʿlmh, "from now and unto eternity".

[2] See Kautzsch, *op. cit.*, § 90h.

concept must avoid drawing conclusions from etymological relationships. Therefore, this part of the study will be concluded here in order to restrict it to an associated contribution to a comprehensive treatment of the word *'ēth*, without gaining an influence in the matter of its actual usage.

CHAPTER SIX

CONCLUSION

A. The Uses of 'ETH: Grammatical Considerations

1. Reviewing the grammatical usage of '*ēth* in the historical perspective, it is obvious that it was not employed as an independent substantive. In the earliest instances, it is consistently used with prepositions in the formation of adverbial expressions, *e.g.*: "at the time of evening" (2 Sam 11: 2), "at the occasion of the giving of Merab" (1 Sam 18: 19), "on such an occasion he would have made known to us such as this" (Jdg 13: 23), "and they smote Moab on that occasion" (3: 29; pp. 21-23, 29 f., 32, 37, 48, 51, 102). This demonstrates that '*ēth* was primarily employed with relationship. It was concerned with indicating the *relationship between occasions*. Therefore, its function is to point to the *juncture of circumstances*, that is, to the *specific occasion* produced by this juncture.

2. Somewhat later, '*ēth* also came to be used to designate the particular occasion itself, at first somewhat indirectly with a pronominal suffix in an adverbial reference, as, "I will take back my grain in its season" (Hos 2: 11; pp. 26, 32). The designation was soon made directly to the occasion, *e.g.*, "when it is time, he does not present himself" (13: 13), "for it is an evil situation" (Am 5: 13b), and then with particular emphasis: "The occasion has come!" (Ezek 7: 7), "that her occasion may come" (22: 3; pp. 27, 85, 88, 102, 107). Thus, the characteristic of indicating a specific juncture of circumstances proved to be desirable in denoting an *occasion of peculiar significance*. In either case, the basic characteristic of '*ēth* appears to be that of referring to a *specific, definite occasion*.

3. Still later instances indicate a further change in the grammatical usage. In some temporal references, '*ēth* is obviously nothing more than a *superfluous addition or conjunction*, so that it loses its character of referring to a definite occasion, *e.g.*, "on the occasion of every day" (1 Chr 12: 23), "it was an occasion when" (2 Chr 24: 11), "time after time" (1 QS 8: 15; pp. 43 f., 147 f.). The introduction of plural forms gives evidence of a trend toward *objectivization*, apparently first used in Ezek 12: 27 ("for distant occasions", p. 86). In this way, direct designation was made of situations ("in those times", Dan 11: 6),

of experiences ("my situations", Ps 31:16), and even of appointments ("on appointed occasions", Neh 13:31, "their (= festivals) occasions", 1 QS 1:14; pp. 31, 76 f., 80, 146).

4. Further, in contrast to the singular late construction *bāʿēth hazzoʾth* (Est 4:14; cf. 1 QS 9:20; see pp. 43, 148), which involves the peculiar urgency of a present situation, the very frequently used form *baʿēth hahīʾ* refers decidedly to an occasion that is definitely to be *distinguished from the present*. For instance, the cases in Dt 1-10 make an actualization of the past occasions in the present an impossibility (pp. 64-66, 71 f., 74 f.).

5. The contexts of the instances of *ʿēth* frequently demonstrate that it is *not primarily concerned with the temporal aspect* of the particular occasion. References to a natural or customary occasion indicate primarily the *definiteness of the orders of nature and custom*, e.g., "in the season of harvest" (Jer 50:16), "at the occasion of their coming forth to draw (water)" (Gen 24:11; pp. 25 f., 28, 32). Emphasis may also be placed upon a *certain quality*, *activity* or *experience* that forms the content of the occasion, e.g., "on the occasion of healing" (Jer 8:15), "the occasion of their punishment" (46:21), "the occasion of favor" (Ps 69:14; pp. 79, 81, 91). The primary indication may also be directed to the *substantiation of the reality of an occasion* by means of emphasizing an oath, a past historical event, or a foretold future occurrence, e.g., "according to this situation—tomorrow" (1 Sam 9:16), "on that occasion" (Dt 1:9), "on the occasion when I punish them" (Jer 6:15; pp. 40, 64, 82).

6. Later cases of *ʿēth* also frequently point up the *fact* of an occasion more than its temporality. For example, "it is the occasion of peoples" (Ezek 30:3, p. 107) stresses the fact of the divine intervention and "for the final Situation" (Dan 8:17, p. 112) the fact of the End. Further, "man does not know his occasion" (Ecc 9:12, p. 116) points to the definite fact of death, and "an occasion for every matter" (3:1, p. 125) to the fact of the given occasion. This tendency to refer to the *definiteness and quality of an occasion* rather than to its temporal aspect speaks against the usual interpretations that wish to see in *ʿēth* the reference to a temporal moment.[1] An occasion may be critical or decisive, but according to the *peculiarity of its content* and not because of a peculiarity in its temporality.

---

[1] See esp. Delling, "καιρός", pp. 459 f., and *Das Zeitverständnis des Neuen Testaments*, p. 49; Vollborn, *op. cit.*, pp. 6 ff.; Knight, *op. cit.*, pp. 201 ff.; Ebeling, *op. cit.*, pp. 346 ff.

B. The Uses of ʿēth: Semantical Considerations

1. Turning now to the semantical considerations, it has already been seen that the rendering *"occasion"* for ʿēth has proven itself applicable in nearly all cases, serving well as a general designation. The word "occasion" may indicate temporality, as is mentioned in the *Oxford English Dictionary* as the eighth definition: "A case of something happening; the time, or one of the times, at which something happens; a particular time marked by some occurrence or by its special character." However, the other definitions show that the basic meaning is of somewhat other nature, as the first: "A falling together or juncture of circumstances favourable or suitable to an end or purpose, or admitting of something being done or effected; an opportunity." [1]) Such a *juncture* forms the basic characteristic of ʿēth, rather than temporality.

Thus, ʿēth is a very appropriate word for indicating the *relationship of events*, e.g., "as on this occasion" (Jdg 21:22), "about the occasion of her dying" (1 Sam 4:20; pp. 37 f.,). This basic aspect made it also exceptionally applicable in referring to a *definite occasion*. It seems that the earliest usage in the OT employed it in this manner for the definite occasion of a *higher order*—that of regular natural occurrences (*e.g.*, "as on this occasion—the coming-to-life", Gen 18:10; "at the occasion of the breeding of the flock", 31:10) and that of expected activity of social custom (*e.g.*, "the occasion of gathering the flock", Gen 29:7; "at the occasion of the going forth of the kings", 2 Sam 11:1; pp. 23-25, 28).

2. This indication of a definite occasion made ʿēth a very appropriate expression for other situations. It was therefore suitable in a formula used with oaths and promises (see 1 Sam 9:16, p. 162), as well as to such special occurrences as death (see 4:20, above) and birth ("at the occurrence of her giving birth", Gen 38:27, pp. 41 f.). Then it also came to be used in early historical prose in reference to a *certain definite occasion of the past* in the form baʿēth hahīy' (Jdg 3:29; Gen 38:1, *etc.*, pp. 48, 59, 162). This is in distinction to the practice of historical poetry, which was content to employ expressions of a more indefinite nature (*cf.* the use of 'āz and yāmīym in Jdg 5; see p. 52). It was then only natural that this term be appropriated by the prophets in reference to the definite occasion of the divine intervention, as in Mic 3:4 and Jer 6:15 (see pp. 82, 84). This practice was

---

[1]) Vol. VII, Oxford: 1933, p. 42.

then extended to the definite occasions of man's natural destiny ("not yet at your occasion", Ecc 7:17), of the fate of a people ("at the occasion of the End-punishment", Ezek 21:30), and of the divinely given opportunity ("everything he has made beautiful on its occasion", Ecc 3:11), as well as to occasions of appointment (Neh 13:31; 1 Qs 1:14; pp. 107, 117, 126, 162).

3. In this perspective, then, it would be incorrect to assign a basic meaning to ʿēth that can be applied only to a limited number of cases, and that particularly in later texts, as von Orelli's and Ratschow's definition "the right time", Vollborn's "determined moment", Delling's "decisive moment", and Marsh's "time of opportunity".[1]) It is likewise a poor representation of the facts to relate the late occurrences of the plural forms to a sequence of "times", whether in the historical sense, as done by Delling, Marsh and Eichrodt, or in the personal sense, as done by von Rad.[2]) In the plural, ʿēth never implies a sequence, but only the *plurality of occasions*, as the *events* experienced by David (1 Chr 29:30), the Psalmist (31:16), Job (24:1), or the lawyers (Est 1:13), or repeated situations (Neh 9:28; pp. 80, 86 f., 162).

4. It has not, however, been a mistake to emphasize the peculiarity of ʿēth in referring to the *content* or *concreteness of the occasion* (von Orelli, Pedersen, Delling, H. W. Robinson, Vollborn, Marsh, Boman, Knight, von Rad, Muilenburg, Ebeling).[3]) When the juncture of circumstances is indicated, it is obvious that a concrete situation is meant, and when a situation is described, it is obvious that its contents or quality is understood. However, it is also evident that this aspect is *dependent upon the use in the context and is not an inherent quality of the word* (see pp. 32 f., 102).

In short, it may be concluded that *the word ʿēth was used in the OT in order to indicate the relationship or juncture of circumstances, primarily in an objective sense and only secondarily in a temporal sense, and to direct attention to a specifically definite occasion or situation.*

---

[1]) Von Orelli, *op. cit.*, p. 48; Ratschow, *loc. cit.*, pp. 380 f.; Vollborn, *op. cit.* pp. 6 ff.; Delling, *loc. cit.*, p. 49; Marsh, "Time, Season", p. 258.

[2]) Delling, *loc. cit.*, p. 52; Marsh, *The Fulness of Time*, p. 28; Eichrodt, "Heilserfahrung und Zeitverständnis im Alten Testament", p. 118; von Rad, *Theologie des Alten Testaments*, II, p. 114.

[3]) Von Orelli, *op. cit.*, p. 63; Pedersen, *Israel*, I-II, pp. 487-491; Delling, *loc. cit.*, p. 49; H. W. Robinson, *Inspiration and Revelation in the Old Testament*, p. 109; Vollborn, *op. cit.*, p. 26; Marsh, "Time, Season", p. 258, and *The Fulness of Time*, p. 28; Boman, *op. cit,*. pp. 111, 117; Knight, *op. cit.*, p. 314; von Rad, *loc. cit.*, pp. 113-116; Muilenburg, *op. cit.*, pp. 235 f.; Ebeling, *op. cit.*, p. 346.

C. The Comparison of Other Temporal Expressions with

ʿēth

Although the limitations of the investigation prevent a comparably detailed study of other temporal expressions, they have been dealt with throughout wherever they showed cause for relationship to the use of *ʿēth*.

1. The words dealing with eternity or the distant extension of time have an important bearing upon the general concept of time, although they do not give evidence of any relationship in *usage* to *ʿēth*, with the lone exception of a contrast in Ecc 3:11 between "distant time" and the "given occasion" (pp. 18, 126).

2. It has been demonstrated how *'āz* may indicate a *significant change or continuation of the situation* (Mic 3:4; Jer 22:22), but always in the sense of *indefinite temporal relationship* (Gen 49:4; Jdg 5:11; 1 Kgs 3:16; pp. 52, 64,88f,). This is similar to the use of prepositions in cases where *ʿēth* might possibly have been used (Gen 21:2; Jos 8:29; Ezra 9:5; p. 33), for they only indicate the fact of relationship which, depending on the content, may be of a temporal nature.

3. An opportunity of comparison has been presented by *qēts* with respect to the *eschatological End*, for which it is used in Daniel as a *terminus technicus* (8:17, etc., pp. 112 f.). The use of *ʿēth* depends upon the context in this reference, although it is appropriate because it indicates a *definite occasion*.

4. Of particular significance is *mōʿēd*, which always reflects its basic meaning of "*appointment*". Similar to *ʿēth*, its use is not primarily temporal, so that the frequently assigned meaning "appointed time" depends entirely on the context and does not belong inherently to the word itself. Indications of this fact are provided by cases where the two words occur together, *mōʿēd* stressing the *aspect of appointment* and *ʿēth* that of *occasion* (secondarily implying temporality), as in Hos 2:11; Jer 8:7; 2 Sam 24:15 (pp. 26-28, 88 f.). The same applies as well to the use of *mōʿēd* with respect to historical, intervening and eschatological references, where the appointed aspect is desired (see Dt 16:6; Hab 2:3; Dan 12:7; pp. 66, 89, 113). Thus it is incorrect for Pedersen to connect it to historical events by seeing a development of the appreciation of the events out of the cultic observances on the appointed festal occasions.[1]) It was much rather

---

[1]) *Loc. cit.*, p. 490.

the *events* that gave meaning to the festivals, while the function of *mōʿēd* relates only to their nature as having been appointed.

5. It is quite natural that *yōm*, with some 2000 instances by far the most frequently used temporal expression in the OT,[1]) should be of major importance for the concept of time. *a*. Apart from the many cases of usage in chronological references, it is ordinarily employed purely for *temporal references* in distinction to *ʿēth*. It usually retains the basic meaning *"day"*, which indicates both *the temporality of the occasion and its localization at a certain time*, e.g., "on that day" (Gen 26:32), "on the day of tomorrow" (30:33; pp. 40, 47). However, *yōm* may also imply a qualitative aspect of the particular occasion, as "on the day of my calamity" (2 Sam 22:19), "the day of evil" (Am 6:3), "on the day of harvest" (Prov 25:13; pp. 25, 90 f.). In some later cases, an *indefinite reference* may be made to the occasion, as "daily" (Prov 8:30), "on every day" (Ps 7:12; p. 45). The plural presents a further peculiarity in referring to an *indefinite period or situation*. In fact, drawing upon one of the several meanings in English, it may well be rendered "time" in this indefinite temporal sense: "it was after a time" (Jdg 11:4), "all the time of David's being in the stronghold" (1 Sam 22:4), "at that time" (2 Sam 16:23), "a time is coming" (Am 4:2), "after a certain time" (Dt 4:30; pp. 52, 55, 57, 69-71, 100). It is therefore impossible that *yāmīym* represent either periods that have been reduced to moments or the individual acts of a greater event.[2])

b. Some cases of *yōm* that refer to *crisis situations* (*e.g.*, "on the day of battle", Am 1:14; "on the day of punishment", Isa 10:3; "on the day of salvation", 49:8; pp. 90 f.) would seem to detract from the one-sided emphasis in this respect given by some interpreters to *ʿēth* (see p. 164). This is particularly true of the expression *yōm yhwh* (Ezek 13:5, *etc.*, pp. 94 f.), which has been singled out by Scott as a prime example of a "transforming moment" where past and future are realized in the present, while Knight refers to it as a "term full of 'substance' . . . a fulness of time".[3]) However, the Day of Yahweh is always *differentiated from past and future events*. Further, it is not itself a substance that is "filled", but is only the *means* of referring to the intervening activity of Yahweh. This is borne out by the considerations of Charles, von Rad and Černý (pp. 92-94). A unique

---

[1]) So Delling, *loc. cit.*, pp. 50 f.

[2]) So, resp., Delling, *ibid.*, p. 49, and Vollborn, *op. cit.*, p. 54.

[3]) Scott, *op. cit.*, pp. 149 f.; Knight, *op. cit.*, p. 315.

usage is represented here, for, since *yōm* indicates the day of Yahweh's devastating battle against his enemies, the expression may be rendered "battle of Yahweh" (p. 95).

c. yōm may also be used with particular significance in *historical* situations, especially in the form *bayyōm hahū'*, which refers to events occurring on the same day (1 Sam 4:12) or, more often, to the historical causal relationship of events (14:18; 22:18; pp. 56 f.). Although the expression is somewhat limited by its temporal character in referring specifically to the occasion itself, it at least indicates the *historical aspect and temporal distinction of the peculiar situation.* "on that day" is also used similarly by the prophets, but always as a temporal reference (Am 2:16; Isa 2:11; p. 97) and never as a designation of the occasion itself. Similar results are also obtained in considering other uses, as *hayyōm* and related expressions for "today". These often refer not merely to the present situation, but also emphasize it as *the occasion for a significant event* (Dt 4:4; 9:1; Jer 1:10, 18; pp. 67 f., 101). Since an oath or command may be reinforced (Dt 4:26, 40; p. 68), it is evident that these expressions are used to stress *the reality of the particular occasion.* Reality expressed temporally means an emphasis on *the historical character*, for the event is thereby attached to a *certain* day—it is *localized* in time and therefore identified as a real occurrence. This also applies to "until this day" (*e.g.*, Dt 2:22), which signifies the reality of a condition until the present, except 11:4, where it is the effect of Yahweh's "signs and deeds" that still bears consequences for the present (pp. 68 f.).

These considerations of other temporal expressions underline the uniqueness of *'ēth*. For, while *yōm*, *'āz* and temporal prepositions indicate nearly always only *the aspect of temporal relationship* and *mō'ēd* only that of *appointment*, *'ēth* refers *directly to the occasion itself.*

D. Considerations toward a Concept of Time in the Old Testament

1. *Event and Time*

a. In reviewing the use of *'ēth* toward determining the nature of the concept of time in the OT, it is basic that it refers *primarily to the juncture of circumstances, the specific occasion.* This conclusion is borne out by the fact that, when it is objectivized, it becomes a designation of the occasion itself. It is therefore a reference to, or a designation of, *an event or condition.*

b. Although it cannot ordinarily be translated properly by the word "time", *ʿēth* is often used in such a way that it *implies* the temporal aspect of the situation. This combination of the temporal aspect with the occasion in one expression demonstrates a unique phenomenon: *there is a very close association between time and the occasion.* It may not, of course, be supposed that time and occasion are identical, as has been said by, *e.g.*, Pedersen with respect to time and its substance.[1]) However, the close association of the two factors indicate that they may be comprehended as belonging together.

c. The fact that *ʿēth* refers to the juncture of circumstances also indicates the third major factor in its character: *it implies definiteness.* Where a juncture occurs, a *fusion of elements* is produced; plurality becomes singularity; the indefinite becomes definite. It is therefore natural that, through its usage, *ʿēth* indicates that an occasion is of definite quality. This attribute is very significant because it means that a definite occasion is given a temporal setting: *a specific event is given a definite place in the category of time.*

2. *Definiteness and Historical Perspective*

a. It is also obvious why *ʿēth* was first employed in connection with events relating to the orders of nature and social custom. The events of nature to which regularity may be ascribed have a definite occasion for their occurrence. Thus, another event may be assigned a definite place in time through association with an occurrence of nature. The accepted events of social custom likewise have their definite occasions.

b. However, it is of particular significance when reference is made to an historical occasion, for this means that *a definite place is given to the event in historical time*: *it is placed into historical relationship with other occasions.* A reference with *ʿēth* may place a following story into an historical setting, relating it historically to the preceding occasion. This means that *the sense for the historical perspective* was very evident, for a word was often chosen to express the relationship that signified a very definite, singular character. Evidence of this fact is also very clearly to be seen in the unusually heavy emphasis laid upon genealogy and chronology in the OT. It is likewise significant that this same word was frequently chosen by the prophets in reference to *the specific, definite occasion of Yahweh's intervention.* This intervention was thereby assigned *a definite, singular place in time.*

---

[1]) *Op. cit.*, p. 487.

c. The applicability of *ʿēth* to definite occasions within the category of time is also seen in other uses where it may refer to the final destiny of a man, of a people, or even of history itself. Then, too, it may be used for the divinely given occasion, for the "right occasion", or for appointed dates.

3. *Historical Relationship*

Although other temporal expressions do not ordinarily exhibit the same characteristics that distinguish *ʿēth*, some of their uses reflect the same manner of thought. *a.* Indefinite though it is, *ʾāz* may indicate temporal relationship between historical events. *b.* The designation for appointment, *mōʿēd*, may be used for temporal situations as an established date. *c.* The most frequent temporal expression, *yōm*, indicates primarily the aspect of temporality. However, the fact that it refers to a certain day means that it also assigns to the particular event *a specific place in time*. In similar manner as the form *bāʿēth hahiyʾ*, the expression *bayyōm hahūʾ* may indicate *a causal historical relationship between events*.

4. *Historical Singularity*

It is therefore evident that the historical writers of the OT, all of whom used either *bayyōm hahūʾ* or *bāʿēth hahiyʾ* or both, were well aware of *the relationship of events to each other in the historical sense*. It is likewise evident that the authors recognized *the definiteness and singularity of certain events*, as the employment of other uses of *ʿēth* and of the emphatic *bayyōm* demonstrates. The appropriation of these expressions in their emphatic sense for significant, definite events through the prophets and their re-appropriation in the prophetic sense in Deuteronomy show that a general appreciation for *the temporal and historical singularity of events* prevailed in the OT. That this conclusion may also be applied to non-historical writings may be defended on the grounds of distinct references to *specific events of experience* (Ps 21:10; 31:16; 105:19; Job 24:1; Prov 15:23; Cant 2:12; Ecc 3:1-8; 7:17; pp. 27, 29, 80, 82, 86, 117-122, 125, 164).

From these considerations, it is obvious that many of the conclusions that have been made in the past concerning the OT concept of time cannot be held. Because the temporal expressions show that *events were given a certain, definite place in the category of time*, they were therefore *temporarily differentiated from each other*. This means that it would have been *impossible to assume a temporal identity of individually different events*.[1])

5. *Temporal Distinction*

The generally accepted recognition of definite places in time for various events is also the presupposition for recognizing *the differences between the tempora of past, present and future*.

a. The Deuteronomist, in respecting the difference between generations and between the present and the past, does not attempt to actualize Moses and his time in the present, but rather tries to actualize the validity of the *principles* of "that occasion" for his "today".

b. The prophets also differentiated between past and present generations and expected God's intervening activity as impending but future. The tenacity with which the prophets held to the occurrence of all event within the range of historical time may also be seen in the fact that they did not regard the decisive intervention by God as an eschatological event, for the history of the divine-human encounter on the finite world stage was to continue.

c. Koheleth also recognized the singularity of temporal occasions as well as the significance of past and future generations for the present, thus advising to learn from them in utilizing the present to the best advantage.

d. Even *the cult* did not attempt to actualize past events in the recitation of the creed or in the present performance of the ritual —that would be "de-historicizing". It only called them to mind with the concept of *corporate personality* and observed their memory because of the continuing effect of their *consequences*.

Therefore, it is untenable that there be represented a concept of the actualization of past or future events in the present situation or that a confrontation with God may transpose man beyond the limits of time.[2])

6. *The Time and Content of Event*

As has been emphasized repeatedly from other sources, the content of the temporal event in the Hebrew view is not to be underestimated. However, the mistake must be avoided that tries to identify the phenom-

---

[1]) Against Pedersen, *loc. cit.*, p. 488, and Marsh, *loc. cit.*, p. 65.
[2]) Against Galling, "Die Geschichte als Wort Gottes bei den Propheten", p. 171; Weiser, *Glaube und Geschichte im Alten Testament*, p. 85; Scott, *op. cit.*, pp. 149 f.; Vollborn, *op. cit.*, p. 5 *et passim*; Marsh, *loc. cit.*, pp. 63-65; von Rad, *loc. cit.* I, p. 131, II, p. 117; Sekine, *op. cit.*, p. 70; Ebeling, *op. cit.*, pp. 350-352.

enon of time with the content of event.[1]) For the Hebrew, time had no substance of its own, but, as is well demonstrated by *ʿēth, yōm* and *ʾāz* in particular, it was merely *a category of reference*. Because it was only an *aspect* of event and could not itself be experienced, it never became a subject of speculation. Even such a meditation as Ecc 3:1-9 is concerned with *the given occasion* and not essentially with time or the temporal aspect. Although, for the Hebrew, *every event had its time and the factors of time and event were inseparably bound together into one concept*, there remained a *differentiation* between the two factors. The *temporal factor* was necessary but remained an "earthen vessel" for the event in the same sense as *space. The essential factor was the content of the event.* As for the events where God was concerned, the essential factor, therefore, was *God himself*, who condescended to the restrictions of time and space, and not the concept of time that experienced the finite dimension of the event.[2])

7. *Event as Decisive Encounter with God*

Finally, time does not present itself for the Hebrew in the guise of a moment of decision. There do occur decisive times and even an occasion when God calls man to a vital decision. But such an occasion, especially as it is portrayed by the prophets, is of singular character and entails a decision for one's entire life. *It cannot therefore be a typical characteristic of the OT concept of time or event, but only of the concept of the decisive encounter of an individual with God.*[3])

The OT is a religious book, and it is therefore not peculiar that God should intentionally be the dominating subject throughout. It is likewise to be expected that the concept of God should dominate the concept of time, at least in so far as it is concerned with religious experience. In any case, the significant word *ʿēth* appears as *a very appropriate expression for a faith that witnessed the confrontation with God and his mighty work in the sphere of finite experience. For it signifies the fact of such an event as an occurrence with a definite, specific place in time.*

---

[1]) So Pedersen, *loc. cit.*, p. 488; H. W. Robinson, *op. cit.*, p. 109; Vollborn, *op. cit.*, p. 5 *et passim*; Marsh, *loc. cit.*, p. 65; Muilenburg, *op. cit.*, p. 236.

[2]) See Barr, *Biblical Words for Time*, p. 144. *Cf.* the distinction made by Karl Heinrich Rengstorf with respect to the Resurrection, that the proper subject of the kerygma is the crucified Jesus (and not the "salvation occurrence"), and that the new day of creation began with the New Creation, who is the Risen Jesus himself (*Die Auferstehung Jesu*, 5th ed., Witten/Ruhr: 1967, pp. 26, 92).

[3]) Against Delling, "καιρός", pp. 459 f., and *Das Zeitverständnis des Neuen Testaments*, p. 61; Vollborn, *op. cit.*, p. 25; Marsh, *loc. cit.*, p. 28, and "Time, Season", p. 258; Eichrodt, *loc. cit.*, p. 116; Knight, *op. cit.*, p. 316; Jocz, *op. cit.*, pp. 223-225; Ebeling, *op. cit.*, p. 349.

BIBLIOGRAPHY

A. PRIMARY SOURCES

Aland, Kurt, Matthew Black, Bruce M. Metzger, Allen Wikgren, edd.: *The Greek New Testament*, American, British and Foreign, National of Scotland, Netherlands and Württemberg Bible Societies, Stuttgart: 1966.

Allegro, J. M.: "Further Light on the History of the Qumran Sect", pp. 89-95, *JBL* 75 (1956).

——: "More Isaiah Commentaries from Qumran's Fourth Cave", pp. 215-221, *JBL* 77 (1958).

Avigad, Nahman, and Yigael Yadin: *A Genesis Apocryphon, A Scroll from the Wilderness of Judaea*, Magnes, Jerusalem: 1956.

Barthélemy, D., and J. T. Milik: *Qumran Cave I, DJD*, I, 1955.

Benoit, P., J. T. Milik, and R. de Vaux: *Les Grottes de Murrabba'at, DJD*, II—*Textes*, 1961.

Burrows, Millar, ed., with John C. Trevor and William H. Brownlee: *Plates and Transcription of the Manual of Discipline* (*The Dead Sea Scrolls of St. Mark's Monastery*, II), American Schools of Oriental Research, New Haven: 1951.

CIS II—see: *Inscriptiones Aramaica Continens*.

Donner, H., and W. Röllig: *Kanaanäische und aramäische Inschriften*, I—*Texte*, Harrassowitz, Wiesbaden: 1962.

Driver, G. R.: *Aramaic Documents of the Fifth Century B.C.*, Clarendon, Oxford: 1954.

Gordon, Cyrus H.: *Ugaritic Manual*, II—*Texts in Transliteration* (*Analecta Orientalia*, 35), PIB, 1955.

Habermann, A. M., ed.: '*Edah we-'Eduth, Three Scrolls from the Judaean Desert, The Legacy of a Community*, Maḥbaroth le-Sifruth, Jerusalem: 1952.

——: *The Scrolls from the Judean Desert*, Machbaroth Lesifruth, Tel Aviv: 1959.

Hunzinger, Claus-Hunno: "Fragmente einer älteren Fassung des Buches Milḥamā aus Höhle 4 von Qumran", pp. 131-151, *ZAW* 69 (NF 28, 1957).

Inscriptiones Aramaica Continens, I (*CIS*, II), 1889-1893.

Kahle, Paul: *Masoreten des Westens*, II, Kohlhammer, Stuttgart: 1930.

Kittel, Rudolf, ed., with Paul Kahle, Albrecht Alt, and Otto Eissfeldt: *Biblia Hebraica*, 7th ed., PWB, 1951.

Kraeling, Emil G., ed.: *The Brooklyn Museum Aramaic Papyri, New Documents of the Fifth Century B.C. from the Jewish Colony at Elephantine*, Yale University, New Haven: 1953.

Lévi, Israel: *The Hebrew Text of the Book of Ecclesiasticus* (*Semitic Study Series*, III), Brill, Leiden: 1904.

Lidzbarski, Mark: *Ephemeris für semitische Epigraphik*, I, Ricker, Giessen: 1902; II, Töpelmann, Giessen: 1908; III, Töpelmann, Giessen: 1915.

Lohse, Eduard, ed.: *Die Texte aus Qumran, Hebräisch und deutsch*, Wissenschaftliche Buchgesellschaft, Darmstadt: 1964.

Milik, J. T.: *DJD*, II—see: Benoit.

Rahlfs, Alfred, ed.: *Septuaginta, id est Vetus Testamentum Graece iuxta LXX interpretes*, 6th ed., PWB (no date).

Sachau, Eduard: *Drei aramäische Papyrusurkunden aus Elephantine*, Königliche Akademie der Wissenschaften, Berlin: 1908.

Schlatter, A.: *Das neu gefundene Hebräische Stück des Sirach* (*Beiträge zur Förderung christlicher Theologie*, I : 5-6), Bertelsmann, Gütersloh: 1897.

Smend, Rudolf: *Die Weisheit des Jesus Sirach hebräisch und deutsch*, Reimer, Berlin: 1906.

Sperber, Alexander, ed.: *The Bible in Aramaic, Based on Old Manuscripts and Printed Texts*, I: *The Pentateuch according to Targum Onkelos*; II: *The Former Prophets according to Targum Jonathan*, Brill, Leiden: 1959.

Strack, Hermann L.: *Die Sprüche Jesus', des Sohnes Sirachs (Schriften des Institutum Judaicum in Berlin*, 31), Deichert, Leipzig: 1903.

Sukenik, Eliezer L.: *Otsar ha-Megilloth ha-Genuzoth*, ha-Universitah ha-Ivrith, Jerushalaim: 1955.

Torczyner, Harry, ed.: *The Lachish Letters (The Welcome Archaeological Research Expedition to the Near East*, I), Oxford University, London: 1938.

Zeitlin, Solomon: *The Zadokite Fragments (Jewish Quarterly Review, Monograph Series*, No. 1), Dropsie College, Philadelphia: 1952.

B. SECONDARY LITERATURE

1. Reference Works

a. Dictionaries and Concordances

Aistleitner, Joseph: *Wörterbuch der ugaritischen Sprache (Berichte über die Verhandlungen der sächsischen Akademie der Wissenschaften zu Leipzig, Philologisch-historische Klasse*, 106:3), Akademie-Verlag, Berlin: 1963.

Barth, Jakob: *Etymologische Studien zum semitischen, insbesondere zum hebräischen Lexicon*, Hinrichs, Leipzig: 1893.

Brockelmann, Carl: *Lexicon Syriacum*, 2nd ed., Niemeyer, Halle: 1928.

Buhl, Frants: *Wilhelm Gesenius' Hebräisches und Aramäisches Handwörterbuch über das Alte Testament*, 17th ed., Vogel, Leipzig: 1915.

Dalman, Gustaf H.: *Aramäisch-neuhebräisches Handwörterbuch zu Targum, Talmud und Midrasch*, 3rd ed., Pfeiffer, Göttingen: 1938.

Deimel, Anton, ed.: *Akkadisch-Šumerisches Glossar (Šumerisches Lexikon*, III:2), PIB, 1937.

——: *Šumerisch-Akkadisches Glossar (Šumerisches Lexikon*, III:1), PIB, 1934.

Delitzsch, Friedrich: *Prolegomena eines neuen hebräisch-aramäischen Wörterbuchs zum Alten Testament*, Hinrichs, Leipzig: 1886.

Delling, Gerhard: "καιρός, ἄκαιρος, ἀκαιρέω, εὔκαιρος, εὐκαιρία, πρόσκαιρος", pp. 456-465, *TWNT*, III, 1938.

Dillmann, August: *Lexicon Linguae Aethiopicae*, Giessen: 1864 (repr.: Ungar, New York: 1955).

Donner, H., and W. Röllig: *Kanaanäisches Glossar (Kanaanäische Inschriften*, III), Harrassowitz, Wiesbaden: 1964.

Gelb, Ignace J., Benno Landsberger, and A. Oppenheim: *The Assyrian Dictionary of the Oriental Institute of the University of Chicago*, 7, Augustin, Glückstadt: 1960.

Gesenius, Wilhelm: *Thesaurus philologicus criticus Linguae hebraeae et chaldaeae Veteris Testamenti*, I, II, Vogel, Leipzig: 1840.

Gordon, Cyrus H., *Ugaritic Manual*, III—*Glossary (Analecta Orientalia*, 35), PIB, 1955.

Grimm, Jacob and Wilhelm: *Deutsches Wörterbuch*, Leipzig: I, 1854; XIV, 1960.

Koehler, Ludwig, and Walter Baumgartner: *Lexicon in Veteris Testamenti Libros*, Brill, Leiden: 1958.

König, Eduard: *Hebräisches und aramäisches Wörterbuch zum Alten Testament*, 7th ed., Dieterich, Leipzig: 1936.

Levy, J.: *Chaldäisches Wörterbuch über die Targumim und einen großen Theil des rabbinischen Schriftthums*, II, 3rd ed., Breslau: 1867 (repr.: Melzer, Köln: 1959).

Lisowsky, Gerhard: *Concordantiae Veteris Testamenti Hebraicae atque Aramaicae*, PWB, 1958.
Noeldeke, Th., and A. Mueller: *Delectus Veterum Carminum Arabicorum*, 1890 (repr.: Harrassowitz, Wiesbaden: 1961).
Oxford English Dictionary, Clarendon, Oxford: 1933.
von Rad, Gerhard: "'Der Tag' im AT", pp. 945-949, "ἡμέρα", *TWNT*, II, 1935.
Sasse, Hermann: "αἰών", pp. 197-209, *TWNT*, I, 1933.
von Soden, Wolfram: *Akkadisches Handwörterbuch*, 1-4, Harrassowitz, Wiesbaden: 1962.
Wehr, Hans, ed.: *Arabisches Wörterbuch für die Schriftsprache der Gegenwart*, 2nd ed., Harrassowitz, Leipzig: 1956.

b. Grammars

Bauer, Hans, and Pontus Leander: *Grammatik des Biblisch-Aramäischen*, Halle: 1927 (repr.: Olms, Hildesheim: 1962).
Bergstraesser, G.: *Wilhelm Gesenius' hebräische Grammatik*, 29th ed., Vogel, Leipzig: 1918.
Brockelmann, Carl: *Grundriss der vergleichenden Grammatik der semitischen Sprachen* (*Porta Linguarum Orientalium*, XXI), Reuter & Richard, Berlin: 1908.
——: *Hebräische Syntax*, NVBE, 1956.
Dillmann, August: *Grammatik der äthiopischen Sprache*, 2nd ed., ed.: Carl Bezold, Tauchnitz, Leipzig: 1899.
Friedrich, Johannes: *Phönizisch-punische Grammatik* (*Analecta Orientalia*, 32), PIB, 1951.
Kahle, Paul: *Der masoretische Text des Alten Testaments. Nach der Überlieferung der babylonischen Juden*, Hinrichs, Leipzig: 1902.
Kautzsch, E.: *Wilhelm Gesenius' Hebräische Grammatik*, 28th ed.; Vogel, Leipzig: 1909.
König, Fr. Eduard: *Historisch-comparative Syntax der hebräischen Sprache*, Hinrichs, Leipzig: 1897.
——: *Historisch-kritisches Lehrgebäude der hebräischen Sprache, mit steter Beziehung auf Qimchi und die anderen Auctoritäten*, I, 1881; *—, mit comparativer Berücksichtigung des Semitischen überhaupt*, II, 1895, Hinrichs, Leipzig.
von Soden, Wolfram: *Grundriss der Akkadischen Grammatik* (*Analecta Orientalia*, 33), PIB, 1952.

c. Translations

Burrows, Millar: *The Dead Sea Scrolls*, Viking, New York: 1955.
Dupont-Sommer, A.: *Les écrits esséniens découverts près de la Mer Morte*, Payot, Paris: 1959.
Holy Bible, The, Revised Standard Version (Division of Christian Education of the National Council of the Churches of Christ in the United States of America), Nelson, New York: 1952.
Maier, Johann: *Die Texte vom Toten Meer*, I—*Übersetzung*, Reinhardt, München: 1960.
Rabin, Chaim: *The Zadokite Documents*, Clarendon, Oxford: 1954.

2. Commentaries

Bardtke, Hans: *Das Buch Esther*, *KAT*, XVII: 5, Mohn, Gütersloh: 1963.
Bentzen, Aage: *Daniel*, 2nd ed., *HAT*, I:19, 1952.
Benzinger, Immanuel: *Die Bücher der Könige*, *KHCAT*, IX, Freiburg i. B.: 1899.
Bertheau, Ernst: *Das Buch der Richter und Ruth*, 2nd ed., *KEHAT*, 6, 1883.
Bertholet, Alfred: *Hesekiel*, *HAT*, I:13, 1936.

Bonkamp, Bernhard: *Die Psalmen nach dem hebräischen Grundtext*, Visarius, Freiburg i.B.: 1949.

Briggs, Charles Augustus, and Emilie Grace Briggs: *A Critical and Exegetical Commentary on the Book of Psalms*, *ICC*, 16:1, 4th imprint, 1927; 16:2, 4th imprint, 1951.

Budde, Karl: *Die biblische Paradiesesgeschichte*, Töpelmann, Giessen: 1932.

——: *Die Biblische Urgeschichte* (*Gen. 1-12, 5*), Ricker, Giessen: 1883.

——: *Das Buch der Richter*, *KHCAT*, 7, Freiburg i.B.: 1897.

Burney, C. F.: *The Book of Judges*, 2nd ed., Rivingtons, London: 1920.

Caird, George B.: "The First and Second Books of Samuel", "Exegesis", *IB*, II, 1953.

Cassuto, U.: *A Commentary on the Book of Genesis*, I—*From Adam to Noah, Genesis I-VI 8*, tr.: Israel Abrahams (*Mēʾadam ʿad Noach*, Jerusalem: 1944), Magnes, Jerusalem: 1961.

Cornill, Karl Heinrich: *Das Buch des Propheten Ezechiel*, Hinrichs, Leipzig: 1886.

Delitzsch, Franz: *Biblischer Commentar über den Propheten Jesaia*, 3rd ed., *BCAT*, III:1, 1879.

——: *Das Buch Iob, Biblischer Commentar über die poetischen Bücher des Alten Testaments*, *BCAT*, IV:2, 1864.

Dillmann, August: *Die Bücher Numeri, Deuteronomium und Josua*, 2nd ed., *KEHAT*, 13, 1886.

——: *Die Genesis*, 6th ed., *KEHAT*, 1, 1892.

Driver, Samuel Rolles: *The Book of the Prophet Jeremiah*, Hodder & Stoughton, London: 1906.

——, and George Buchanan Gray: *The Book of Job*, *ICC*, 15, 1921.

——: *Deuteronomy*, *ICC*, 5, 1895.

——: *Notes on the Hebrew Text and the Topography of the Books of Samuel*, 2nd ed., Clarendon, Oxford: 1913.

Duhm, Bernhard: *Das Buch Hiob*, *KHCAT*, 16, Freiburg i.B.: 1897.

——: *Das Buch Jesaia*, 3rd ed., *GHAT*, 3:1, 1914.

——: *Die Psalmen*, 2nd ed., *KHCAT*, 14, Tübingen: 1922.

Eberharter, Andreas: *Das Buch Jesus Sirach oder Ecclesiasticus*, *HSAT*, VI:5, 1925.

Ehrlich, Arnold B.: *Randglossen zur hebräischen Bibel*, I, Hinrichs, Leipzig: 1908.

Ewald, Heinrich: *Das Buch Job* (*Die poetischen Bücher des Alten Bundes*, 3), VR, 1836.

——: *Die Propheten des Alten Bundes*, I—1840, II—1841, Krabbe, Stuttgart.

——: *Die Psalmen* (*Die poetischen Bücher des Alten Bundes*, 2), VR, 1835.

Fohrer, Georg: *Das Buch Hiob*, *KAT*, XVI, Mohn, Gütersloh: 1963.

——: *Ezechiel*, *HAT*, I:13, 1955.

Galling, Kurt: *Die fünf Megilloth*, see: Haller.

Gesenius, Wilhelm: *Der Prophet Jesaia*, I, II, Vogel, Leipzig: 1821.

Gordis, Robert: *Koheleth—the Man and His World*, 2nd ed. (*Texts and Studies of the Jewish Theological Seminary of America*, XIX), Bloch, New York: 1955.

Gray, George Buchanan: *The Book of Isaiah, 1-39*, *ICC*, 21, 1912.

——: *The Book of Job*, see: Driver.

——: *Numbers*, *ICC*, 4, 1912.

Greßmann, Hugo: *Die älteste Geschichtsschreibung und Prophetie Israels*, *SAT*, 2:1, 1910.

——: *Die Anfänge Israels*, *SAT*, 1:2, 1914.

Gunkel, Hermann: *Genesis*, 3rd ed., *GHAT*, I:1, 1910.

Haller, Max, and Kurt Galling: *Die fünf Megilloth*, *HAT*, 1:18, 1940.

Harper, William Rainey: *Amos and Hosea*, *ICC*, 28, 1905.

Herkenne, Heinrich: *Das Buch der Psalmen*, *HSAT*, 5:2, 1936.

Hertzberg, Hans Wilhelm: *Die Bücher Josua, Richter, Ruth*, 2nd ed., *ATD*, 9, 1959.

Hertzberg, Hans Wilhelm: *Der Prediger, KAT*, XVII:4, Mohn, Gütersloh: 1963.

Hirsch, Samson Raphael: *Die Psalmen*, Hermon, Frankfurt: 1924.

Hitzig, Ferdinand: *Der Prophet Jeremia*, 2nd ed., *KEHAT*, 3, 1866.

Hölscher, Gustav: *Das Buch Hiob, HAT*, 1:17, 1937.

Holzinger, Heinrich: *Genesis, KHCAT*, 1, Freiburg i.B.: 1898.

———: *Numeri, KHCAT*, 4, Tübingen: 1903.

Horst, Friedrich: *Die zwölf kleinen Propheten*, see: Robinson.

Hupfeld, Hermann, and Wilhelm Nowack: *Die Psalmen*, I, II, 3rd ed., Perthes, Gotha: 1888.

Kaiser, Otto: *Der Prophet Jesaja, 1-12*, 2nd ed., *ATD*, 17, 1963.

Keil, Carl Friedrich: *Biblischer Commentar über den Propheten Jeremia und die Klagelieder, BCAT*, III:2, 1872.

———: *Die Bücher der Könige*, 2nd ed., *BCAT*, II:3, 1876.

———: *Die Bücher Samuels*, 2nd ed., *BCAT*, II:2, 1875.

———: *Josua, Richter und Ruth*, 2nd ed., *BCAT*, II:1, 1874

———: *Leviticus, Numeri und Deuteronomium*, 2nd ed., *BCAT*, I:2, 1870.

Kissane, Edward J.: *The Book of Isaiah*, Browne & Nolan, Dublin: 1960.

Kittel, Rudolf: *Die Bücher der Könige, GHAT*, I:5, 1900.

Köberle, J.: *Der Prophet Jeremia*, 2nd ed., *EAT*, 2, Stuttgart: 1925.

König, Eduard: *Das Buch Jesaja*, Bertelsmann, Gütersloh: 1926.

———: *Das Deuteronomium, KAT*, 3, Deichert, Leipzig: 1917.

———: *Die Genesis*, 3rd ed., Bertelsmann, Gütersloh: 1925.

Kraus, Hans-Joachim: *Psalmen, BKAT*, 15:1, 2, 1960.

Leupold, H. C.: *Exposition of Ecclesiastes*, Wartburg, Columbus, Ohio: 1952.

Marsh, John: "The Book of Numbers", "Exegesis", *IB*, II, 1953.

Marti, Karl: *Das Buch Daniel, KHCAT*, 18, Tübingen: 1901.

———: *Das Buch Jesaja, KHCAT*, 10, Tübingen: 1900.

———: *Das Dodekapropheton, KHCAT*, 13, Tübingen: 1904.

Mauchline, John: "The Book of Hosea", "Exegesis", *IB*, VI, 1956.

May, Herbert G.: "The Book of Ezekiel", "Exegesis", *IB*, VI, 1956.

McCullough, W. Stuart: "The Book of Psalms", "Exegesis", *IB*, IV, 1955.

Mitchell, Hinckley G., John Merlin Powis Smith, and Julius A. Bewer: *Haggai, Zechariah, Malachi and Jonah, ICC*, 30, 1912.

Montgomery, James A., and Henry Snyder Gehman: *The Books of Kings, ICC*, 10, 1951.

Moore, George F.: *Judges, ICC*, 7, 1895.

Myers, Jacob M.: "The Book of Judges", "Exegesis", *IB*, II, 1953.

Noth, Martin: *Das Buch Josua, HAT*, 1:7, 1938.

Nowack, W.: *Die Kleinen Propheten*, 3rd ed., *GHAT*, III:4, 1922.

Oettli, Samuel: *Das Deuteronomium und die Bücher Josua und Richter, KKHS*, München: 1893.

Paton, Lewis Bayles: *The Book of Esther, ICC*, 13, 1908.

Peters, Norbert: *Das Buch Jesus Sirach oder Ecclesiasticus, EHAT*, 25, 1913.

Porteous, Norman W.: *Das Danielbuch*, tr.: Walter Beyerlin and Rudolf Walz, *ATD*, 23, 1962.

Procksch, Otto: *Die Genesis*, 3rd ed., *KAT*, 1, Deichert, Leipzig: 1924.

———: *Jesaia*, I, *KAT*, 9, Deichert, Leipzig: 1930.

———: *Die kleinen prophetischen Schriften vor dem Exil, EAT*, 3, 1910.

Rabast, Karlheinz: *Die Genesis*, EVB, 1951.

von Rad, Gerhard: *Das erste Buch Mose. Genesis*, 6th ed., *ATD*, 2-4, 1961.

———: *Das fünfte Buch Mose. Deuteronomium, ATD*, 8, 1964.

Ringgren, Helmer, and Artur Weiser: *Das Hohe Lied. Klagelieder. Das Buch Esther, ATD*, 16:2, 1958.

——, and Walther Zimmerli: *Sprüche. Prediger, ATD*, 16:1, 1962.
Robinson, Theodore H., and Friedrich Horst: *Die zwölf kleinen Propheten, HAT*, I: 14, 1938.
Rudolph, Wilhelm: *Chronikbücher, HAT*, 1:21, 1955.
——: *Esra und Nehemia samt 3. Esra, HAT*, I:20, 1949.
——: *Jeremia*, 2nd ed., *HAT*, I: 12, 1958.
Schilling, Othmar: *Das Buch Jesus Sirach (Die Heilige Schrift für das Leben erklärt— Herders Bibelkommentar)*, VII: 2, Herder, Freiburg: 1956.
Schmidt, Hans: *Die großen Propheten, SAT*, 2:2, 1915.
Schulz, Alfons: *Das Buch der Richter und das Buch Ruth, HSAT*, 2:4, 5, 1926.
Scott, R. B. Y.: "The Book of Isaiah, Chapters 1-39," "Exegesis," *IB*, V, 1956.
Sellin, Ernst: *Das Zwölfprophetenbuch, KAT*, 12, Deichert, Leipzig: 1922.
Simpson, Cuthbert A.: "The Book of Genesis", "Exegesis", *IB*, I, 1952.
Skinner, John: *Genesis*, 2nd ed., *ICC*, 1, 1930.
Smend, Rudolf: *Die Weisheit des Jesus Sirach erklärt*, Reimer, Berlin: 1906.
Stärk, W.: *Lyrik, SAT*, 3:1, 1911.
Steuernagel, Carl: *Das Buch Josua*, 2nd ed., *GHAT*, I: 3:2, 1923.
Strack, Hermann L.: *Die Genesis*, 2nd ed., *KKHS*, A: I, 1905.
Taylor, William R.: "The Book of Psalms", "Exegesis", *IB*, IV, 1955.
Tuch, Friedrich: *Commentar über die Genesis*, 2nd ed., ed.: A. Arnold, Verlag der Buchhandlung des Waisenhauses, Halle: 1871.
de Vaux, R.: *La Genèse, SBtf*, 1, 1953.
Volz, Paul: *Der Prophet Jeremia*, Deichert, Leipzig: 1922.
——: *Weisheit, SAT*, 3:2, 1911.
Weiser, Artur: *Das Buch Hiob*, 4th ed., *ATD*, 13, 1963.
——: *Das Buch des Propheten Jeremia, 1-25, 14*, 4th ed., *25, 15-52, 34*, 3rd ed., *ATD*, 20-21, 1960.
——: *Das Buch der zwölf kleinen Propheten*, I, 4th ed., *ATD*, 24, 1963.
——: *Die Psalmen*, II, 5th ed., *ATD*, 14, 1959.
de Wette, W. M. L.: *Commentar über die Psalmen*, 5th ed., ed.: Gustav Baur, Mohr, Heidelberg: 1856.
Wolfe, Rolland E.: "The Book of Micah", "Exegesis", *IB*, VI, 1956.
Wolff, Hans Walter: *Hosea, BKAT*, XIV: 1, 1961.
Wutz, Franz: *Das Buch Job (Eichstätter Studien*, III), Kohlhammer, Stuttgart: 1939.
——: *Die Psalmen*, Kösel, München: 1925.
Zapletal, Vincenz: *Das Buch der Richter, EHAT*, 7:1, 1923.
Zimmerli, Walther: *Ezechiel, BKAT*, 13, 1956-1961.
——: *Sprüche. Prediger*, see: Ringgren.

3. Monographs

Barr, James: *Biblical Words for Time (Studies in Biblical Theology*, 33), SCM Press, London: 1962.
——: *The Semantics of Biblical Language*, Oxford University, London: 1961.
Boman, Thorleif: *Das hebräische Denken im Vergleich mit dem Griechischen*, 3rd ed., VR, 1959.
Botterweck, Johannes G.: *Der Triliterismus im Semitischen erläutert an den Wurzeln gl kl ḳl (Bonner Biblische Beiträge*, 3), Hanstein, Bonn: 1952.
Bultmann, Rudolf: *Geschichte und Eschatologie*, tr.: Eva Krafft (*History and Eschatology*, University Press, Edinburgh: 1957; *Gifford Lectures*, Edinburgh: 1955), Mohr, Tübingen: 1958.
Cassuto, U.: *The Documentary Hypothesis and the Composition of the Pentateuch*, tr.: Israel Abrahams (*Tōrāh hats-Tseʿōdōth u-Sīdōram shel Siphrēy hat-Tōrāh*, Jerusalem: 1941), Magnes, Jerusalem: 1961.

Černý, Ladislav: *The Day of Yahweh and Some Relevant Problems* (*Práce z Vědeckých Ústarů*, LIII), Nákladem Filosofické Fakulty University Karlovy, Praze: 1948.

Charles, R. H.: *Religious Development Between the Old and The New Testaments* (*The Home University Library of Modern Knowledge*, 94), Oxford University, London: 1914.

Cohen, Marcel: *Le système verbal sémitique et l'expression du temps* (*Publications de l'École des Langues Orientales Vivantes*, 5th series, XI), Imprimerie Nationale, Paris: 1924.

Cullmann, Oscar: *Christus und die Zeit. Die urchristliche Zeit- und Geschichtsauffassung*, 3rd ed., Evangelischer Verlag, Zollikon-Zürich: 1962.

Dietrich, Ernst Ludwig: *Shūb shebūth. Die endzeitliche Wiederherstellung bei den Propheten* (*BZAW*, 40), Töpelmann, Giessen: 1925.

Driver, G. R.: *Problems of the Hebrew Verbal System* (*Old Testament Studies*, 2), T. & T. Clark, Edinburgh: 1936.

Eichrodt, Walther: *Theologie des Alten Testaments*, I, 5th ed., 1957; II, 4th ed., 1961, Klotz, Stuttgart.

Eissfeldt, Otto: *Ewigkeit im Alten Testament. Geschichtliches und Übergeschichtliches im Alten Testament* (*Theologische Studien und Kritiken*, 101/2), EVB, 1947.

Frankfort, Henri: *Kingship and the Gods. A Study of Ancient Near Eastern Religion as the Integration of Society and Nature*, University of Chicago, Chicago: 1948.

Greßmann, Hugo: *Der Messias* (*Forschungen zur Religion und Literatur des Alten und Neuen Testaments*, 43, NF 26), VR, 1929.

——: *Der Ursprung der jüdisch-israelitischen Eschatologie*, VR, 1905.

Gunkel, Hermann: *Schöpfung und Chaos in Urzeit und Endzeit. Eine religionsgeschichtliche Untersuchung über Gen 1 und Ap Joh 12*, VR, 1921 (repr.: VR, 1894).

Heidel, Alexander: *The System of the Quadriliteral Verb in Accadian* (*Assyriological Studies*, 13), Chicago: 1940.

Hempel, Johannes: *Altes Testament und Geschichte* (*Studien des apologetischen Seminars*, 27), Bertelsmann, Gütersloh: 1930.

Hurwitz, Solomon, and Theodore Halévy: *Root-Determinatives in Semitic Speech. A Contribution to Semitic Philology* (*Contributions to Oriental History and Philology*, VI), Columbia University, New York: 1913.

James, E. O.: *Myth and Ritual in the Ancient Near East*, Thames & Hudson, London: 1958.

Jocz, J.: *The Spiritual History of Israel*, Eyre & Spottiswoode, London: 1961.

Knight, George A. F.: *A Christian Theology of the Old Testament*, Knox, Richmond: 1959.

Loretz, Oswald: *Qohelet und der Alte Orient. Untersuchungen zu Stil und theologischer Thematik des Buches Qohelet*, Herder, Freiburg: 1964.

Marsh, John: *The Fulness of Time*, London: 1952.

Messel, N.: *Die Einheitlichkeit der jüdischen Eschatologie* (*BZAW*, 30), Töpelmann, Giessen: 1915.

Mowinckel, Sigmund: *Psalmenstudien*, II, Oslo: 1922 (repr.: Schippers, Amsterdam: 1961).

Munch, Peter Andreas: *The Expression Bajjôm Hāhūʾ. Is It an Eschatological Terminus Technicus?* (*Avhandlinger utgitt av Det Norske Videnskaps-Akademi, Oslo*, II:2), Dybwad, Oslo: 1936.

Noth, Martin: *Überlieferungsgeschichte des Pentateuch*, 2nd ed., Kohlhammer, Stuttgart: 1948.

——: *Überlieferungsgeschichtliche Studien*, 2nd ed., Niemeyer, Tübingen: 1957.

von Orelli, Conrad: *Die hebräischen Synonyma der Zeit und Ewigkeit genetisch und sprachvergleichend dargestellt*, Lorentz, Leipzig: 1871.

Pedersen, Johannes: *Israel. Its Life and Culture*, I-II—1926, III-IV—1940, Branner og Korch, Copenhagen.

Pfeiffer, Robert H.: *Introduction to the Old Testament*, 5th ed., Harper, London: 1941.

Procksch, Otto: *Theologie des Alten Testaments*, Bertelsmann, Gütersloh: 1950.

von Rad, Gerhard: *Theologie des Alten Testaments*, I—3rd ed., 1961, II—1960, Kaiser, München.

Ratschow, Carl Heinz: *Werden und Wirken. Eine Untersuchung des Wortes hajah als Beitrag zur Wirklichkeitserfassung des Alten Testaments* (*BZAW*, 70), Töpelmann, Berlin: 1941.

Rengstorf, Karl Heinrich: *Die Auferstehung Jesu. Form, Art und Sinn der urchristlichen Osterbotschaft*, 5th ed., Luther-Verlag, Witten/Ruhr: 1967.

Robinson, H. Wheeler: *Inspiration and Revelation in the Old Testament*, Clarendon, Oxford: 1946.

Rost, Leonhard: *Einleitung in das Alte Testament*, see: Sellin.

Rowley, H. H.: *The Relevance of Apocalyptic. A Study of Jewish and Christian Apocalypses from Daniel to the Revelation*, 2nd ed., Lutterworth, London: 1947.

Scott, R. B. Y.: *The Relevance of the Prophets*, Macmillan, New York: 1944.

Sellin, Ernst: *Einleitung in das Alte Testament*, 9th ed., ed.: Leonhard Rost, Quelle & Meyer, Heidelberg: 1959.

Trendelenburg, Friedrich Adolf: *Logische Untersuchungen*, I-II, 3rd ed., Leipzig: 1870.

Vollborn, Werner: *Studien zum Zeitverständnis des Alten Testaments*, VR, 1951.

Weiser, Artur: *Einleitung in das Alte Testament*, 5th ed., VR, 1963.

——: *Glaube und Geschichte im Alten Testament*, Kohlhammer, Stuttgart: 1931.

Wellhausen, Julius: *Die Composition des Hexateuchs und der historischen Bücher des Alten Testaments*, 3rd ed., Reimer, Berlin: 1899.

4. Articles

Barth, Johannes: "Vergleichende Studien I: über biliterale Nomina", *ZDMG* 41 (1887), pp. 603 ff.

Budde, K.: "Ellä toledoth", *ZAW* 34 (1914), pp. 241-253.

——: "Wortlaut und Werden der ersten Schöpfungsgeschichte", *ZAW* 35 (1915), pp. 65-97.

Ebeling, Gerhard: "Zeit und Wort" (*Das Zeitproblem im 20. Jahrhundert*, Francke, Bern: 1964), *Zeit und Geschichte* (Festschrift: Rudolf Bultmann zum 80. Geburtstag), Mohr, Tübingen: 1964, pp. 341-356.

Eichrodt, Walther: "Heilserfahrung und Zeitverständnis im Alten Testament", *ThZ* 12 (1956), pp. 103-125.

Frankfort, H. and H. A.: "The Emancipation of Thought from Myth", *IAAM*, pp. 363-388.

Galling, Kurt: "Die Geschichte als Wort Gottes bei den Propheten", *ThB* 8 (1929), col. 169-172.

——: "Das Rätsel der Zeit im Urteil Kohelets (Koh 3, 1-15)", *ZThK* 58 (1961), pp. 1-15.

——: "Stand und Aufgabe der Kohelet-Forschung", *ThR* 6 (1934), pp. 355-373.

Gelin, Albert: "Moses im Alten Testament", *Moses in Schrift und Überlieferung* (tr.: *Moïse, l'Homme de l'Alliance*, Desclée, Tournai: 1955), pp. 31-57, Patmos, Düsseldorf: 1963.

Ginsberg, H. L.: "The Structure and Contents of the Book of Koheleth", *Wisdom in Israel and in the Ancient Near East* (presented to H. H. Rowley), *SVT* III, pp. 138-149, 1955.

Hesse, Franz: "Amos 5, 4-6. 14 f.", *ZAW* 68 (NF 27, 1956), pp. 1-17.

Hesse, Franz: "Zur Frage der Wertung und der Geltung alttestamentlicher Texte", *Festschrift*: Friedrich Baumgärtel zum 70. Geburtstag (*Erlanger Forschungen* A: 10), pp. 74-96, Universitätsbund, Erlangen: 1959.

Irwin, William A.: "The Hebrews", *IAAM*, pp. 223-360.

Jacobsen, Thorkild: "Mesopotamia", *IAAM*, pp. 125-219.

Jenni, Ernst: "Das Wort ʿōlām im Alten Testament", *ZAW* 64 (NF 23, 1952), pp. 197-248; 65 (NF 24, 1953), pp. 1-35.

Lauha, Aarre: "Die Krise des religiösen Glaubens bei Kohelet", *Wisdom in Israel and in the Ancient Near East* (presented to H. H. Rowley), *SVT* III, pp. 183-191, 1955.

Marsh, John: "Time, Season", *A Theological Word Book of the Bible*, ed.: Alan Richardson, pp. 258-267, Macmillan, New York: 1950.

Mowinckel, Sigmund: "Der Ursprung der Bilʿāmsage", *ZAW* 48 (NF 7, 1930), pp. 233-271.

Muilenburg, James: "The Biblical View of Time", *HTR* 54 (1961), pp. 225-271.

Pedersen, Johannes: "Scepticisme israélite", *RThPh* 10 (1930), pp. 317-370.

Pidoux, Georges: "A propos de la notion biblique du temps", *RThPh* 2 (3rd series, 1952), pp. 120-125.

von Rad, Gerhard: "The Origin of the Concept of the Day of Yahweh", *JSS* 4 (1959), pp. 97-108.

Ratschow, Carl Heinz: "Anmerkungen zur theologischen Auffassung des Zeitproblems", *ZThK* 51 (1954), pp. 360-387.

Robinson, H. Wheeler: "The Hebrew Conception of Corporate Personality", *Werden und Wesen des Alten Testaments*, *BZAW* 66, pp. 49-62, Töpelmann, Berlin: 1936.

Sekine, Massao: "Erwägungen zur hebräischen Zeitauffassung", *SVT* IX (Congress Volume), pp. 66-82, 1963.

Staerk, W.: "Der Gebrauch der Wendung beʿacharīyth hayyāmīym im at. Kanon", *ZAW* 11 (1891), pp. 247-253.

Stoebe, Hans Joachim: "Gut und Böse in der Jahwistischen Quelle des Pentateuch", *ZAW* 65 (NF 24, 1953), pp. 188-204.

Talmon, Shemaryahu: "The Calendar Reckoning of the Sect from the Judaean Desert", *Scripta Hierosolymitana* IV (*Publications of the Hebrew University*), pp. 162-199, Magnes, Jerusalem: 1958.

Tillich, Paul: "Kairos I", *Der Widerstreit von Raum und Zeit* (*Gesammelte Werke* VI), pp. 9-28, EVS, 1963.

Ungnad, A.: "Zur babylonisch-assyrischen Grammatik", *OLZ* 11 (1908), col. 244-250.

Weiser, Artur: "Psalm 77. Ein Beitrag zur Frage nach dem Verhältnis von Kult und Heilsgeschichte", *ThLZ* 72 (1947), col. 133-140.

Wildberger, Hans: "Jesajas Verständnis der Geschichte", *SVT* IX (Congress Volume), pp. 83-117, 1963.

Wolff, Hans Walter: "Das Geschichtsverständnis der alttestamentlichen Prophetie", *EvTh* 20 (1960), pp. 218-235.